# PRIVATE EYE ANNUAL 2019

EDITED BY IAN HISLOP

Published in Great Britain by
Private Eye Productions Ltd
6 Carlisle Street, London W1D 3BN
**www.private-eye.co.uk**


ISBN 978-1-901784-67-1
Designed by Bridget Tisdall
Printed and bound in Italy
by L.E.G.O. S.p.A

2 4 6 8 10 9 7 5 3 1

# PRIVATE EYE ANNUAL 2019

EDITED BY IAN HISLOP

*"Apparently, there are significant traces of cocaine in the water supply"*

**Exclusive to all newspapers**

# WHAT HAPPENS NEXT?

1. We run headlines saying “What happens next?”
2. Something happens that we didn’t predict.
3. We run more headlines saying “What happens next?”

# TORIES UNVEIL NEW BREXIT VISION

It's time to stress the positives!

# TWITTER FURY OVER NEW DOCTOR WHO

by Our Social Media Staff
**Stormy Teacup**

**THE Twittersphere was in meltdown yesterday, as angry viewers took to social media to complain about Doctor Who regenerating as a woman.**

"Why not trans?" asked literally tens of outraged tweeters who retweeted each other's comments in the early hours of the morning.

Said one furious troll, "For too long, ie ten minutes, Doctor Who has been a woman. What a missed opportunity, BBC! Join the 21st Century, Auntie – or how about Uncle? Or is that too much for you?" #MeWho

Only in the Daily Mail

# Sarah Vain

*It's all about ME!*

HOW sad that the BBC has made Dr Who so "woke"! Guess what? One of her companions is (*yawn*) disabled!

Yes, Auntie, we get it! You're so committed to diversity! Why do we have to have a "positive" disabled character anyway? We already had a delightful disabled character in the form of Davros, a truly inspirational figure that taught us there was no problem too great that it couldn't be solved by the creation of an army of Daleks who wanted to exterminate everyone and *(cont. until the end of time)*

# Trump blames media for stoking violence

by Our Political Terror Staff
**Di Namite**

After pipe bombs were sent to the homes of various opponents of Donald Trump, the president was quick to react, stating publicly, "I todally condemn whoever sent those pipe bombs to Crooked Hillary, cheating Kenyan Muslim Obama, enemy of the people CNN and George Libtard Soros!"

He then indicated those whom he felt were the most obvious perpetrators of the crime, declaring, "The media is clearly to blame. If only TV and newspapers didn't cover my tweets, speeches and rallies, the world would be a far safer place.

"Almost every day there's a story of some new crazy thing I've said. No wonder psychos and nutjobs and others among my loyal supporters read this stuff and are inspired to commit acts of potential terror."

He then went on to tweet at three in the morning, "The failing evil media need to watch their step or someone's gonna get hurt. Like that reporter who got body-slammed by a Republican congressman.

"Did you see that?! Woah! Respect! And I bet some dumb journalist will now report I tweeted that. They deserve to get beaten up. #MediaToo. Sad!"

WARNER

# Could a healthy diet be good for your mind?

SCIENTISTS at the prestigious Institute of Stuff Your Nan Says have concluded that eating a healthy diet of vegetables, oily fish and nuts could be beneficial to the brain. This follows recent studies carried out by the Institute, including:

- Determining a link between eating up all your carrots and seeing in the dark.
- Identifying the lack of benefit felt if you keep your coat on in the house.
- Calculating the correlation between people who don't shut doors and those who were actually born in a barn.

# THAT FACEBOOK/NICK CLEGG JOB INTERVIEW IN FULL

**SHERYL SANDBAG:** Tell us a bit about yourself.

**NICK CLEGG:** Well…

**MARK SUCKERBERG:** No, don't bother, we know it all anyway.

**SANDBAG:** Why should we give you a job?

**CLEGG:** I'm a big fan of Facebook.

**SUCKERBERG:** Have you been on Facebook for long?

**CLEGG:** Well, I've got no friends.

**SUCKERBERG:** So that's a yes, then.

**SANDBAG:** And Instagram?

**CLEGG:** I've got no followers.

**SUCKERBERG:** Excellent.

**SANDBAG:** We're looking for someone with political experience, who knows how to influence elections.

**CLEGG:** Oh yeah, I can do that. Where do you want to lose?

**SANDBAG:** And if Mr Suckerberg were to run for office in America, the top job, would you be happy to play a supporting role, facilitating something that could turn out badly?

**CLEGG:** Have you read my CV? Count me in!

**SANDBAG:** So you're happy to do exactly what you're told?

**CLEGG:** I don't know. Am I?

**SUCKERBERG:** Yes.

**CLEGG:** I agree with Mark.

**SANDBAG:** And you're prepared to carry the can later, when Mark disappears to write his memoirs in the American equivalent of a shepherd's hut?

**CLEGG:** Can't wait.

**SUCKERBERG:** Nick, reluctant though I am to harvest your personal data, why exactly do you want this job?

**CLEGG:** I need the money to pay for my kids' tuition fees.

**FUCKERBERG:** The job's yours.

**SANDBAG:** But you won't find it too taxing.

**CLEGG:** TwoFacebook, here I come!

***Exclusive to all newspapers***

# MOMENT OF TRUTH AS BREXIT HYPERBOLE REACHES CLIMAX IN EXPLOSIVE BOILING POINT ROLLERCOASTER SHOW DOWN

Full boring story, page 94.

THE ALTERNATIVE VOICE

Long-term Private Eye contributor **DAVE SPART** calls for a boycott of Private Eye

**Yet again we see the sickening neoliberal hegemony of the fascist Private Eye as its faux anti-establishment public schoolboys completely persecute and smear the millions and billions of ordinary working and non-working British people who are revolutionising the way this country... and... er... we call for this boycott of Private Eye... due to its manifestly alt-right anti-Corbynist policies... er... in fact even the word "boycott" with the implicit phallocentricity inherent in the word "boy" and its troubling narrative of penetrative male action is deeply problematic and should be replaced instead by the neutral term "personcott", hence we will be personcotting Private Eye and the Guardian and er... er... we have the total support of many hugely popular modern leftist websites and media outlets allied with us, including leftsquelch.org, skwawkybudgie.geocities, and redbloodoftraitor-blairistscum.blogspot, and we will not rest until all of us are united in a positive and friendly campaign to destroy the neo-Blairist agendum of the disgraced Soho junta and its so-called *(That's enough Spart. Ed.)***

*"You seem a mite familiar, stranger"*

# LABOUR PLEDGE

We want to transform Britain into a very different country
Yes, Venezuela


## THE EYE'S MOST READ STORIES

### Sophisticated fraud costs UK residents £500m a year

The public was urged to be vigilant in the wake of increasingly sophisticated attempts to fleece them of their cash with emails that look like they are from their bank, but are in fact, from their bank.

"These bankers have decades of experience in fleecing customers with dodgy insurance policies, worthless pensions, crippling mortgage interest rates and disastrous investments," said one fraud expert. "You must not fall for their patter."

Fraud experts advise that once you confirm that the email in question offering you an investment opportunity of a lifetime is, in fact, from your bank, you should not open it and delete it immediately.

## That New Patisserie Valerie Menu In Full

*Books (cooked)*

*Tarte aux Fraudes*

*No Profiteroles*

*All-the-money's-scone*

*Sourdough*

*Poached Cheques*

*You'd-better-inject-some-cash-by Sundae*

*Mille-ions-missing feuille*

*Porridge?*

## The Eye's Controversial New Columnist

*The columnist who wants a squeaky Brexit*

This week I am very angry about the BBC and the preposterous liberties they take with factual accuracy when it comes to their dramas. I have noticed between naps that a lot of people are calling into question how television drama is becoming more unrealistic in the name of "shock value", and I heartily agree. Take, for example, the big-budget serial thriller "Fireman Sam". I have followed this electrifying tale for many years now, and have noted that a ridiculous amount of fires are started in one tiny village, Pontypandy, and all by one small child, Norman Price. It is completely unrealistic that he can keep getting away with his reign of terror for so long, and I can only conclude he is being ignored by the police because he is a "useful idiot", used to distract attention from the real arsonist at large, Fireman Sam himself. For it is only by setting these fires that he can get the funds for all his wondrous gadgets: his firetruck, jeep, helicopter, and speed boat, all on sale in good toyshops now. I have been waiting for someone to twig this, but everyone is so stupid that they never do. I now only watch it for the helicopter. And don't get me started on Postman Pat! There's a man who's up to no good and *(cont. p94)*

Exclusive to the Daily Mail

# PRINCESS EUGENIE'S FAMILY TREE REVEALS EMBARRASSING PARENTS

GENEALOGISTS have traced Princess Eugenie's family tree back an incredible one generation, to reveal she is directly related to a pair of highly embarrassing parents.

One was called Sarah, a minor children's author, and the other, Andrew, a dubious sailor.

Sarah was famous for toe-curling, embarrassing romantic liaisons and money problems, Andrew for being an unsavoury Lothario with links to dodgy businessmen and a rich American paedophile.

Luckily, some generations back, they did find someone a bit less embarrassing in Eugenie's family tree – a millionaire thief and slave trader named Edward Lascelles.

# Jeremy Corbyn *WRITES*

**HELLO! It's me again. I read a newspaper the other day. Sorry everyone! But it wasn't really my fault. Geoff sometimes brings in old papers to line his compost bins and I accidentally glanced at a headline.**

It said 'Where is Jeremy Corbyn?"

What a silly question! I'm in my shed, of course! Typical lazy journalism! Never bothering to find out the facts!

But the thrust of the article seemed to be that, with the biggest political crisis since Suez and the government on the point of collapse, they seem to think I should be DOING something! Well, pardon me!

My leadership style is easily explained. My political heroes are the strong, silent types. I'm particularly fond of Leonid Brezhnev, particularly during the year 1982 when he commanded a very large communist utopia even though he was slightly incapacitated, due to being dead. Now that's the leadership I admire! A leader who was unbending (due to rigor mortis) and unblinking (due to the replacement glass eyes). A leader who sends a strong message and that message is "Don't bother me with trivialities everyone, I'm having a little lie down!"

I had an exciting moment yesterday. I felt my hand and it was so cold with no pulse that I thought for a second I was actually dead! "This is it!" I thought. "I'm making history here! The first leader of a British socialist party to rule while completely deceased!"

Imagine my disappointment that it wasn't my hand at all. In the darkness of my shed I had just mistakenly gripped an interestingly shaped carrot.

But fingers (and carrots) crossed, there's still time for my demise before the election, whenever that will be. I'm sure someone will tell me if I DO become prime minister? Or perhaps I might just find out when I peer inside Geoff's compost bin and see a fragment of *Daily Mail*.

Who knows?

Cheerio!

# GLENDA SLAGG
## Royal Wedding Special!!!!!!!

■ **DID you see the Royal Wedding??!?!? Me neither!!!! Like everyone else in Britain, I had better things to do than watch Princess Freebie getting hitched to the Tequila-toting toff!?!?!? What does she become now??!? Princess Margarita??!? (Geddit???!) And talk about D-List celebs on the guest list??!! Jimmy Carr is no George Clooney!!!?? And Kate Moss is no Kate Middleton!!???! *(How do you know this, if you weren't watching? Ed.)* And what was Fergie wearing??!! With her red hair and her green dress she looked like a stuffed olive??!?! No offence!!?!? Just saying!!! And Cara Delevingne, who turned up dressed as Jacob Rees-Mogg!!?!! No, I'm glad I missed the whole thing and stayed at home watching television!?!?!?**

■ THE Royal Wedding!??! What a triumph for Team York, Princess Eugenius and the Titan of Tequila himself, Jack Daniels??!!!? *(Is this right? Ed.)* And what a guest list!!!! TV funnyman, Jimmy Carr???! Sexy supermodel, Kate Moss??? And top hats off to eyebrow-raising(!!!) Cara Delarue for cross-dressing as Lord Snooty!??! And, best of all, the Dazzling Duchess of Fergiana, showing her inimitable style and class by coming along as a gherkin with a cherry on top!!???!

■ **ROYAL Wedding goodybags!??! Baddybags, more like!!??! What an insult to the hardworking members of the general public who had taken the day off to attend the great event and were fobbed off with a packet of crisps, a Windsor Castle biro, a chocolate euro and a free copy of the Evening Standard to keep out the rain!!?!?! Talk about cheap!??!!**

■ ANYONE want to buy a brilliant Royal goodybag??!! I bought one for £500 on eBay and now I can't shift it!!?? Come on, Joe and Joanna Public, it's full of fantastic treasures, including a historic packet of crisps, a priceless Windsor Castle biro, not to mention an entire euro made from chocolate and a rain poncho that doubles as London's favourite evening newspaper. That's gotta be worth a couple of quid??!? Pleeeease!!!?

***Byeee!!***

"This means nothing to me"

# DIARY

## DAME JOAN COLLINS IN INTERVIEW

"Where's the glamour, where's the CLASS?" asks Joan Collins as she slides onto the velveteen couchette at London's legendary Claridge's Hotel, throwing scatter-cushions to the winds. "It's *disparued*, as we say in France, where, as you know, I maintain an iconic abode on the legendary Cote d'Azur."

Eighty-five years young, Dame Joan goes from strength to strength, ever more in demand for her inimitable style, class and waspish wit.

Only last month, she filmed an advertisement for the iconic Harpic White and Shine Original Bleach brand. "They tell me it's one of the most successful campaigns they've ever run on mid-morning television for a mid-priced bathroom cleaner," she tells me, proudly.

"It's so stupid of the young these days to try to save a few pence on budget brands. Where is their style, their glamour, their *panache*? Gianni Versace used to swear by Harpic White and Shine, and so did Diana Vreeland, bless her. And I'll give you the most marvellous fashion tip, darling: if your shoulder pads are looking a little soiled, then the teensiest dab of Harpic White and Shine Original Bleach will breathe new life into them!"

How does she do it? In the new year she's back on tour with her one-woman show, *Joan Collins Unbuttoned*, in which she promises to tell all about her desperately romantic *affaires d'amour* with Hollywood superstars, including Alistair Sim, Oliver Hardy, Mr Pastry, Lord Charles and little Arthur Askey. She once even enjoyed a romantic liaison with Ted Rogers, host of the legendary "3-2-1" – a fling that turned sour only after Roger's up-and-coming sidekick, Dusty Bin, came between them.

"Young actresses today are so sordid and untoward with their common little kiss-and-tell stories. I'm not like that, darling, never have been, never will be. Some things are meant to be secret. My lips are sealed. And that's why I would never go public with the names of men I went to bed with – and we're talking now of world-class superstars like Terry Scott, top-of-the-bill star of *Terry and June*, and masterchef Johnnie Cradock, before Fanny finally got her big fat teeth into him."

For many years, she remained tight-lipped about her turbulent affair with moustachioed lothario Neville Chamberlain. Ever discreet, she devoted barely 150 pages of her steamy 1973 memoir *With His Little Piece of Paper in His Hand* to her tryst with the dashing former British Prime Minister.

But nowadays she is more relaxed, recalling the brush of his moustache over her youthful cheek. "Neville was a modern man, who used his sexuality to get what he wanted," she recalls, blushing ever so slightly. "And the time has now come to admit that I used rather a lot of him in my portrayal of Alexis in Dynasty."

It helps that Joan's uncompromising glamour and dedication to elegance also happen to coincide with the fashion mood of the moment. Our fashion editor assures me that Joan circa Dynasty 1981 is THE look for 2019 – think animal prints, sequins, big earrings, shoulder pads.

"I've never relied on a stylist. I do my own make-up, my own hair. You see a lot of young actresses and they look wonderful on the red carpet, but the next day they look like something the cat's brought in. I'm not going to name names. Let's just call them Keira and Scarlett and Reese and Angelina for short."

Joan is equally vehement about the current tendency of young models and actresses to flaunt their bodies. "Have these young tarts never heard the word 'allure?'" she says. "They strip off at a moment's notice! In my day, we would always keep our clothes on, no matter what, unless we were hard at work filming Hollywood classics like *The Stud*, *The Bitch*, and *Confessions of a Window Cleaner*, or posing for tasteful *en plein air* studies by world-renowned photographers."

*As told to*
CRAIG BROWN

---

# BREXIT REALITY CHECK

As everyone gets more and more confused about what on earth is going on with the Brexit negotiations, Private Eye offers a complete guide to everything you need to know.

**Those technical terms you hear every night on the news – what do they mean?**

**1 The Norway Option**
You leave Britain to go and live in Norway where they enjoy all the benefits of being in the single market without being in the EU.

**2 Canada-plus**
You leave Britain to go and live in Canada. The plus here is that you won't hear anyone going on about Brexit.

**3 Chequers Plan**
The only idea Mrs May has been able to come up with. Although everyone else agrees that it is totally unworkable, she can't think of anything else. Basically, what it means is that you have to leave Britain because Corbyn has moved into Chequers.

# CHINESE INTERPOL CHIEF DISAPPEARS

## AGENCY ISSUES PHOTO OF POSSIBLE ABDUCTION OR MURDER SUSPECT

**Man know only as President X**

# WHY AREN'T MY CHILDREN DRINKING AS MUCH AS ME?

by A. Pissedoldhack

**SO, I see from the newshpapers that the kids these days aren't drinking. Whassobloody wrong with having a drink, eh?**

When I look at my kidsh, I see them there, sipping on their bloody elder-deldy-delderflower cordials, and I say to them, "Kidsh. You've got the whole thing wrong. Why don't you want to be like me? Whassowrong with being like your old man? Why don't y'wanna have a nice time every night like me and your mother with a nice bottle or three of thish – thish whatever I'm having now, I think it'sh wine? Eh?"

And they look at me like I'm shome kind of disgrasheful loser.

Well, if they think they're getting their handsh on my fabuloush houshe when they're such a bunsch of bloody po-fashed do-good-ooder prigsh, they've got another thinksh coming. *(You're fired, and possibly in the Priory. Ed.)*

R.I.P.
ANDRÉ PREVIN
KBE, PIANIST, COMPOSER, 4 OSCARS, 10 GRAMMYS, CONDUCTOR OF LSO, RPO, LA PHILHARMONIC, ETC ETC
AND APPEARED ON THE MORECAMBE AND WISE SHOW!!
BIRCH

# NEW GUIDELINES FOR GIRL GUIDES & BOY SCOUTS

**Boys that identify as girls to go to Girl Guides**

**Girls that identify as boys to go to Boy Scouts**

**Men that identify as paedophiles go to either**

# NO-DEAL BREXIT PREPARATION LATEST

## BRITAIN READIES FLEET OF ALTERNATIVE FERRIES FOR CALAIS CROSSING

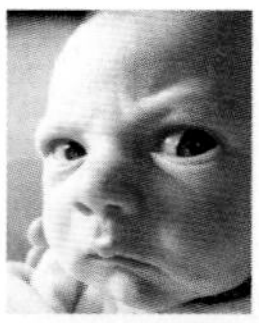

## The Eye's Controversial New Columnist

*The columnist whose first words were "fake news"*

This week I am very angry about Project Fear again. The idea that the UK would be paralysed in the event of a "No Deal" is a ridiculous one. To those who say that the south east of England is going to have to be turned into one big lorry park – I say nonsense! Just this morning I took every single lorry I own (Lego, Duplo, Meccano, Postman Pat's van, Fireman Sam's fire engine, Bob the Builder's quad bike, even Lunar Jim's space buggy) and placed them end to end across the living room floor and was struck, even when space was taken up by the sofa and the cat, how many vehicles a relatively small area could accommodate. So much for Project Fear! As I surveyed my collection, I could see nothing that remotely resembled "chaos"! So I am telling you now there is nothing to fear from "No Deal". In fact, when my father and mother return from hospital (broken leg, minor rib fractures) I will tell them too and proclaim another common-sense victory for *(cont. p94)*

# GOOD NEWS FOR BRITAIN: FACEBOOK PAYS MORE TAX THAN EVER BEFORE

by Our Social Media Expert **Kat Video**

**THERE was delight among the common taxpayers of the United Kingdom at the news that the social media giant Facebook was finally facing up to its moral responsibilities and paying substantially more tax than last year.**

According to reports, Facebook's tax bill has spiralled from 2017's amount of "Sweet FA" to this year's all-time high of "Bugger All".

Said one Treasury minister, "This is a major breakthrough for the accountability of global tech giants. We were expecting to receive 'Diddly Squat', so to get any amount above 'Zilch/Zippo/Nada' amounts to a major coup for our hard-working team."

This news represents payback time for the British public, who are at last getting something in return for the billions of pounds' worth of personal data which they've freely handed over. In fact, the full amount could almost pay for the cost of a trainee accountant to look at their books.

A spokesman for Facebook said, on his way to the bank, "Ha ha ha ha ha ha ha ha."

**2030: Talks on tackling rising sea levels finally begin**

## A Doctor Writes

AS A doctor, I'm often asked, do vaginal eggs work? The answer is of course, yes. They work extremely well for Gwyneth Paltrow, who has made a great deal of money out of them.

What happens is that the patient recognises Gwyneth from a film, a magazine, or from her marriage to the bloke from Coldplay. Then, believing that anything a celebrity says must be true, the patient inserts a vast sum of money into Ms Paltrow's bank account, causing heightened pleasure and extreme well-beingness, but only for Ms Paltrow.

Having been consciously uncoupled from their hard-earned money, the patient, or *publicus generalis gullibiliensissimus,* to give them their full medical description, feels renewed stress which then needs alleviating with another product from the "Goop" range, such as Moonshine Dust, Karmacleanser or the Colonic Vegetable Steamer™.

If you think you have more money than sense, you may be interested in my clinic, in which I sell snake oil for the very reasonable price of £300,000 per fluid ounce, which I guarantee will be just as effective as any old Goop Ms Paltrow has to offer.

*© A Doctor, 2018.*

# France's Best-Loved Entertainer Joins 94 Club

By Lunchtime O'Bituary

THE singer, songwriter and actor Charles Aznavour has become a member of the legendary 94 Club after dying at the tragically early age of 94.

Aznavour, who showed enormous promise through his long career, was known at one point as the French Sinatra, achieving fame through his best-selling recording of the song "She". He wrote songs for Edith Piaf and appeared in numerous iconic films, including the Oscar-winning *Tin Drum*, but was sadly taken from this world just after his 94th birthday. Who knows what he might have achieved had he lived? His three wives and six children can only speculate as to what the future might have held had not his time on earth been so cruelly cut short.

Aznavour thus joins such other distinguished luminaries of the 94 Club as the legendary journalist W.F. Deedes, the novelist Anthony Powell, the celebrated food writer Egon "Toast" Ronay, the detective-story writer Baroness P.D. James, the playwright George Bernard Shaw, the American First Lady Nancy Reagan and Miss Google Withers, the inventor of the internet *(surely "actress"? Ed.)*

## tripadvisor Istanbul ★★★★★

Review by Mustapha al-Ibi and Sheiki al-Ibi

We are two innocent tourists from Saudi Arabia, with no connection at all to the Crown Prince or his security forces, who just wanted to visit the famous tourist sites of old Istanbul, particularly the fabulous blue mosque with its 123m minarets and the great grey cell in the basement of the Saudi consulate.

**Places of interest**

**The cell in the Saudi consulate**

We didn't stay long because we come from Saudi Arabia and the weather was far too hot for us in Turkey, I mean we're just not used to it. We had a fun afternoon posing for typical tourist holiday snaps in front of CCTV cameras.

In one of them I wore a fake beard just for a laugh, along with the clothes of a journalist whom I've never met, or killed. We were just in town on a chopping spree, sorry, bloody Saudi predictive text.

# New Press Standards Campaign Group Launched

A NEW campaign group dedicated to curbing the intrusive behaviour of the press has been set up in Saudi Arabia.

Known as "Hacked Up", the group is led by campaigner Crown Prince Mohammed Bin Salman, the famous star of *No Weddings and One Funeral*, and is committed to stamping out any sort of investigative journalism or criticism of the country's regime in the press.

"What I get up to in my public life is entirely my own business," said the crown prince, who is a renowned liberal moderate. He continued, "I am a paragon of virtue, and it's not just me saying this, it's the entire Saudi Press, unless they want to die."

Jamal Khashoggi was unavailable for comment, but President Erdogan of Turkey was cautious about the journalist's disappearance from the Embassy in Istanbul, saying, "A lot of people are blaming the Saudis but, let's be honest, with my record on press freedom, we can't be sure it wasn't me." *(Rotters)*

# US-SAUDI ARMS SALES TO CONTINUE

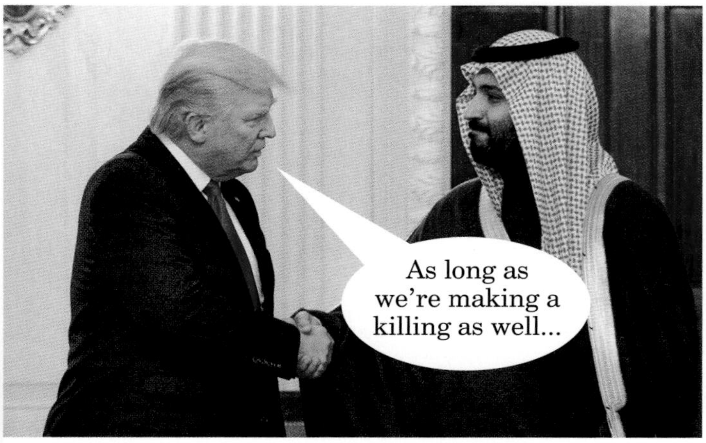

As long as we're making a killing as well...

# Man and woman on radio to be replaced by woman

by Our Broadcast Correspondent **Beeby C. Bashir**

BRITAIN has been convulsed by the news that a radio programme presented by a man and a woman will now be presented just by a woman, albeit a different woman from the first woman.

When the first woman joined the man, who had previously presented the show alone, a lot of people were extremely annoyed about it, saying that women couldn't possibly know the first thing about talking inbetween the songs on a radio station.

Meanwhile, the man who was joined by the woman, but who is now leaving, has said it's got nothing to do with the fact that he was joined by the woman, although his views on the second woman who will be replacing both him and the first woman are not known.

The first woman said she was sad the man was leaving, although she herself is leaving, and the second woman said she was happy to be joining, even though the other two had left.

## On other pages

- Does this spell the end of BBC radio as we know it?
- Is the whole corporation in crisis?
- Can we get any more desperate?

# BRITAIN TO CONTINUE SELLING BRIMSTONE TO HELL

by Our Trade Staff **Ian Ferno**

**AN embarrassed prime minister last night admitted that Britain will continue to trade with the Devil despite his alleged involvement in recent wrongdoings, including breaking all of the Ten Commandments – particularly the one about not killing people.**

The Crown Prince of Darkness has denied all charges and vowed to get to the bottom of who was responsible for all the evil in the world.

"Meanwhile," he said, "I expect Britain to supply me with as much brimstone as I need to keep the infernal regions aflame for all eternity."

Mrs May explained that this was a bad time to try and renegotiate the one foreign trade deal that she actually had in place.

"Yes, I know it doesn't look too good," the prime minister said. "The Devil has his bad points – particularly at the end of the fork we sold him – but supplying brimstone gives us influence in how hell is managed. It allows us to encourage Crown Prince bin Al-Zebub to adopt more moderate policies, such as allowing women to drive themselves to Hell in a handcart."

According to *Hell-o* magazine, the Devil buys not only brimstone and forks from Britain, but the British military provides training for his army of demons in crowd control, suppression of the damned and eternal torment techniques.

Concluded Mrs May on her way to church, "It's a good deal. Better a Faustian deal than no deal at all. And it's not as if we've sold our soul. Oh yes – so we have."

**Student Revolutionaries**

*"Of course, everyone's entitled to their own opinion"*

## PHILIP GREEN SCANDAL
# MORE WOMEN COME FORWARD

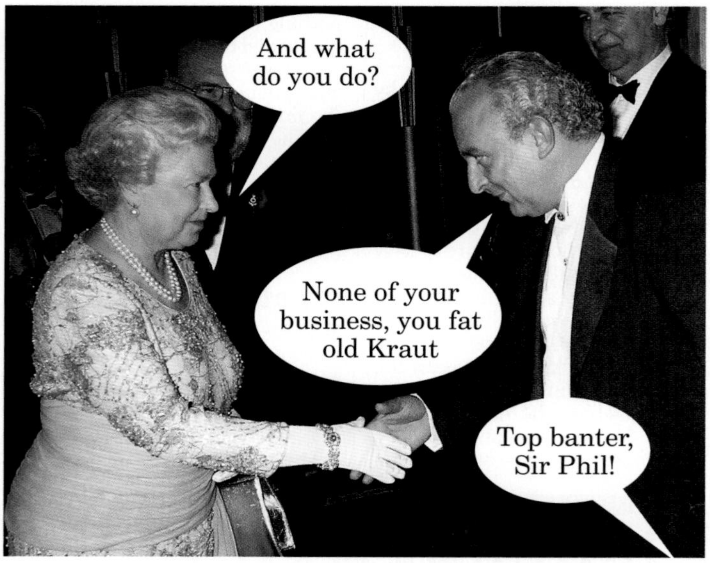


And what do you do?
None of your business, you fat old Kraut
Top banter, Sir Phil!

*More tales from the Mister Men*
## The Mystery Man

Mr Gropey was in a foul mood.

Only a few days before, nobody had known that Mr Gropey was gropey, because his picture had only appeared in newspapers in silhouette.

"That was because there was an injunction out, and we couldn't reveal his identity," said Mr Brown-Trouser, the Editor. "We thought about colouring him in green, but that would have been too much of a give-away and we didn't want to end up in court."

"I wish I could get my hands on whoever accused me of being gropey," said Mr Gropey.

But then, suddenly, Mr Orange used Parliamentary Privilege in the House of Lords to reveal that Mr Gropey was none other than Mr Green.

At this, Mr Green turned extremely red, saying, "I'm a model employer. I employ loads of them and I'm a hands-on boss! These accusations make me livid!"

"Is that because you've been exposed as Mr Gropey?" asked Mr Nosey, the journalist.

"No, you nosey twat! It's because I've spent half-a-million quid on lawyers trying to keep my name out of the papers, and now it's bloody everywhere! What greedy bastards lawyers are," said Mr Greedy/Gropey/Green *(cont. Court 94)*

# WORLD REACTS TO SAUDI OUTRAGE

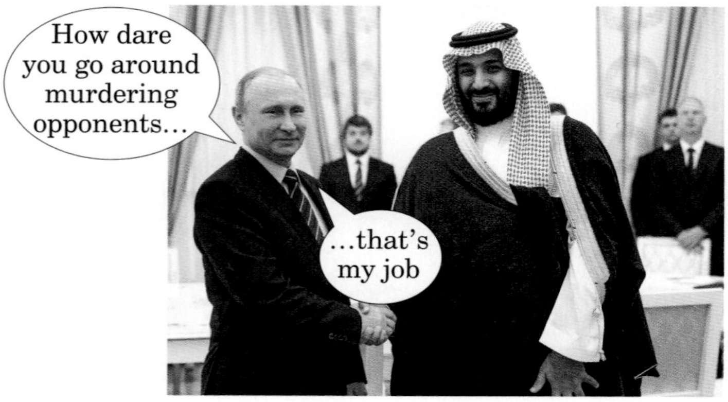


How dare you go around murdering opponents...
...that's my job

**Exclusive to all newspapers**

# HOW SIR PHILIP BULLIED ME, BUT I FORGOT TO MENTION IT AT THE TIME

by **All Hacks**

I'LL never forget the moment the phone rang and there, on the end of the line, was Sir Philip Green.

"Listen, you stupid bastard, if you run a piece about me bullying you, I'll have you killed."

I was so shocked by this verbal intimidation with clear overtones of misogyny, racism and hate crimes that there was only one response possible.

"Ha! Ha! Ha! Sir Philip," I replied. "You are such a laugh. Can I come to your next party?"

And that was the moment I determined that the appropriate course of action was to do nothing at all, thus sending a clear signal that *(cont. p94)*

# POETRY CORNER

**Lines on the 20th birthday of internet search engine Google**

So. Happy Birthday,
Google,
You started
In 1998.

How did I know that?
I googled it.
But then you know that,
Just like you know when
My birthday is and
Where I live and
What I had for
Breakfast.

Are you sure
You didn't start
In 1984?

E.J.Thribbot
(17½ milliseconds to generate this poem)

HOW DO YOU PLEAD?
WEALTHY

## Schillings signs non-disclosure agreement with itself

■ The top law firm that took £500,000 from Sir Philip Green in order to keep his name out of the newspapers has obtained an NDA forbidding any of its employees from mentioning the fact that this wasn't very good value for money and made them look quite ridiculous.

Anyone breaching this agreement will face immediate legal action from the top firm Pounds, Schillings & Even More Pounds.

OI, YOU — YESH, YOU! YOU WANT SOME, DOOYAH?!
ROB MURRAY

*"Don't look now – here comes Cider-man"*

# *DIARY*

## ALAN YENTOB MEETS TRACEY EMIN

*St Pancras Station. Rachmaninov's Piano Concerto 2, Opus 18, plays portentously.*

**ALAN YENTOB** (*voiceover*): Do you remember the first time you saw the iconic work of Tracey Emin? The wild abandon with which she first broke through has given way to a more mature, reflective voice. A voice that has something vitally important and iconic to tell us all.

*Workmen in cranes at St Pancras erect a large neon sign saying "I want my time with you" in squiggly writing.*

**YENTOB**: Tracey, this strikes me as one of your most powerful and iconic pieces, both painful yet curiously hopeful. What exactly were you trying to convey with it, what was on your mind when you conceived it?

**TRACEY EMIN**: It's like this is a famous station and since childhood I've always like had this I don't know kind of real feeling that stations and platforms and whatever are like places where trains go in and out of and people are on them or off them depending whether they've like bought tickets or not and that's a feeling that's never left me.

*Yentob continues to nod, looking surprised and intrigued.*

***

**YENTOB**: So who is the real woman behind this painfully honest and iconic confessional work and does she still have the power to SHOCK and INSPIRE like she did when she first came to our attention twenty-five years ago?

*Old footage of Tracey drunk in studio discussion.*

**TRACEY**: I don't give a fucking fuck about the fucking – oh, what the fuck, fuck this for a fuck –

**SERIOUS ART CRITIC**: It's impossible to ignore Tracey and that's, in a very real way, why she's impossible to ignore. You have to engage with her on her own terms, which are, in a very real way, the terms upon which you have to engage with her.

***

*Yentob and Tracey walking along street in Margate. Birds are flying around.*

**YENTOB** (*voiceover*): It's June 2018 and I'm receiving an iconic tour of Margate from its most famous daughter.

**TRACEY**: That's the sea and that's a house and that's more sea and that's a road and that's a shop and that's an amusement arcade.

**YENTOB**: An amusement arcade! Did you go in there much?

**TRACEY**: Not much, no.

**YENTOB**: Hey! What on earth is that? It looks… extraordinary. And powerful. Powerful and extraordinary. And… strangely unsettling.

**TRACEY**: It's a seagull.

**YENTOB**: There's something… iconic… about its wings. And the way it flies. It's clearly some sort of bird. Have you always felt this, I don't know how you'd describe it… connection… with what you call "seagulls"?

**TRACEY**: You like get used to them I s'pose like the way they're sort of gulls so they fly but they're also SEAgulls, so they swim too or like not exactly swim but sort of paddle about a bit.

***

**YENTOB** (*voiceover*): Emin shares her instinctive affinity with Margate with that most quintessential of British artists, JWM Turner. And now, Turner is receiving the ultimate accolade of having his works exhibited as a backdrop to Tracey Emin's powerful and iconic bed. For me, it's quite uncanny to observe the symmetry between Turner's seascapes and Tracey's bed.

**TRACEY**: Like you have the white of the sheets well offwhite more like then you have the white of the waves and then there's blue in the sky and there's a bit of blue –

*Yentob nods enthusiastically.*

– on that box of Kleenex or whatever by the bed I mean I can't really believe all these like connections it's just brilliant.

**YENTOB** (*looks sympathetic*): And – as I understand it – the bed's got an awful lot of pain in it.

**TRACEY**: Yeah there's a lot of pie in it, I was really into Fray Bentos steak and kidney back then, so that's like definitely what that mark must be.

*Cut to Nicholas Serota.*

**SEROTA**: My Bed is a tremendously… powerful… piece, calling to mind Goya and Van Gogh and Schiele. And if you get up very close to it, you can see these splashes that can best be described as human evacuations, and they have a sort of… raw urgency… about them which is, to my mind, really compelling. When one looks at the bed, one sees the bed looking back at one, asking one where one is in the world, and who one is, and why one exists, and one thinks to oneself she's not only pressed buttons and pushed the envelope but also – in a very real way – she's changed the sheets, or, paradoxically, not changed the sheets, and that is, to my mind, every bit as powerful.

***

**YENTOB** (*voiceover*): In the late Eighties and early Nineties, the British art scene experienced an iconic renaissance when a group of young turks were busy reconfiguring the very definition of art. From now on, they wanted it to combine the searingly honest with the powerfully intellectual:

*Old footage of Tracey disco dancing in a T-shirt with the slogan "Have You Wanked Over Me Yet?"*

**TRACEY**: So like I made a tent with everyone I'd ever slept with in it like it was so important because it was saying like I had sex with all these people and everyone I could think of was on that list and what it was saying was that I had sex with them all not all at the same time but all at different times and like that was a really important statement because those times are never going to happen again so they're in the past and not the future so it was a way of saying that the past and the future are not the present so there was all these different like layers that people could relate to.

**YENTOB** (*nods*): And how many names were in that iconic tent, Tracey? How many men had you actually… slept… with?

**TRACEY**: A hundred and two.

**YENTOB** (*nods vigorously*): A hundred and two? That's very iconic, very urgent, very… numerous.

**TRACEY**: My vision, my thoughts and my whole nature want to connect with something not only in me but not in me by which I mean outside me so what I'm doing is really a dialogue between myself and whatever it is that isn't myself, or at least would be myself if it was myself which it is in a way like it's really personal.

**YENTOB**: A hundred and two... Imagine!

*Back to St Pancras Station. Tracey Emin surrounded by photographers.*

**YENTOB**: She's been made a CBE, is Professor of Drawing at the Royal College of Art and was in the vanguard of guests at the recent prestigious marriage of Princess Eugenie at St George's Chapel, Windsor. Like William Blake and Johann Sebastian Bach, William Shakespeare and Plato, Tracey Emin's searingly honest work has explored this rich seam of human existence for three iconic decades now, tracing the line that connects our primal passions with our deepest desires. And, for me, there's only one word for it. Iconic.

*Closing titles to Rachmaninov's Prelude Opus 2, No 5.*

*As told to*

CRAIG BROWN

# Forgotten Moments In Music History

It was time for Brian to get a round

It was a little bit funny, the feeling inside...

So, do you come from the land down under?

# PRESIDENT HAILS 'MASSIVE TURNOUT'

by Our Armistice Staff
**Poppy Cock**

PRESIDENT Trump last night denied reports that his visit to American war graves had seen a poor turnout by the president.

"No way did I not appear," he said from his hotel room. "My presence was huge. Bigger than any visit of Obama's. It was bigly big."

Photographs of the event suggested that Trump was not there at all, with French President Macron and German Chancellor Merkel embracing at the solemn ceremony at Compiègne.

But a spokesperson for the White House dismissed the images as fake news. "They're just trying to make President Trump look bad," she said, "which is unnecessary. He can do that himself."

President Trump added, "Contrary to failing media reports, I went to pay my respects to those who lie in France. Namely, myself."

## TRUMP MISSES ARMISTICE CEREMONY DUE TO 'RAIN'

## THE Sun SAYS

**HOW low can you go? Shame on you, Mr so-called Portuguese policeman, for making money out of Madeleine McCann, when that's exactly what we want to do by putting her on the front page. Haven't her parents suffered enough? No!**

How dare a national newspaper try to capitalise on a foreign detective trying to capitalise on such a tragic incident. Just how much money can anyone expect to make out of such disgraceful behaviour?

We don't know but we're determined to find out. We should be ashamed of ourselves. But we're not. Sometimes words aren't enough to express our feelings, so here's lots of pictures of Maddy. See pages **2, 4, 5, 6, 94**

# Let's Parlez Franglais!

**Numéro 94**

## Armistice Jour Le 100th anniversaire

**Président Macron:** Bienvenue à Normandy, Monsieur Trump. Donnez-moi un hug!

**Président Trump:** Ne touchez-moi pas, Monsieur FrenchFry. Je ne vous fancy pas! Je don't even fancy votre wife – elle est trop agée pour moi!!

**Président Macron:** Would vous voulez visiter les battlefields avec les cimetières américains?

**Président Trump:** Non, il est raining! Et je ne peux pas work un parapluie! Fact! Quel crummy country et quel useless Président – vous cannot même controller le weather! Loser!

**Président Macron:** Keep votre hair on!

**Président Trump:** Mon hair est le whole problem!!

**Président Macron:** Calmez-vous down! Nous sommes here en Flandres pour promoter La Paix! Peace dans notre temps!

**Président Trump:** Peace off!!

**Président Macron:** Ça c'est why nous avons besoin d'une Armée Européenne – pour défendre notre selves contre vous!

**Président Trump:** Vous êtes très rude et je will slag vous off sur le Twitter!

**Président Macron:** Vous must cesser les insultes!

**Président Trump:** Makez-moi!

**Président Macron:** OK!

**Président Trump:** Vous et l'armée de qui?!

**Président Macron:** Avec l'armée Européenne, comme j'ai already dit – commandée par-moi, General Emmanuel Napoleon Macronaparte!!

**Président Trump:** C'est la guerre!!

**Président Macron:** C'est la guerre to end toutes les guerres!!

**Président Trump:** Vous êtes even plus mad que moi! J'aime ça dans un Président!

**Président Macron:** C'est l'entente cordiale!

*(Les deux stateshommes solemnellement shake mains et put leur différences aside jusqu'à la next fois.)*



## RYANAIR GUIDE TO ACCEPTABLE BAGS

*"Can we lose the cow?"*

# US MIDTERM ELECTIONS – HUGE WIN FOR NO ONE

by Our Political Staff **Jon Sopelopera**

**IN what is being widely hailed as a turning point in American political history, the 2018 mid-term elections delivered an extraordinary result, which left political commentators in a state of shock.**

Neither side did particularly well, or particularly badly, leaving both parties claiming a victory for themselves and a defeat for the other side.

The Republicans held the Senate, the Democrats took the House, commentators took a deep breath and pretended they had any idea what it meant.

Said one, "Mark my words, the country is split between those who don't know what's going on, and those who don't have a clue."

Said another, "I disagree, the country's united down the middle, there is now a widespread consensus that we are heading into a brand new phase of uncertainty."

Matters were further complicated when President Trump announced that he had won, which immediately convinced commentators that he had lost. However, it turned out that he might have been half-right.

"It's impossible to know who's speaking the non-truth anymore," said one reporter before being ejected from the White House. Truly, these are confusing times.

# Pundits discover main reason why democrats triumphed in midterms

by Our American Election Expert **Gerry Mander**

AFTER intensive research and sifting of the voting patterns, leading US psephologists have pinpointed the reason why Democrats triumphed in the 2018 mid-terms, seizing control of the House.

"We've tracked it all back to Kevin Bates of Macclesfield," said one leading poll expert. "Kevin did a tweet last week to his 209 followers which read: *'I hope the Yanks vote against Trump this time. He seems a right c*nt'.*

"Despite all the political ads, the rallies and the intensive campaigning, it was this social media post, which was retweeted seven times from Cheshire in England, that made Americans from coast to coast realise how they had to vote to stop Trump.

"It started a blue wave which resulted in the Democrats flipping the house."

"I'm extremely happy that I caused this," said Kevin, reclining on his faux-fur DFS original sofa. "The tweet was just a spur-of-the-moment thing.

"I was going to put up a photo of my slippers, because they looked like they were smiling, but instead I went for the Trump tweet, which made an impact far beyond my wildest dreams. I'm so glad because, when all is said and done, he is a bit of a c*nt really."

# 'I HAD TOTAL BREAKDOWN' SAYS SEXTING MINISTER

by Our Political Staff **Philippa Screen**

**THE disgraced MP at the centre of the sexting scandal described yesterday how he had recently suffered a manic episode of aberrant behaviour.**

He was, he said, engaged in his normal activities, texting barmaids and promising them money for racy images when he "completely lost it and became a Conservative minister".

He told unsympathetic reporters, "I don't know what came over me. I think it was the stress of having to send thousands of raunchy phone communications every day that caused me to flip and take a senior post in Theresa May's government."

He continued, to raised eyebrows, "I hope I will be forgiven for this uncharacteristic lapse and will be allowed to resume my career as a serial saucy sexter."

He concluded, "The whole minister thing is over. It was just something I had to do at the time. Now, if you'll excuse me, Daddy has got some naughty pics to send."

## What You Missed

### Radio 4am

**Presenter**: And now, for some more historical context, we are going over to Jim Middle-of-the-Naughtie for the conclusion of his campaign diary.

**Naughtie** *(for it is he)*: Not since the Republican senator Barry Ditchwater was challenged here in New Dworkin in the legendary mid-term elections of 1954 by the then unknown senator Conrad F. Paintdry has any contest been so keenly fought, bringing back memories, not just of Governor Snoozeburger's epic retention of the Democratic vote in Fortywinks Idaho in 1938, but also the extraordinary events of 1898 when Republican, Mortimer J. Yawnfest, declared himself the winner in Little Dozing, Nebraska, when only two years previously he had lost to the Democratic front-runner, General T.D.S. Baugh, known to all as "Collosal" after his unexpected landslide victory in Great Dullerware, Michigan, over the popular House majority leader Hamilton P. Slumber, the surprise choice for GOP candidate over Senator Z.Z. Zed…

**Presenter**: Thanks, Jim. We're all asleep now. Job done.

*(Cont. 94 kHz)*

**All channels**

*"Midterm wave Trump House Senate flyover blue-collar caravan employment turnout divided second-term base one thing is certain: I don't have a clue what it might all mean"*

# BREXITEER DYSON TO MANUFACTURE NEW INVENTION IN SINGAPORE

It's a moral vacuum
You suck!

**Daily Mail,** Friday, November 16, 2018

# IS THIS THE MOST BIASED BBC REPORTING EVER?

by Our Media Staff **Antie Beeb**

**IT's been called the most disgraceful example of partisan journalism in the history of the media. Namely, this piece about the BBC's biased journalism.**

It's an appalling attack on the BBC, clearly driven by a political agenda and not even pretending to be balanced in any way.

It is an affront to fair, decent and honest newsgathering, which is why we demand that those responsible, ie ourselves, be given a sackful of money by the Mail so that we can carry on putting the boot into a commercial rival who takes digital traffic away from our highly respected online clickbait platform which *(cont. p94)*

# MAY'S IRISH BORDER FORCE BEGINS TRAINING

# SUPERMODELS

KERBER

## From The Message Boards

**Members of the online community respond to the major issues of the day...**

**Businessman offers personal eulogies**

Guys, I see that an American company is selling custom-made holograms so people can deliver a 'personal eulogy' at their own funerals. CEO Carl Minardo has already created one, in which he thanks assembled mourners and toasts himself with a martini. I always fancied playing a tape recording at my funeral, with a muffled voice shouting 'Let me out, I'm not dead!' but my daughter Charlotte declares this 'typically pathetic'. I fear if I were really buried alive, she would cock a deaf 'un anyway! – **Bogbrush**

Hey Shitbrush, the thought of your funeral certainly made me smile. – **King of the Hill**

Thanks, and g'day, my Antipodean friend! – **Bogbrush**

It was the thought of your death that amused me, dipshit, not your funeral antics. – **King of the Hill**

Loving the banter Kingy! – **Bogbrush**

As a member of the consensual cannibal community, I won't have a funeral because there will be no body to bury. It will instead be consumed in its entirety during my 'nose to tail' memorial dinner (ethically reared and responsibly sourced) in keeping with the principles of biological and ecological upcycling. – **Meat isn't necessarily murder**

*Comment deleted by user* – **Tim the househusband**

Tim, how can you, a father of teenage daughters, say such an awful thing? – **Emily**

Any funeral nonce comes near my girls I swear Ill do time – **Family man**

I would like to apologise to the forum and my daughters Remain (2), Daisy (13) and former daughter Poppy (15, who self-identifies as recreationally transgender) for any offence or distress caused my previous post (now deleted). I intended to indicate my support for ecologically responsible lifestyles, but unfortunately the autocorrect facility changed the word 'upcycling' to 'upskirting'. – **Tim the househusband**

lolz course it did #timthehouseperv – **hatfield gooner**

post up the pix timmy! – **Danny Daz**

I have reported the above posters to the moderators. – **Tim the househusband**

#timthehousegrass – **hatfield gooner**

tim i will do a hologram for your funeral it will say my names tim im a grass and a nonce and a shithouse then i will tear open your compostable cardboard coffin and kick your fucking head in – **stokie steve**

Lovely sentiments mate, I will do the same for Bogbrush. – **King of the Hill**

Great stuff guys! – **Bogbrush**

# HEIR OF SORROWS
## A Short Story Special

by Dame Sylvie Krin, author of *Duchess of Hearts* & *You're Never Too Old*

*THE STORY SO FAR: Prince Charles is seventy and is publicly celebrating this historic milestone...*

"THIS is marvellous," enthused the septuagenarian Birthday Boy, "I'm here surrounded by all my old friends."

Charles was alone in the greenhouse at Highgrove, in the midst of his beloved collection of pot plants.

"I'm sorry about this, chaps, but I'm going to have to keep my opinions to myself when I'm King."

Suddenly, Camilla arrived to disturb his convivial conversation. "Stop skulking around in here, Chazza, and come back to the party."

"But..." Charles remonstrated, "it's all so loud and boisterous and the young people are playing those awful gramophone records... and that ghastly fellow with Princess Eugenix is handing out Tequila Slammers... urgh!"

The future king's consort was, however, having none of this curmudgeonly display. "Don't be such a party pooper. They are about to bring in the cake – specially baked by Abdul from TV's Bake Off."

Charles's face fell as further details of the elaborate celebrations organised by the younger Royals were revealed. First, he had had to dance with someone called Snoggya from *Strictly Come Dancing*. Then there was a supposedly amusing speech from some vulgar comedian called Jimmy Carrtax. Then embarrassing selfies with ladies called Cara De La Rue and Amal Clooneytunes. I mean, who were they? Why were they here? What was wrong with the surviving members of the Three Degrees – if there were any...?

Camilla finished her Duchy Original Organic Mint 'n' Cannabis-flavoured vape and dragged the protesting Prince towards the Michael Ball Room from where the heavy pounding of top Grime Artist Stormzy Daniels could be heard vibrating through the Louis de Bernières chandeliers...

As they entered the vast chamber, an enormous cheer erupted from the throng. Charles briefly flushed with pride until he realised that Princess Meghan of Markle

had just arrived outside by helicopter on the Islamic Multi-faith lawn where Sir Alan Fitztitchmarch, the Interviewer Royale, was bowing low and asking how she felt about her father-in-law being "so old".

As the Duke and Duchess of Sussex made their way through the French doors to be greeted by the enthusiastic guests, Charles wondered for the 100th time that evening what on earth he was doing there? Was this a fitting climax to a lifetime of devoted public service, promoting worthwhile causes such as environmentalism, traditional architecture and holistic spirituality thingie in a very real sense...

But it was too late for such introspection. A giant cake in the shape of the infamous "monstrous carbuncle" extension to the National Gallery was wheeled in by Prince Wills and Kate Middleclass, whose mother, the proprietor of Middleclass Party Solutions PLC, had kindly given them a 10 percent discount on the colourful balloons which, for some reason, read *"Happy 80th Vera!"*

A piano struck up the tune "For he's a Jolly Good Fellow of the Royal Society of Water Colourists", played by none other than Sir Ben Elton John, accompanied on the tambourine by his partner David Soft Furnishings. The whole room joined in raucously and then suddenly, from out of the multi-tiered confection, burst Her Majesty the Queen, wearing full court regalia, including the Grand Medal of Sovereign Order of the Amazon Prime. As the room fell to its knees, Her Majesty's regal tones rang out over their bowed loyal heads.

"Happy Birthday, Charles. We are going to give you the present you have always longed for. At last, we shall give you your heart's desire. The Crown."

The guests gasped as one and Charles felt his heart leap to his mouth. This was it. The Day of Destiny had arrived. The ancient monarchy was joining the modern age. And was that the London Trans Police Community Voice Choir singing? *Vivat T. Rex! Zadoc Tor Who! God Save the Burger King!*

But instead of handing over the elaborate glittering gold and silver coronet inlaid with Philip Green Emeralds, Ruby Waxes and the famed Sebastian Kohinoor Anne Diamond, Her Majesty merely presented her son and heir with a box set of Season 2 of the award-winning Netflix Royal Drama (starring Clare Foy as the young Olivia Colman).

Everyone began to laugh and suddenly Charles was back at school at Gordonsbrown with the assembled bekilted boarders mocking him and calling him the "Prince of Wallies".

"WAKE up, Your Highness, wake up!" The alarmed tones of Sir Alan Fitztightly, the Royal Equerry, jolted Charles from his deep slumber.

"You've fallen asleep in the bath, Sire."

And so he had. Charles shook his head, relieved to find himself in familiar surroundings. Thank goodness, it had all been a dream! He dried his furrowed brow on the towel proffered to him by Sir Alan with its distinctive "His 'n' Heirs" logo.

"I was having the most terrifying nightmare... there was only one word for it... it was..."

"There's no time for that, sire, you're due downstairs at your 70th party in 5 minutes. The guests are all here and Mrs Middleclass has done a wonderful job with the balloons..."

Charles looked confused and the words of the Bard of Bohemia flashed through his brain.

"Is this the real life? Is this just fantasy? Caught in a landslide – no escape from reality". Yes, Sir Frederick of Mercury had hit the nail on the head, as he so often did. How very true. How very, very, very true.

*(To be continued...)*

## Who should replace Posh Spice for The Spice Girls Reunion Tour?

**A coat hanger**

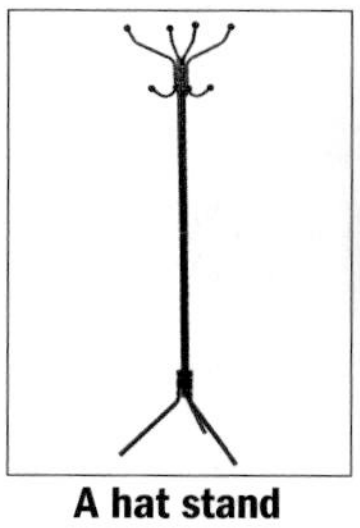

**A hat stand**

**Grumpy Cat**

**Mr Miserable**

**Une Misérable**

**A can of Bitter Lemon**

**Jacob Rees-Mogg**

**Posh Spice, again**

# Arron Banks fury over data breach fine

ARRON BANKS has insisted that, despite a £135,000 fine from the Information Commissioner's Office for data from one of his insurance businesses being used for pro-Brexit marketing, he is committed to data security.

"I am absolutely determined that all my data, most noticeably my clandestine meetings with Russian officials, and the real source of my £8m Brexit donation, must remain totally secret and out of the public domain," Mr Banks told reporters, as staff in his office frantically wiped his hard drives in anticipation of a raid by the National Crime Agency.

"My personal data protection is paramount to me and it always will be."

Asked whether he accepted the Information Commissioner's findings, he said, "I reject every claim. How else would my insurance businesses make money?"

*"The police will be an hour, the fire service fifty minutes, and the ambulance thirty minutes... I can have a pizza with you in about ten, though, if you fancy it?"*

## Film highlights

### Mary Poppins Returns

Foreign nanny Mary Poppins is sent straight home by arch-Brexiteer Mr Banks, who tells her to fly out by the next umbrella and, spit-spot, she's gone.

Mr Banks is left to get on with his uniquely successful insurance business, which works like magic, turning tuppence (safely invested in the Banks) into eight million pounds or possibly roubles, which come out of his bottomless carpet-bag.

"How does he do this?" ask all the children, the Electoral Commission, and a cartoon penguin called Andrew Marr. He sings: "It's Supercalifragilistic-Brexitalitrocious," before telling the Serious Crime Agency that they are trying to fly a kite and he's not going to help out.

Don't miss the cameo by lovable cockney geezer Nigel Bert Farage who smokes like a Chim-Chiminee, Chim-Chiminee, Chim-Chim Cheree, and leads everyone in a rousing chorus of "A spoonful of bitter helps the rest of the pint go down".

**SPOIL ALERT:** *Mr Banks spoils the referendum.*

### The Boy From Brazil

Classic thriller in which Adolf Hitler is cloned by scientists in Brazil, and the child Führer grows up to become leader of a fascist government.

When an attempt to assassinate him fails, Jair Bolsonaro becomes even more popular, and is elected by millions to the highest office in the land, with terrifying consequences for such demographics as homosexuals, transsexuals and heterosexuals. He is not without his critics in South America, as several ex-SS officers, hiding in their luxury villas in the jungle, find his views a little too extreme for their liking.

However, in a moving romantic phone call, President Trump declares that he knows a good guy when he sees one.

**EYE RATING:** *Brazil? They're all nuts.*

**Daily Mail,** Friday, November 30, 2018

# DUCHESS DING DONG!

by Our Royal Staff
**May Kittup**

**The honeymoon's over and the gloves are off! What started as frosty froideur has now become open warfare!**

I can exclusively reveal that the relationship between feisty, independent Meghan and staid, frumpy Kate has reached an all-time low. The tell-tale signs are only too obvious to seasoned Royal watchers like myself:

- As clear evidence of the big bust-up, Prince William, Prince Harry and their wives are going to live in their own houses, instead of all together in a Royal flat, like in *Friends*.
- Meghan has desperately got pregnant, instead of remaining childless, clearly only to upstage Mother of Three, Kate.
- Kate's displays of public affection towards her new sister-in-law are fooling no one and hide an obvious urge to pull Meghan's hair out and call her unpleasant names until she cries.
- The Cambridge/Sussex rivalry extends to both of the Duchesses wearing clothes in public, which has fuelled their mutual hatred to a level described as "Mega-thermonuclear" by one palace insider (myself).
- In a deliberate snub to her sister-in-law, Meghan has let it be known that if the baby is a boy, she will **not** call it "Kate".

**So, let battle commence in the War of the English Roses – although one of them is American.** ***(This is rubbish. More, please. Ed.)***

## The Mail Says

# PUT 'EM AWAY LIZ, WE'VE ALL HAD ENOUGH OF THEM!

**Just how much of Liz Hurley's cleavage does anyone want to see? Let's find out with 17 saucy pics of Liz's bikini bouncers! What a disgrace! Phwoooar! It's them again! Give us a break** *(Cont. p2-94DD)*

# PENGUIN TIMES

*Giving the news in Black and White*

## SHOULD WE STEP IN AND HELP HUMANS?

WE'VE all seen the footage, the desperate plight of millions of powerless Brits, trapped deep in a harsh unforgiving hole, facing certain doom, with no idea how to get out.

Should we, as penguins, let nature take its course and leave them to their fate?

Is it our duty, as intellectually and morally superior creatures, to waddle in and help them escape in some way?

Or should we let them jump over a cliff, in slow motion, with stirring music and a commentary by David Attenborough?

At the moment, their future looks cold and bleak. Should we save them from Brrrrrrrexit? No, it's none of our business – we're penguins.

## CALIFORNIA FIRES – TRUMP POINTS FINGER OF BLAME

by Our Disaster Staff **Ian Ferno**

**AS the President of the United States visited the areas around Los Angeles that have been devastated by forest fires, he refused to blame climate change and instead hit out at local firefighters.**

"If you guys had been properly equipped, tooled up with semi-automatic machine guns, that fire would never have got as far as it did.

"Even an idiot knows that you have to fight fire with fire. In fact, forget machine-guns, you could have taken out that fire with a flame-thrower."

Mr Trump later tweeted about a conversation he'd had about forest management with the president of Narnia, saying, "If I'd have been there, I'd have picked up a rake and charged straight at those bad-guy flames! They hate rakes!! Cowards!!! #MakeFireGrateAgain!!!!"

## JOHNSON EMBRACES DUP

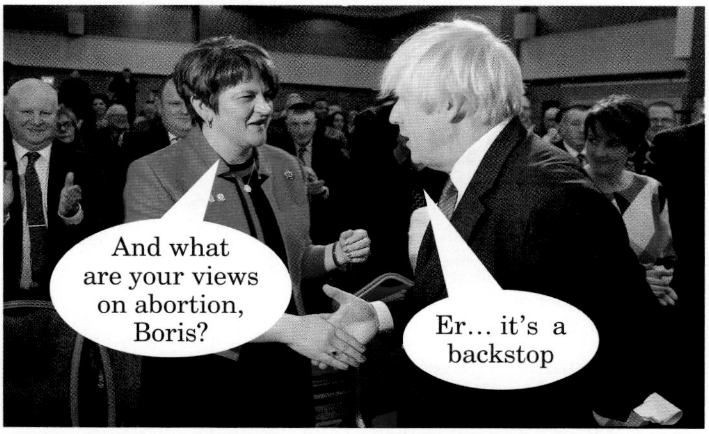

And what are your views on abortion, Boris?
Er… it's a backstop


## THE EYE'S EXCLUSIVE GUIDE

### How to save huge amounts of money on Black Friday and Cyber Monday

**1.** Don't buy any pointless rubbish you don't need

**2.** Er…

**3.** That's it.

## The Eye's Controversial New Columnist

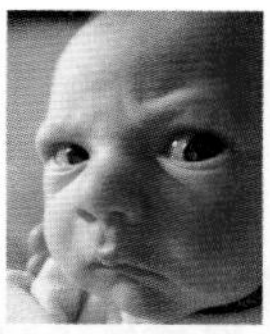

*The columnist who threw all the toys out of his pram when he saw they had European kitemarks*

This week I am very angry about casting actors in roles that should have been played by minorities. At first glance, this might not seem like a cause close to my heart, but hear me out. Everyone complains about Jack Whitehall being cast as a gay man, but no one talks about the most heinous example of all – Emma Bunton has the gall to announce that she is going back on tour with the Spice Girls as "Baby" when she is nothing of the sort. I remember when Ms Bunton came on the scene in 1996 purporting to be a "baby", when she was plainly not, and have followed her for 22 years now becoming progressively less like a baby with every passing year. There are any number of real babies who can play her part, just as someone who is a genuine red-head can play the part of "Ginger". It is all very well complaining when disabled characters are played by able-bodied people, but when it comes to babies, it seems that everyone can have a go. I'm almost as cross as when I watched *Look Who's Talking* and was told that the baby was played by a man called "Bruce Willis". This was a bigger shock than *The Sixth Sense*, when Mr Willis turned out to be *(cont. p94)*

## POETRY CORNER

**In Memoriam Peter Boizot, founder of Pizza Express**

So. Farewell
Then Peter Boizot,
You weren't Italian or
Even very French,
As you came
From Peterborough,
But you brought Italy
Into our lives
And stomachs.

Yes, you made
An awful lot
Of dough
Balls, but you also
Made us happy
With your Pizza
Peroni Jazz combo.
Mmmm, nice.

Four Seasons,
American Hot,
Margherita,
And the one where
You gave 25p to
Save Venice.

As Keith says,
"Venice is still there",
But sadly,
You aren't.

E.J. Thribb (17½ inches, before "entrepreneur" Luke Johnson took you over and made the plates smaller)

♫ I'll tell you what we want, what we really, really want... ♫
Ken Pyne

# Nursery Times

Friday, Once-upon-a-time

## FLU EPIDEMIC SWEEPS THROUGH NURSERYLAND COMMUNITY

by Our Health Staff **Little Boy Flu**

A catastrophic shortage of flu vaccine in Nurseryland has seen an entire population of dwarves stricken by the seasonal virus.

Up to seven dwarves, all working in the diamond mining industry, have become victims of the dreaded influenza.

Said Ms Snow White, a spokeswoman for the dwarves, "It began with Sneezy, and before long, spread to Sneezy, Sneezy, Sneezy, Sneezy, Sneezy and, eventually, Doc."

Doc (now Sneezy as well)

responded to allegations that he had shown a lack of foresight in not stocking up with enough vaccine, stating, "Ok, I admit we were short. But then, what's new?"

The dwarves are now a sad sight, coughing, wheezing and singing *"Hi ho, hi ho, it's off work we go".*

### Late News

Grand old Duke of Rees-Mogg admits he didn't have 10,000 men, or even 48, when he led them up the hill to post a letter to the 1922 committee.

## GAMBLING CRISIS HITS NURSERYLAND – 10 APPALLING CASE STUDIES

● Christopher Robin loses house at Pooh Corner after betting on Pooh-sticks Online.

● Jack and Jill tumble after ill-advised trip up William Hill.

● Goldilocks resorts to porridge theft to fund gambling habit.

● Witch lures Hansel and Gretel with oven betting game.

● King in Counting House has no regrets about setting up online Casino.

● Bookies clean up after

controversial hare-tortoise race upset.

● All Tinkerbell's wishes are granted after she sets up Betfairyland.

● Emperor loses shirt to little boy in New Clothes gamble.

● Humpty jumps off wall, thanks to spiralling gambling debts after betting on all the king's horses.

● Little Bo Peep loses whole flock in gambolling disaster.

*(That really is enough. Ed.)*

*"Ah'm tired o' runnin', Jake"*

## WHAT SHOULD HAVE HAPPENED ON THE ANDREW MARR SHOW

I don't know about you, Andrew, but I'm a democrat

No, you're not. You are an unelected peer, rewarded with a seat in the House of Lords for whitewashing the Labour Party over anti-Semitism

Oh yes, so I am

## A CHILD'S GUIDE TO THOSE ONLINE BETTING COMPANIES IN FULL

**BET 365**
We don't mind if you're 3, 6 or 5, just have a go. You can bet 24/7 – though we'd rather you were 7 than 24 'cos that way you'll get addicted younger.

**BET 265**
Top punter Denise Coates won £265 million by betting on the public getting easily addicted to online gambling. What are the odds on that? No wonder she's addicted to it!

**LADBROKES**
If you're a young lad, preferably under 10, you'll be broke in seconds.

**BETWAY TOO YOUNG**
Does what it says on the tin! Takes your pocket money and turns it into millions – for us!

**BETFAIR**
No, it isn't, sonny. Just hand over the money, and don't tell mum and dad.

## Outrage as minister resigns on principle

by Our Political Gambling Correspondents **Fred Bet** and **William Hill**

The Westminster village was reeling today as word spread that Tracey Crouch, a member of Theresa May's government, had resigned from office for reasons of conscience.

Said one MP, "This is a poor show, and not the sort of behaviour we expect from our senior politicians. She didn't grope anyone, bully anyone, nor was any porn found on her computer. She merely had a strong moral view about fixed-odds betting terminals."

The row blew up when the

government reneged on its commitment to introduce a cap on the stakes, and sports minister Ms Crouch handed in her notice.

"It's unbelievable!" added another. "What are the odds on that?!"

Speaker John Bercow summed up the situation, saying, "Ms Crouch is completely unfit to hold any post in this administration. If she's going to put scruples above self-interest, and leave in a dignified fashion, rather than be dragged kicking and screaming out of her office, then she's just embarrassing the rest of us."

Ms Crouch was available for comment and not hiding behind any spokespeople.

# That May Letter In Full

10 DOWNING STREET
LONDON SW1A 2AA

THE PRIME MINISTER — 24 November 2018

Dear every man, woman and child in Britain, from the moment I became your Prime Minister, I have had only one purpose – to carry out your wish to leave the European Union and take back control of our laws, our money and our borders. That is why I and our European friends have come up with a deal that does exactly that.

Under this Withdrawal Agreement, the United Kingdom takes back full control of our laws (from the hated ECJ), our money (to spend on our own NHS) and our borders (including Northern Ireland and Gibraltar). And then immediately hands it all back to the EU for an unspecified period, for safekeeping.

Only under this arrangement can Britain remain the most happy and prosperous country in the world.

What's not to like?

Your friend,

*(Indecipherable signature)*

# EUROPE'S RESPONSE TO MRS MAY'S PLEAS FOR HELP

I fart in your general direction, your mother was a hamster and your Brexit smells of elderberries

# A Doctor Writes

AS A doctor, a lot of patients come to me and say, "Doctor, I spend a lot of time online, googling possible medical symptoms, is there anything wrong with me?"

The simple answer to this is: "Yes, but not in the way you're thinking. There is probably nothing wrong with you at all, but if you keep googling illnesses, you'll soon believe there is."

What usually happens is this: you feel a slight twinge in your knee, look up the symptoms online and within seconds of browsing on medical websites, you conclude you are just minutes away from total organ failure.

You will experience palpitations, sweat profusely and search for "Online will-making services".

These are classic symptoms of *googleitis hypochondriam nervosa* or *Browser's Syndrome*.

If you feel a twinge in your knee, the recommended treatment is in fact quite straightforward. Simply go and see a doctor and report your symptoms. The doctor will reply with the reassuring words: "Hang on while I google that."

*© A doctor@ symptomcheques.com*

# Film highlights

## Nightmare on Threadneedle Street

BBC2 Horror season

Terrifying standard-of-living slasher pic that will have you hiding behind your sofa, if it hasn't been repossessed already.

Mark Carney (played by an on-form Freddie Kruger) wages a campaign of fear, haunting the dreams of homeowners and businessmen alike with his scream-inducing, hair-raising, no-deal Brexit economic forecasts.

You won't be able to sleep anymore once you find out what's lurking under your mattress – no money at all.

He leaves a terrifying blood-red line going down the wall on all profit charts and the chills don't stop there. House prices, retail sales, the pound – all will head remorselessly downwards on a one-way trip to hell.

**EYE RATING:** *Overly optimistic*

**MOGG RATING:** *Hysterical poppycock*

# Dave Snooty — YES, HE'S BACK!

I'M BORED SHEDLESS! I WANT TO COME BACK AS FOREIGN SECRETARY!
WHAT MAKES YOU THINK YOU'D BE SUITABLE?
I'M AN OLD ETONIAN AND I'M USELESS!
THAT'S THE WORST IDEA YOU'VE HAD SNOOTY, SINCE THE REFERENDUM!
YAR-EU!!!
JOE PUBLIC ESQ
BOOT!
REMAIN IN YOUR SHED AND LEAVE US ALONE!
I WANT TO START A NEW CHAPTER ...
ME-ME-ME-MOIRS
JACOB REES-SNOOTIER
OK. CALL IT 'THE END'

# YES, IT'S GILETS JAUNESON

No plan and ready to create chaos. Follow me!

## *EYE* EXCLUSIVE

THE ALTERNATIVE VOICE

**DAVE SPART** on the riots in Paris

**Yet again we see the sickening spectacle of a fascist dictator brutally shutting down peaceful democratic protest by responsible and sensible protestors who made their point clearly and calmly and even had the decency to protest wearing health and safety acceptable clothing proving that their demonstration was in the same spirit as those other peaceful protests of 1968, 1848 and 1789... er... the peaceful leftist movement sensibly demanded an end to brutal imperialist fuel taxes which would have helped the fight against the global climate change death spiral... er... anyway the point is that movement was regrettably hijacked by violent right-wing protestors against whom all violence would be justified so hurrah for the gendarmes who mowed them down... er... anyway the protestors were nonetheless justified in burning loads of cars to ensure those very cars could no longer benefit from any prospective savings on their fuel tax... er... anyway yet again Macron has channelled the fascist Napoleon (bad Napoleon who invaded Russia, not good Napoleon who fought royalist tyrant brutes of the quasi-dictatorial British feudal nepotocracy) and will reap a whirlwind when peaceful yet violent lefto-anarcho-brutalists sweep him from his throne and once and for all stop him suppressing our far-right anarchist comrades... er... er...**

## British street protests

■ HALF a million people take to the streets to protest, carrying amusing signs which will get shared thousands of time on Facebook. This amiable, peaceful gathering is so good-humoured and reasonable that the politicians have no option wbut to totally ignore its demands.

## French street protests

■ TENS of thousands of people take to the streets, carrying not very amusing Molotov cocktails.

This furious, violent gathering soon descends into such an orgy of destruction that the politicians have no option but to agree to its demands.

# Let's Parlez Franglais!

### Numéro 94

## Président Macron et Les Riots

**Macron** *(pour c'est lui standing outside Le Palais d'Elysée)*: Pourquoi would anyone veut quitter l'Europe? With moi en charge, tout va bien!

*(Une voiture explodes dans flammes et les gendarmes chargent aux protestors avec les jackets hi-vis)*

**Protesteur un**: A bas Macron! Down avec le fuel tax extortionaire!

**Macron**: Vraiment, la Grande Bretagne est mad comme un serpent! Après le Brexit, il y aura le trouble sur les rues.

**Protesteur deux**: ...de Paris!!

**Macron**: Non, non! De Londres! Le Royaume Uni est un pays divisé et toxique!

**Protesteur trois**: Ah, Monsieur le Pot, ou should that être Président Kettle?

**Macron** *(channelling le late Michel Vainqueur dans l'advertisement)*: Calmez-vous down, cheri. It's seulement un tax nécessaire. Allez-vous chez vous! Vous should être ashamed de vous-même.

**Protesteur un**: Je ne peux pas aller chez moi parce que ma voiture est on fire...

**Macron**: Non, non, la vie est en rose!!

**Protesteur deux**: ...et vos pantalons brûlent aussi!



## What should Nigel Farage's new party be called? You decide...

1. FUKIP
2. The National Farage Party
3. The Nigel Front
4. The British Nigel Party
5. The National Fruitcake Party
6. The Nigel Farage Watneys Party Seven
7. The Publican Party
8. Nigel's Delicious Xmas Party Recipes
9. The Children's Party *(entertainer: Nigel the Clown, very reasonable rate)*
10. Party McParty Face.

**Simply register your vote and then get furious when you win!**

## FARAGE QUITS UKIP

*"It's full of extremists"*

## POPE QUITS CHURCH

*"It's full of Catholics"*

## BEAR QUITS WOODS

*"It's full of shit" (see Farage)*

# PROPOSED QUESTION FOR SECOND REFERENDUM

**Q** Do you think there should be a referendum on having a second referendum?

*"If anyone wants me, I'll be in the detail"*

# MEGHAN MARKLE – ESTRANGED DAD SEEKS TO REKINDLE RELATIONSHIP

by Our Royal Correspondent **E. Bay Ocction**

**FURIOUS at being shut out of his daughter's life for constantly selling stories about her, Thomas Markle, the estranged father of the Duchess of Sussex, says he's making one last attempt to build bridges by selling every last piece of correspondence between them to the tabloids.**

"These letters, notes and emails from Meghan show her deep love and affection for me," said Thomas Markle, cashing a rather substantial cheque.

"Particularly moving are the sections where Meghan pleads with me to stop being a blood-sucking leech, feeding off her new-found fame, and begs me to never make the content of these letters public.

"The public needs to see these letters in full to know the deep affection I have for the most special thing in my life – my bank account."

Asked about the Markle spat, a Palace spokesman chuckled quietly to himself and said waspishly, "What do you expect when you let Americans join the family?"

# FAREWELL, GEORGE BUSH SENIOR

I love presidents' funerals – bring on the next one


## ME AND MY SPOON

THIS WEEK

**CAROLE MIDDLETON**

*Reprinted with kind permission from the Daily Spoonograph*

**May I just say how beautiful and young you look, Mrs Middleton?**

Thank you very much.

**Do you have a favourite spoon?**

I do. It's any spoon from the Middleton Party Spoon Collection, which retails at a very reasonable £949.49 for six plastic metal-style spoons.

**You've got terrific legs for a woman your age...**

At £949.99 these spoons are incredible value. And will really get your party going, even if the guests don't include my son-in-law, who happens to be the heir to the throne. But I don't want to talk about William, my daughter Kate, or my grandson George, who's also a future King.

**Your hair is so glossy too, and you look even younger and more petite in real life than you do in the amazing photos that we see everywhere...**

The Middleton Right-Royal Party Spoon Collection is even better than the standard Party Spoon Collection. The spoons come in quality silver-effect plastic, with a Royal crest featuring a lion and a spoonicorn. And they really are a snip at £9,494.99.

**You're so perfectly tanned and you have such a thin waist – how do you do it?**

You'll find that all our spoons in the Middleton Party Spoon range are multi-purpose. They've been specially designed with both handle and scooping mechanism for a variety of spooning functions, including stirring tea, transporting sugar from bowl to cup, and even putting jam on your scone. I can particularly recommend the Deluxe Middleton Top-of-the-Range range in gold-standard plastic, retailing at just £94,949.99.

**Did your love of plastic spoons begin when you were an air hostess?**

I told you not to mention that! Your nearest exits are there, there and there.

NEXT WEEK: *Holly Willoughby – Me and my Holly.*

# POETRY CORNER

**In Memoriam**
**Windsor Davies, actor**

So. Farewell
Then Windsor Davies.
You were in *Z Cars*,
*Dr Who* and many
Other TV shows
Of yesteryear.

But you were most
Famous for the part
Of Sergeant Major
"Shut Up" Williams in
*It Aint't Half Hot*
*Mum*, with your
Famous catchphrase,
"Oh dear, how sad,
Never mind."

Now you have
Been silenced.
Oh dear, it is
Sad and we
Do mind.

And wherever
You're going,
We hope it ain't
Half hot mum.

E.J. "Lah-di-dah" Thribb
(17½ series)

## News in brief

# Pippa content 'still as thin as ever'

■ Bikini pics of Pippa Middleton taken on holiday in St Barts just 11 weeks after she gave birth have revealed that the stories about her are as thin as ever.

Said a friend of Pippa's, "That's literally the whole story, she's on the beach on holiday... it's actually scarily thin and devoid of real content... I hope the editors responsible for running it don't have some sort of disorder which means they're addicted to scarily thin content in 2019 and *(cont. p94)*

# Nursery Times

Friday, Once-upon-a-time

## OWL AND PUSSYCAT RESCUED AT SEA

by Our Migration Staff **Little Boat Peeple**

NURSERYLAND was shocked by an upsurge in the number of migrants desperate to get to the Land Where the Bong Tree Grows.

The latest refugees were revealed to be an owl and a pussycat who had clearly paid bird and cat traffickers large sums of money (plenty, wrapped up in a five-pound note) to provide a poorly-equipped, pea-green boat to make the hazardous journey.

The boat was overloaded with the couple's possessions, including honey, quince, mince, a runcible spoon and a small guitar.

Coastguards said that they were fortunate that the silvery moon provided plenty of light and they were alerted to the presence of the boat by the sound of an owl singing.

But not everyone was delighted that the avian/feline rescue mission had been successful.

"We've got quite enough birds over here already," said one furious resident. "Only last week we had four-and-twenty of them, black ones, smuggled here in a pie! And as for cats – down the well, that's the best place for them."

## GOVERNMENT WARNS OVER SUGAR DANGERS

by Our Sugar Correspondent **Pelham Fairy**

AUTHORITIES in Nurseryland have yet again cautioned residents over the risks associated with sugar consumption.

They pointed to a recent case of a brother and sister, known only as Child H and Child G, who nearly died after eating half a gingerbread house covered in sweets and candy.

A spokesman said, "Our research shows that this kind of sugar consumption can easily result in being put in the oven and eaten by a witch. We recommend that youngsters switch to something more organic, such as curds and whey – though there are associated risks with this diet, such as spiders coming down, sitting beside you and frightening you off your tuffet."

## CHINA SENDS WATER BUFFALO OVER MOON

by Our Chinese Leader Writer **Chairman Moo**

THE Nurseryland space race hotted up, as the land of Old Cathay announced it had successfully launched a water buffalo over the moon.

The Chinese authorities claimed the moon as Chinese territory and arrested the man in the moon for incorrect thinking, and sent him to be rehabilitated. The Little Dog laughed, but not for long as he too was arrested for subversion.

"He's in the soup – make no mistake," said his friend the cat with the zhonghu.

The rice bowl was unavailable for comment, as it had run away with the chopstick before being arrested for *(cont. p94)*

# New high-speed train plans

by Our Rail Staff
**Victoria Station-Mitchell**

HS2 have announced plans to make the new high-speed link cheaper by slowing the trains down.

When accused of being mad, a spokesman said, "This makes perfect sense – if the trains go slower then we don't have to build all the high-speed stuff and so it's much cheaper. It's win-win for everyone!"

To capitalise on the success of this idea, the company is planning a further refinement – not just slower trains, but no trains at all.

"It's the logical next step," said the spokesman. "It will save millions in rolling stock and commuters will know exactly where they stand – on the platform waiting for a non-existent train.

"An added bonus is that the lack of trains means that there will be no delays, no cancellations, no strikes, no complaints about the buffet, and no lack of seats for Labour leaders who sit on the floor. HS2 is going to be the most efficient rail operator in the world."

### Late News

- HS2 admit paying consultants £600m for money-saving ideas.

**New proposed route for HS2**

*Exclusive to all newspapers*

# STUDY FINDS TEENAGE GIRLS WHO SPEND ALL DAY ON SOCIAL MEDIA TEND TO BE MORE DEPRESSED

On other pages

- Bears "much more likely to relieve themselves in wooded areas"
- Popes who are appointed to head the Church "have a preponderance towards Catholicism"

# 'Screen time should be rationed'

IN a major new study carried out by children, it was revealed today that spending too much time glued to screens is bad for parents.

"I have never actually seen my parents without an iPhone or an iPad in their hands. They have them on the sofa while watching the telly, at the dinner table and even when they go to bed," said one worried nine-year-old.

"I worry what damage that is doing to their ageing, mushy, middle-aged brains."

The study found that parents who spend all day updating their Facebook, Instagram and Twitter accounts with snippets from their "perfect family life", in the hope of impressing people they used to go to school with, tend to be more depressed than parents who don't judge their entire self-worth as adults on meaningless clicks on social media.

# PROJECT FEAR LATEST

# STOCKPILE THIS MAGAZINE NOW!

**Nightmare shortages of satirical periodicals forecast for No-Deal Brexit**

**PRIVATE EYE TO BE EVACUATED TO CANADA**

# CROSS-PARTY CONSENSUS

I'm not listening to my party
And I'm not listening to mine

# Why can't they agree on Brexit?

## Despairing politicians attack 'useless public'

by Our Political Staff
**Laura Laura-Laughs**

A CLEARLY fed-up House of Commons collectively attacked what they called the "hopeless, bickering, divided and self-interested electorate" for failing to come up with a clear vision of what they wanted out of Brexit.

Said one MP, "They've had years since the referendum to work out what they voted for and they still can't come to any sort of consensus."

Said another, "Frankly, I've lost confidence in the public. I know technically it's their decision, but honestly, I'm not sure they're up to it."

Yet another added, "I don't want to be rude, but they're bringing democracy into disrepute. Half of them say one thing, half of them say something completely different. They don't listen to each other. Surely it can't be too much to ask them to sit down, knock some heads together and work something out."

With the country in gridlock, there are now calls for an Electorate of National Unity, in which people from all sides can actually sit at dinner without throwing roast potatoes at each other because Uncle Ted wants to have things back as they were before all this malarkey, and his nephew keeps calling him a racist fascist Northern gammon, while Auntie Maureen just wishes everyone would keep their voices down, be nice and adopt plan B until dessert, preferably with no argument about whether crème brûlée is a betrayal of British puddings or whether Spotted Dick is just colonialist nostalgia on a plate – oh no, put the knives down, lads, it's all kicking off... *(continued until 2094)*

# Jeremy Corbyn *WRITES*

**HELLO! It's me again. Well, it's all go here! After a quiet couple of years, Team Corbyn is now a hive of activity!**

Refusing to meet with people, knocking back requests to negotiate, ignoring pleas to clarify our position on key issues of the day! Phew! Let me tell you, folks, doing nothing gets more and more exhausting with every passing day!

Is it me or is it just getting harder these days to keep out of politics? Time was, I was in a league of my own, following my own conscience with my trusty placard, sleeping bag, Thermos and wigwam, ready to join any protest against any government.

But now, with the Prime Minister wasting a whole two years on her Brexit deal and having nothing to show for it, I can feel the title of "Most Consistent But Ineffectual Politician in British History" slipping away!

I'm ashamed to say, I panicked a bit last week and tabled a Motion of No Confidence, which I knew wouldn't achieve anything, just to say, "I'm still here, Mrs May, and I'm just as consistent and ineffectual as you are"!

So since that little fracas in the Commons, I'm on the alert for Theresa tricking me into doing something positive. For example, this invitation to come to Number 10 for "talks" is a classic trap!

For a start, the invitation was very easy to resist. As you know, I'm very picky about the people I meet! But Theresa May knows my weakness! The lengths she will go to in order to get a face-to-face with old Jezza!

Suddenly she is willing to tear up the Good Friday Agreement, plunge Northern Ireland into a warzone and make a united Ireland more likely... now I'm tempted!

She's only got to start firing a machine gun into the air at the Remembrance Day parade and sending out the whips to kneecap Dominic Grieve and I'll be sorely tempted to be at Number 10 for tea and biccies!

Cheerio!

# BREXIT CHAOS – CAMERON SPEAKS

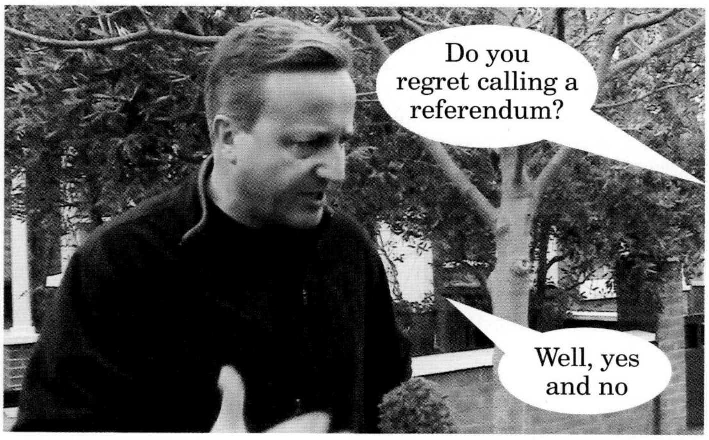
Do you regret calling a referendum?
Well, yes and no

CANNABIS NOW LEGAL IN CANADA
Cordell

"Hey, we should totally move to Canada"

"Dude, we're in Canada"

## Exclusive to all papers
# AN APOLOGY

**IN recent years, we may have given the impression in our coverage of traffic collisions that this newspaper was in some way opposed to people driving when they were well into their nineties, on the grounds that this might increase the chances of an unwelcome traffic incident. Headlines such as DOZY NANA IS DEATHTRAP IN A DATSUN, or GET OFF THE ROAD, GRANDPA, YOU'RE A BLOODY MENACE and PRISON FOR ALL NONAGENARIAN BOY RACERS NOW may have added to this regrettable impression.**

**We now realise, in the light of Prince Philip suffering a car crash, in which two reckless women and a baby brutally slammed into the Duke of Edinburgh's car, that there is not a jot or tittle of truth in our previous articles. In order to correct any unfortunate misinterpretation, we have this week run a series of stories including BAN MUMS FROM DRIVING FORD KIAS NOW, ANOTHER WOMAN DRIVER TRIES TO BUMP OFF OUR GRACIOUS DUKE and FOR CHRIST'S SAKE, LET THE NATION'S BELOVED GREAT-GRANDFATHER DRIVE WHEREVER HE MAY PLEASE. We hope that makes things clear and we apologise for any confusion that we may have caused.**

Advertisement

***HAVE YOU BEEN INJURED in an accident or car crash with a member of the Royal family that wasn't your fault?***

## Then you could be entitled to nothing... that's right, absolutely NOTHING!

- **Not an apology from Prince Philip**
- **Not a phone call from the palace**
- **Not even a bunch of flowers**

Contact **Direct Line of Succession** today and we can organise for you to receive absolutely nothing from the Royal family* almost immediately.

We'll process your claim that the 97-year-old Royal was somehow to blame for the accident and settle on our decision to award you nothing within minutes.

So pick up the phone today... (with your non-broken arm obviously) and discover how little you're worth!

**One more interview with the Sunday Mirror and we know a swan who'll break your other arm.*

# POETRY CORNER

**In Memoriam Chewbacca**

So. Farewell
Then Peter Mayhew,
Better known as
"Chewbacca" of
*Star Wars* fame.

"Mwaaaaargh!",
That was your
Catchphrase.

*"That was the
Wookie that was"*
Will be your
Epitaph.

E.J. Thribb
poeticsolutions.com

## Film highlights
All channels

**Driving Miss Lizzy** (2019)
Charming period drama in which an elderly chauffeur drives his employer around the deep south of Norfolk.

Don't miss the climactic scene where Lizzy shouts "Help!" and tries to get out.

## School news

**St Vegetables (formerly St Cakes)**

Obesity Term begins today. There are 137 overweight boys in the school and 142 overweight girls. R.P. Gastric-Band (Scoffers) is Bread Boy. J.T. Slimmington-Pill (Thinners) is Bread Girl. Weightwatchers will be held in the gymnasium (formerly the Tuck Shop) every morning at 9am, supervised by Mrs Thinny Woodall O.C. The 26-mile school run will take place every afternoon, beginning at Tubby's Yard, through Bloater's Meadow, ending up at the Old Fattery. The new Sports Master is Mr L.P. O'Suction who joins St Vegetables from the prestigious public school, Non-Eton. The school production of *Salad Days* will replace the *Life of Pie* on February 26th. Tickets from the Welsh bursar, Mr Dai Betes.

## ME AND MY SPOONS

**TIM MARTIN**
Wetherspoons Boss

**What kind of Spoons do you like?**

I like my Spoons British. You won't find my Spoons in France or Germany or Spain or bloody Brussels. Though I wouldn't mind a Spoons in Gibraltar or one in the Falklands.

**Aren't you worried about the impact of Brexit on your Spoons?**

Yeah – I'm worried what I'm going to do with all that extra lolly. My Spoons are going to be full of people celebrating their new-found wealth.

**Or drowning their sorrows?**

You're barred.

**Aren't your Spoons very cheap and very tacky?**

I resent that! Only the carpet's tacky because it's had so much cheap booze spilt on it. Are you looking for a fight? Because you've come to the right place!

## THE RECRUITMENT ADVERT THAT CAPITA DID NOT RUN

# *DIARY*

JIMMY PAGE VS ROBBIE WILLIAMS

***From the diary of Jimmy Page***

Another sleepless night, thanks to Mr Robbie So-Called Williams.

My log book informs me that at 03.30am, 03.47am, 04.19am and 05.43am, and subsequently at 06.22am, I was convinced I could hear the sound of a person or persons constructing an underground sports and leisure centre beneath the neighbouring garden, *even though the local authorities have expressly forbidden Williams and/or his family and/or employees from engaging in this and/or similar activities.*

Inevitably, when I looked through my binoculars, I could see no activity, which is the way these people work. The guy has no scruples whatsoever about taking elaborate steps to cover-up all his illegal night-based building operations.

But he's not going to win. As a wise man once said, for evil to triumph you've just got to sit back and do nothing while someone builds extensions next door.

***From the diary of Robbie Williams***

What d'you know? I spotted old Pagey-boy peering at me through those bloody binoculars of his all the way through the night, specifically at 03.30am, 03.47am, 04.19am, 05.43am, and 06.22am. I was hiding in a bush and making banging noises, just to get on his goat!! Blimey, you'd think an old geezer like that would have something better to do with his life than stay up all night fussing about his next-door neighbour!

***From the diary of Jimmy Page***

Had some of my old mates round for a few hands of cribbage, just to take my mind off it.

Jeff Beck, Keith Richards and Eric Clapton all love coming to play round my place, as my cribbage board is one of the oldest and most expensive in the world, a real collector's piece, believed to be by Jezemiah Cribbage himself, and the spillikins are hand-crafted in Brazilian green onyx by a follower of Ferdinand Preiss, no less. Not that that would mean anything to Mr "Let Me Entertain You" next door, who has no sense of history.

Cribbage is a great way to relax and catch up with old friends. "Can you honestly believe it?" I say to Jeff, while the other two are mulling over their next moves. "The guy calls himself an 'entertainer'. Entertainer! Could have fooled me! 'Let me entertain you'. Yeah, go on, mate – entertain me! Jump out your top floor window! Give us all a fuckin' laugh!

"Entertainer? Him? What's the world coming to? In our day, the word 'entertainer' was restricted to only the very few. Jimi. Janis. Keith Moon. Bob 'The Bear' Hite. We'd never use it to describe a fat bloke waddling about on stage waving his arms around and singing crap songs in a flat voice, no fuckin' way!"

"Your go, Jimmy," says Keith. Keith has a bit of a cough.

"Strepsil, mate?" I ask, reaching for my silver Strepsil case with its William Morris interior. These days, I have all my Strepsils hand-crafted for me, by Mariella von Strepsil at the Strepsil workshop in Bonn. I find it makes all the difference.

***From the diary of Robbie Williams***

There's all these reports saying I got 46 bedrooms or whatever that I don't need, but that's total pants 'cos what they don't realise is a dozen are for staff. Well, I call them staff but they're like mates who do things for me for money and they need their own kitchen and sitting rooms and saunas because we can't have them hanging out with us, and they all have cars, which – dur! – need garages, so obviously that means the house is way too small and so we need a mega-extension, do the math.

But for Old Pagey next door, it's all just "me-me-me". This is the way it goes, right? My guys bung in a planning application and seconds later his guys go all queeny, saying oooh, deary fucking me, it'll make Old Pagey's house fall down or whatever. Question: why don't he just buy himself a decent house which won't fall down when the bloke next door's banging a nail in the wall?

If you ask me, he's just jealous. Listen, I've had seven number one hit singles, I've sung with Kylie, I'm attracting a whole new audience as a family entertainer on The X Factor. I'm living the fuckin' dream – and it's tearing him apart. And answer me this, mate. When was the last time Led Zeppelin was asked to the wedding of Princess Eugenie?

And the guy can't take a joke, that's a fact. This afternoon, he was back up there, peering through his lens, so I went out into the garden, dropped my trousers and gave the old bum a bit of an airing! Then I looked back at him through my telescope and he wasn't laughing, just scowling. Entertainment? He doesn't know the meaning of the word!

***From the diary of Jimmy Page***

Today at 15.22pm, I took three photographs of Williams' bottom, for future use. At 15.57, I took a further six photographs of him on his first-floor balcony talking to a man wearing a suit and tie and carrying something, maybe a clipboard. Looked to me like an architect or surveyor. Or could be a hit-man.

What's Williams scheming now? Looks like he's planning to extend his balcony so he can construct some kind of permanent outdoor stage, which'll mean he'll want a 700-seat auditorium in his garden, with an array of amplifiers, sound systems, mixers, lighting facilities, bars, burger and/or hot dog stands, the lot. But it's *expressly forbidden*!

***From the diary of Robbie Williams***

I was thinking about it all night. So, after breakfast, I called the architects. Told 'em to draw up plans to burrow right through to below Old Pagey's house and build an underground all-nite disco and entertainment centre, with extra-thin ceilings, 'cos they say he's deaf.

***From the diary of Jimmy Page***

To my horror, one of my prized china figurines has developed a crack at its base. It's irreplaceable – an exquisite piece, crafted in Belgium, of myself and Mr Robert Plant motoring a vintage Rolls Royce into a hotel swimming pool, believed to be somewhere in Los Angeles. There's only one person to blame – that fat good-for-nothing oaf next door doing his infernal press-ups!

My doctor suggests a period of rest. So I head straight for my Stannah Stairlift to Heaven, and press to ascend.

*As told to*
CRAIG BROWN

# EU-phemisms

*"Time is running out to do a deal"*

**Soon there won't be a European economy to argue over**

*"The EU will not be engaging in constructive negotiations at this point in Brexit"*

**Why start now?**

*"The EU has done everything it must to prepare for the economic consequences of Brexit"*

**Work out who to blame**

*"The parliament will not stop the real work of the EU"*

**Claiming expenses, employing relatives, misappropriating funds...**

## EYE FOCUS

# We reveal the secret woman in Boris' life

SHE'S been kept out of the limelight and Boris is saying nothing about her, but at last the Eye can reveal exactly who she is.

Yes, it's Mrs Zaghari-Ratcliffe, the once-bubbly teacher who didn't catch Boris' imagination. Friends say that the ex-Foreign Secretary and the Iranian prison inmate have a lot in common – they have both, for example, just been on a strict diet, and lost a lot of weight.

Both of them are keen Leavers, him from Europe, and her from prison, and neither of them are too worried about the deal, so long as they get out.

He's always in her thoughts, and she's not in his at all. It's touching. Both are now talking about marriage – Boris, who's about to embark on his third to some fruity woman who used to work for the Tory party, and Mrs Zaghari-Ratcliffe, who thought her first one might entitle her to some protection from the former British Foreign Secretary instead of him landing her in it and *(cont. p94)*

# GLENDA SLAGG

### Fleet Street's Prime Amazon!! (Geddit? As in Female Warrior, Stoopid!!?)

■ **JEFF BEZOS!!!! Dontchahatehim!??!! He's the world's richest man – well, not any more!!? Now that Mr Amazon, aka Baldy Bezos, has dumped his loyal missus and run off with a Foxy (Geddit??!!) lovely from TV's La La Land, he's got to deliver a $55 billion package round to his ex-wife's place!!?! Serves you right, Jiltin' Jeff – specially since Mrs TV Totty was the wife of your Bezzy friend!!?! In fact, why don't you just Bezz off??!!?!**

■ JEFF BEZOS!! Dontchaluvhim?!! OK, he's ditched his wife and asked Alexa for a divorce!!?!?! (That's the virtual assistant, stoopid!!?) Who wouldn't, if you were the world's richest and therefore most attractive nerd??!! Good luck to you, Bonker Bezos, and to your new glamorous gal from the land of guacamole!!?! The geeks shall inherit the earth – well, half of it, anyway, since the rest goes to his ex!!???

■ **JEFF BEZOS?! *(You've done this. Ed.)* At least he ran off with someone his own age!?? Fancy someone a little bit older, Jeff??! I'll *stay* in for you especially, Jeff!! Don't go next door or *(You're fired. Ed.)***

***Byeee!!***

# Those Boris 'n' Carrie pet names in full

**YOU DECIDE what Britain's top loved-up political couple should call each other**

**Names for Him**

Bozzie Bear
Bozzie Bare
Bozzie Bare-Faced Liar
Bozzie Bore
Bozzie Bastard
Bozzie McBozface
Bozzie RRS David Attenborough

**Names for Her**

Little Otter
Little Rotter
Otterly Shameless
Carrie-on-With-Somebody-else's Husband

*(That's enough. Ed.)*

## What You Won't Read in the Spectator

### High life
*Tacki*

How dare pipsqueak leftie Owen Jones suggest on television that the Spectator provides a platform for extremist right-wing rants and allows its columnists to flirt with racism?

I expect this pathetic allegation was only allowed on the BBC (the Bagel Broadcasting Corporation) because Mr Jones is Jewish. And with a name like Owen, would it be too fanciful to suggest that, like his famous namesake, the Olympic runner Mr Jesse Owen, he is actually black?

No wonder, with such obvious cultural bias, Jones is allowed on the BBC (Bolshevik Broadcasting Collective) in order to be rude to the Spectator's publisher, the estimable Mr Brillo Pad, and to cast aspersions on Mr Pad's ability to criticise other European magazines for encouraging right-wing populist movements like the excellent Golden Dawn, who this poor little Greek boy happens to think are the best fascists since *(cont. every week since 1694)*

# Diane Abbott – Question Time racism

by Our Television Correspondent
**Ray Cist**

Diane Abbott has accused *Question Time* of racism after she alleged that she was invited on to the show and ridiculed.

"Someone deliberately tampered with my microphone. They turned it on, meaning people could hear what I was saying.

"The BBC and Fiona Bruce clearly had an agenda to ensure I'm not seen as a serious politician, first by inviting me on to the show and, secondly, by allowing the general public to hear me defending Jeremy's Brexit strategy of not having one," Diane Abbott wrote in a furious Facebook post.

"This is out and out racism, other politicians may not have twigged what *Question Time* was up to, but I quickly put two and two together and got three thousand six hundred and fifty-nine."

Momentum drew parallels between the racism Diane Abbott endured taking a seat on the *Question Time* panel to that which Rosa Parks experienced when she took a seat on a bus in Montgomery, Alabama, in 1955.

"Just as Rosa was unceremoniously carted off to jail, Diane was unceremoniously carted off to the Green Room for some mediocre white wine served at room temperature and then railroaded into a BBC cab home."

## GRAYLING TRANSPORT LATEST

Clap your hands if you believe in ferries

# Sajid Javid blamed for new immigrant crisis

by Our Home Affairs Staff **Phil Boat**

THE Home Secretary found himself under fire this week after he was accused of being personally responsible for large numbers (10) of migrants illegally landing on the beaches of Kent.

One critic said, "Mr Javid must take the blame for this flood (15) of desperate asylum seekers. They have quite clearly taken one look at Mr Javid and decided that if someone as useless as him can get to the top in Britain, then there's hope for all of them."

Said one Iranian, "Britain is obviously a land of unparalleled opportunity where even the most hopeless son of an immigrant will be given a government hand-out in the form of a Cabinet minister's salary."

When asked to comment, Mr Javid said, "It is not my fault that evil people smugglers are using me as an enticement to come to Britain. All I want is a better future for myself, preferably as Prime Minister. If you'd like me to comment further, you'll find my door is always closed."

WE'RE LOOKING FOR THOSE LITTLE WHITE FLOWERED ROCKERY PLANTS

Alyssum seekers

## DOVER PREPARES FOR BREXIT CHAOS

We're trucked!
Do a U-turn!
The government is promising jam tomorrow AND jam today!

# GRAYLING 'DEFENDS CONTRACT'

by Our Chris Grayling Correspondent **Des Aster**

TRANSPORT Secretary Chris Grayling has defended awarding a £13.8m ferry contract to a company that has no ferries nor any experience of operating them, saying he's merely learning from the lessons of the past.

"Whilst operating the rail network, I've awarded contracts to run train services to companies which have trains, and look at the unmitigated disaster that has been," said the strange, bald, robot man, yesterday.

"So, to avoid the possibilities of ferries running late or being cancelled due to adverse weather, I've awarded the contract to a company with no ferries, meaning problem solved.

"Anyone who has followed my government career from being Prisons Minister to Transport Secretary will know I approve of people being given jobs to which they are totally unsuited."

Meanwhile Seaborne Freight Ltd has apologised after it was revealed that it took its terms and conditions from a pizza delivery firm.

"In our defence, there is no way in the world we would be mistaken for a pizza delivery firm, as they are able to deliver," said a Seaborne Freight director, stuffing a suitcase full of £13m of government money and heading for the airport.

A spokesman for Seaborne Freight, however, later confirmed that it was in talks with the pizza delivery firm to purchase a significant number of mopeds which it planned to modify with floats to enable them to make the Channel crossings in April.

### Late news

Chris Grayling has been forced once again to defend the awarding of a new ferry contract, this time to Gerry and the Pacemakers.

"I can assure you, all due diligence was carried out before the decision to award £13m of public money to the Merseybeat band, based solely on the fact they had a chart-topping hit in 1964 with their iconic song, Ferry Across the Mersey.

"Gerry and the Pacemakers' long association with ferries means, to my mind, they are every bit, if not more, qualified to run a ferry service than Seaborne."

**LATE CHRISTMAS GNOMEMART**

It's the

**SEABORNE FREIGHT SHIP IN A BOTTLE**

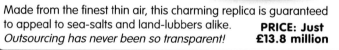

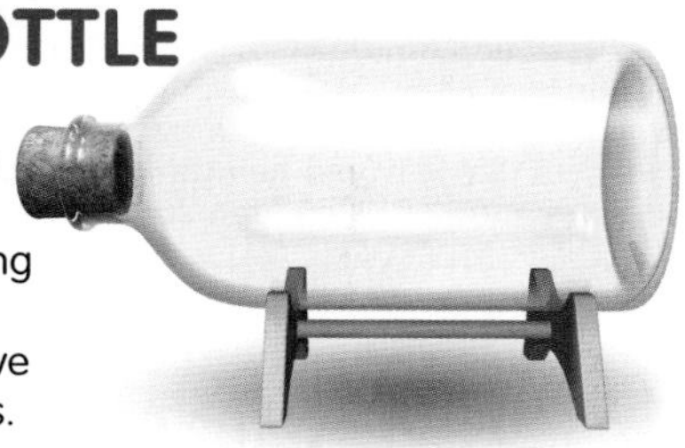

CELEBRATE the government deal of the Century, with this fantastic 125th scale model of the actual ferry that is going to save Britain and keep our economy afloat after we leave the EU and adopt WTO tariffs.

Made from the finest thin air, this charming replica is guaranteed to appeal to sea-salts and land-lubbers alike.

*Outsourcing has never been so transparent!*

**PRICE: Just £13.8 million**

# We managed just fine in the war, say people who weren't there

PEOPLE who have no idea how horrible wars are have used the Second World War as a perfect example of how Britain is capable of surviving the odds.

One 70-year-old, born four years after the war ended, said, "We took on Hitler and the Nazis single-handedly and won, didn't we? So why shouldn't we do it again?"

When it was pointed out that Britain wasn't single-handed and was actually fighting alongside quite a lot of other countries, the septuagenarian declared that this was "treason" and that anyone who disagreed should "shut up".

Someone born quite a long time after the end of the Korean War, but who has been watching the History Channel for the last 30 years, said, "Let's not forget how good the war was for this nation. By the end of it, Britain was economically broken, people had suffered half a decade of hardship, and the nation was completely in hock to the Americans. Why wouldn't we want to do it again?"

# AS BREXIT EMERGENCY MEASURES BITE, WILL BRITAIN RESORT TO MARTIAL LAW?

No. Because we haven't got any troops.

# People's Vote group to split in two

THE pressure group pushing for a second referendum has decided to become a metaphor for the very thing that it is campaigning against, namely the divisive issue of leaving Europe.

Said its leader, Brian Paradox, "Roughly half of us see ourselves as simply a pressure group for a second vote, the other half feel like we're the nucleus for a new centre party, and we can't agree, so I'm leaving and those bastards are remaining.

"Wankers, gits, bastards, traitors, enemies of the People's Vote!" Meanwhile, deputy leader Chris Irony said, "I'm remaining. Brian just doesn't get it. This is a once-in-a-generation opportunity. What a wanker, git, bastard, traitor, enemy of the People's Vote!"

# VOTERS REACT ANGRILY TO IDEA OF SNAP ELECTION

by Our Political Staff **Jon Snowmageddon**

**THE population of the United Kingdom let out a collective groan last night at the suggestion that there might be a June election to cement the government's Brexit withdrawal position.**

One woman, interviewed on television, seemed to sum up the entire nation's mood. When asked about the possibility of another ballot, she turned to the camera and said memorably, "Oh God. Not another excuse for broadcasters to show that clip of Brenda from Bristol again."

She added, "I can't bear it and I think I speak for everyone."

The public's weariness at seeing this clip yet again is believed to have persuaded top government strategists that it would be unwise to call yet another election in 2019 and that they would do better to hold another referendum instead. *(Oh God. Not another one. Ed.)*

## Late News

## BRENDA FROM WINDSOR REACTS WEARILY TO ELECTION RUMOUR

HER Majesty the Queen is said to be deeply bored at the thought of Theresa May appearing yet again to inform her of the dissolution of parliament.

Brenda's previous media appearances have made her a big star amongst TV audiences who are fed up with British politics.

"Brenda tells it like it is," said a woman from Bristol called Brenda who *(cont. 2094)*

# Those Brexit Withdrawal Agreement amendments in full

**PRIVATE EYE's guide to the constitution-breaking innovations that have made Parliament the most exciting British spectacle since the opening of the Millennium Dome**

**The Cooper-Boles amendment**
No-deal off the table (defeated)

**The Parker Bowles amendment**
Camilla to become Queen (defeated)

**The Parker Knoll amendment**
No-deal off the sofa (defeated)

**The Malthouse compromise**
Backstop out of the deal (passed)

**The Maltwhisky compromise**
Who cares, let's have another (passed out)

**The Maltby compromise**
No hand on the knee, Mr Green (pass defeated)

**The Spelman amendment**
No-deal on or off table (passed and ignored)

**The Spellcheck amendment**
No-deel onn th taple (past)

**The Corbyn amendment**
Customs Union, extension of Article 50 and Tony Blair to be tried as war criminal (passed it)

**The Grieve conundrum**
New film based on the novels of Robert Ludlum, in which Jason Bourne comes out of retirement and faces his biggest challenge yet, to come up with a functional compromise amendment to see off the plans for world domination by sinister right-wing organisation ERG. *(That's enough amendments. Ed.)*

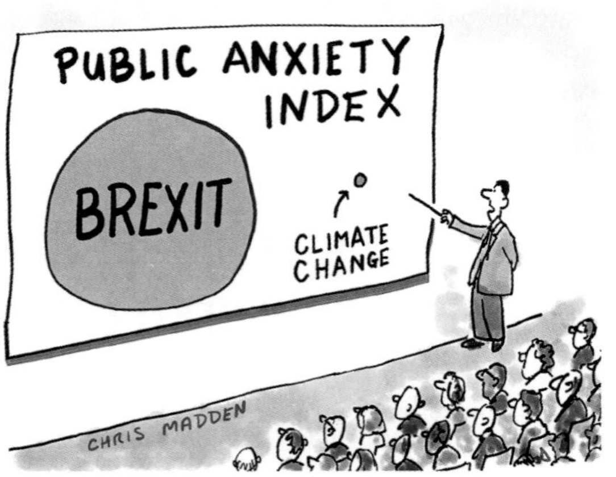


# MEETING WITH A MONSTER

*"It was chilling. He was completely without remorse. He made my flesh creep," said serial killer, Bernard Giles.*

## News in brief

# How Could We Have Guessed?

■ The film community has expressed astonishment at claims by former model and actress Christina Englehardt that she had a relationship with 41-year-old Woody Allen when she was a 16-year-old in the 1970s.

"If only we had had even a tiny hint of Woody Allen's disturbing obsession with extremely young girls from his acclaimed movies down the decades; films such as 1979's *Middle-aged man lusts after sexy young girl*, 1992's *Much older middle-aged man lusts after sexy young girl* and 2009's *Very old man lusts after sexy young girl*," said all movie buffs.

"I certainly never got any sense that Woody was weirdly obsessed with young girls when I attended his wedding at the age of 52 to his 27-year-old step daughter," said one prestigious movie critic.

Could this mean that Woody Allen's latest film *Extremely old man lusts after sexy young girl* may now never be released?

**Judith Kerr's wake**

# Notes&queries

## Who or what is Huawei?

● Huawei is a traditional shout of encouragement in the North East of England, as in "Huawei the lads" (or nowadays I expect we have to say "Huawei the lasses"!). Sunderland FC (and no doubt Sunderland Ladies FC!!) have adopted this as their official slogan. For any Southerners reading (!!!), it roughly translates into received pronunciation as "I'll have a fishy on a little dishy".
*The Reverend Geordie Greggs-Vegan-Roll (Tyne and Huaweir).*

● I'm afraid the good Reverend is Huawei with the fairies on this one. "Huawei" is the Pacific island that was the location for the long-running US police and surfing procedural TV drama *Huawei Five-0*, starring Steve McGarrett as "Book 'im Danno" Dyer. Guest stars included the young Judi Dench, who played McGarrett's girlfriend and can be seen in the canoe – third paddler on the left in the title sequence – featuring the famous theme music by Piers Moronione.
*The Hon. Lulu Grass-skirt (Honolulu).*

● Aloha pedants! You've got this one completely wrong. "Huawei", pronounced "Who are we?", is a giant Chinese communication firm that produces mobile phone technology. They originally got their name from a long-running joke which went as follows: "Knock knock. *Who's there?* Huawei. We're the Chinese government masquerading as a commercial firm in order to spy on the whole world." The humour is possibly lost in translation from the original Mandarin, but Chinese friends assure me that it is a very funny joke, but best not told in the presence of any Chinese authority figure or indeed any Huawei handset.
*Ai Huawei-wei (Tate Modern).*

# Queen's appeal for 'calm' provokes angry Twitterstorm

MPs and members of the public erupted in fury yesterday over the Queen's "unfortunate" and "outrageous" plea for the nation to "calm down".

Addressing a recent meeting of the Sandringham Women's Institute, the Queen had suggested to the 40 ladies present that it was "a good thing for people to behave with courtesy to each other and should treat other people's views with respect".

This was widely viewed as a "wholly unacceptable political intervention by the Queen" in the debate over Brexit, and "an insult to Parliament".

Said one MP, "It is not for the Queen to give us all lectures on how to behave. This woman tells us that we should respect other people's views. She should keep out of politics and learn when to keep her silly mouth shut."

Despite repeated calls, the Queen was last night unavailable for comment.

# POETRY CORNER

**Lines on the retirement of John Humphrys from Radio 4's 'Today' programme**

So. Farewell
Then John Humphrys.

I'm sorry, I'm going
To have to stop
You there.
We've run out
Of time.

Yes, that was
Your catchphrase,
And now we can all
Say it to you.

E.J. Thribb (17½ times more money than my female co-poets)

**EXCLUSIVE TO THE SUNDAY TIMES**

# Ratcliffe leaves sinking ship

by Our Maritime Staff
**Tim Shipshape**

Billionaire rat, Sir James Ratcliffe, last night admitted that he was making plans to desert the RMS *Brexitanic* and swim to Monaco.

"It's purely a business matter," said the entrepreneur rodent, "and not because I want to avoid paying tax or going down with the *Brexitanic*."

Asked why he had constantly maintained that the *Brexitanic* was "unsinkable" and destined to "sail into the sunlit uplands", he replied, "I was advised by top vermin accountants, PriceWaterlogged, that jumping off the ship and scuttling off to Monaco was fiscally prudent and would in no way make me look like a total rat."

Sir James Ratcliffe was recently knighted in acknowledgement of his classic "rats-to-riches story".

Sir James concluded, "I still have a lot of confidence in the *Brexitanic*, but sadly it's every rat for himself" *(cont. 2094)*

## WHAT NEXT FOR THE JIHADI BRIDE? YOU DECIDE

**I'M A CELEBRITY**

**STRICTLY COME DANCING**

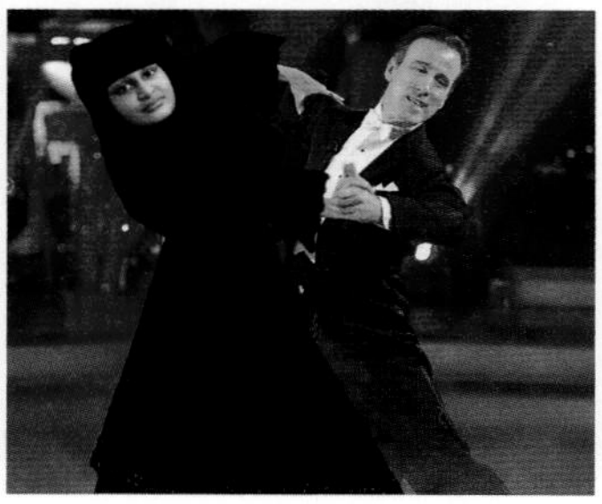

**LOVE ISLAND**

**HAVE I GOT NEWS**

# The Caracas Times

Friday, 8 February 2019

NEWSPAPER MOTTO: YOU DON'T HAVE TO BE CARACAS TO WORK HERE, BUT IT HELPS

# Venezuela demands Britain holds elections, as Mayduro clings on

by Our Man in London
**Guaido Fawkes**

THE Venezuelan government last night threw its weight behind Opposition leader Jeremy Corbyn, saying it was time for a proper socialist to run Britain.

The President said, "Britain's in chaos, teetering on the brink of civil war, with shortages looming in the shops, and martial law a real possibility. It is time to topple the hated leader, Mayduro. She has no legitimacy. The last election was a farce, and she has only rigged a majority by paying bribes to the DUP."

The British government furiously hit back, saying they wouldn't be told how to run their chaos by the likes of Venezuela. "They're just after our oil," said Mayduro, "and they're wasting their time, because it's run out."

Jeremy Corbyn has meanwhile declared himself the legitimate Prime Minister, and has been recognised by a number of international super-powers, such as Cuba, Mexico and Hamas.

*The Guardian* Friday February 8 2019

## Letters

May we, the undersigned, express our total and utter disgust at the totally sickening and utterly predictable stance taken by the so-called Guardian newspaper with regard to the entirely legitimate and utterly blameless Marxist-Leninist-Chavezist-Madurist-Corbynist government of Venezuela which is being cynically undermined by reactionary-Trumpist-Blairist-neo-Liberals in the media like the hated Guardian who are acting merely as the useful idiots and friendly running dogs of the fascist imperial interventionist military industrial complex led by the hated US who are totally and utterly and sickening responsible for the entire made-up Venezuelan crisis which has been orchestrated merely to discredit the forces of international socialism and has nothing whatever to do with the heroic and inspirational government of Venezuela and er…

**Dave Spart** *(Co-chair Vuvuzela Solidarity Campaign),* **John McSpart MP, Emma Spart Coad MP, Kate Osaspart MP, Tariq Sparti***(writer and playwright),* **Owen Spart** *(journalist and campaigner),* **Andy de La Spart** *(actor),* **Michael Manspart QC, Linton Kwesi Spart** *(poet),* **Ken Leninspart** *(former Mayor of London and expert on inter-war Zionism in Germany)* and **37 other signatories**

*"All those in favour of allowing pets in the office?"*

# POETRY CORNER

**Lines written to celebrate the 55th birthday of His Royal Highness Prince Edward, Earl of Wessex**

So. Happy Birthday
Then Prince Edward.

You are called the
Forgotten Royal.

But not today.

As a birthday present,
Your mother has
Made you
Earl of Forfar.
Keith's mum gave
Him a jumper.

To be honest,
I think Keith got
The better deal.

E.J. Thribb (57½)

# OSBORNE BUYS £3M CHALET

I'm not flaunting my wealth... I only bought one

*"I'm one of the modern Royal fans"*

**Mail on Sunday** SPECIAL

# We name the vile trolls behind the Hate Campaign that has upset Meghan and sickened the nation

**IT WILL SHOCK our readers to discover that these are all outwardly respectable people with seemingly responsible jobs. But, in reality, they sit alone in darkened rooms, maliciously spreading filth and poison about an innocent woman.**

Yes! At last we can reveal the people behind the vicious obsessive attacks on the Duchess of Sussex. We are proud to drag these lowlifes out from the shadows and expose them for what they are. Award-winning journalists. *(Brilliant! Ed).*

**Liz Jones,** Columnist and banana expert

**Ted Verity,** Editor Mail on Sunday

**Paul Dacre,** Editor-in-Chief, Mail Online

# DIARY

## PETER HITCHENS: MY LIFE IN FILM

**MARY POPPINS** I would welcome a film which taught children a proper respect for the rule of law, but I am sorry to say that *Mary Poppins Returns* is not it.

Instead, it portrays an obvious drug dealer who trades under the preposterous "street" name of "Mary Poppins" who descends on a respectable family and puts vile hallucinogenic drugs in the children's water.

They then think they can fly, dance on rooftops and so forth. The whole thing would be laughable if it were not so terrifying.

In the real world, the wide-eyed children would trip off the edge of the roof and plummet to their deaths.

And Poppins herself would be under lock and key for the rest of her natural days.

Once in prison, she would no doubt seek diversion in various "lesbian" relationships, of the type so fashionable among Hollywood liberals.

Let's not deny it. Prisons today are hotbeds of lesbian activity. And it's not like in the old days. Sad but true: today's spineless prison governors refuse to interrupt these unseemly goings-on between women who should know better by playing regular renditions of the National Anthem over loudspeakers.

**JAWS** Once again, that outstanding film *Jaws* has been blacklisted for an Academy Award.

Many people have been unable to see it, as the state-run BBC – impervious to what people really want – refuses to show it every night.

So let me tell you a bit about it.

Jaws is the name given to a shark who is not afraid of a hard day's work.

This doughty shark takes the bold decision to teach the loafers, crack-fiends, sun-worshippers and pseudo-intellectuals a short, sharp lesson in reality by waiting until they are frolicking in their expensive swimwear in the water and then biting them in two.

Not a message they're likely to forget in a hurry.

But, needless to say, it's a message that hasn't gone down well with the liberal elite of Hollywood.

Unbelievably, the last time *Jaws* won an Oscar was over 40 years ago.

Every single year since then, I have sent an urgent telegram to the President of the Academy of Motion Picture Arts and Sciences demanding that it should be honoured again.

And how has this pseudo-Marxist organisation responded to my telegram?

Right first time.

By masterminding a cover-up and pretending they haven't received it.

**THE FAVOURITE** The chattering classes just love lapping up old tripe.

That's the only reason I can think why my local cinema was packed last week for an evening presentation of *The Favourite*.

The mixture of four-letter words, same-sex love and historical inaccuracy was enough to put me off my ice cream.

And that's another thing.

Why can you no longer buy a decent choc-ice at your local cinema?

The PC brigade are at it again!

Has no one informed the film-makers that Queen Anne was far too busy building attractive country houses to go cavorting naked with women while yelling vulgar four-letter words at the top of her voice?

The fact is that today's film-makers have no respect for the accuracy.

**BOHEMIAN RHAPSODY** Why has the new film *Bohemian Rhapsody* had so many people flocking to see it?

The answer is simple.

False pretences.

Like many others, I queued expecting to learn something about Dvořák and Janáček, two composers of works of a freeflowing nature, both from Bohemia.

I was hoping that the late, great Sir Malcolm Sargent might put in an appearance.

Not a bit of it.

Instead, we were faced with some of the most sinister and disturbing footage ever shot.

It involved ugly caterwauling, depravity, and scenes of a sexual nature.

An androgynous man called Frederick Mercury boasted to his mother that he had just killed a man.

"Put a gun against his head, pulled my trigger, now he's dead."

Yet this repellent admission was greeted with cheers of adulation from a stadium full of "fans" dressed in jeans, T-shirts and worse.

Are we now expected to greet cold-blooded murder with hoots, hollers and cheers?

Any cinema-goers who enjoyed this pernicious claptrap should hang their heads in shame, return their ice-creams to the box office and ask themselves one question.

Is this what the world has come to?

*As told to*
CRAIG BROWN

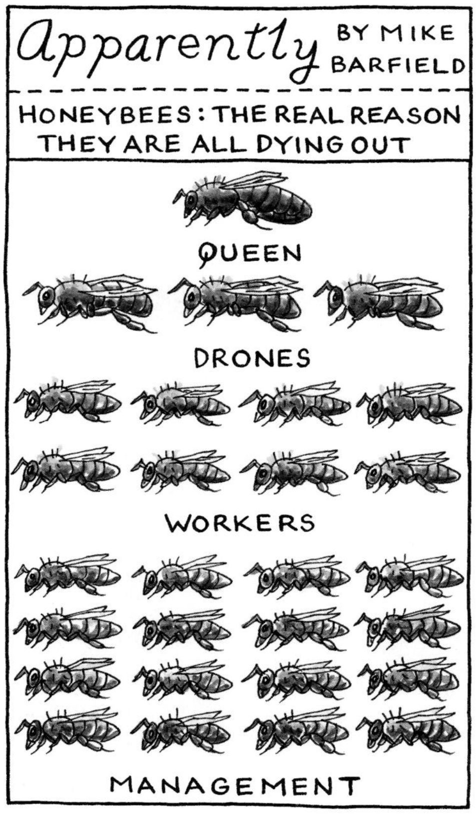


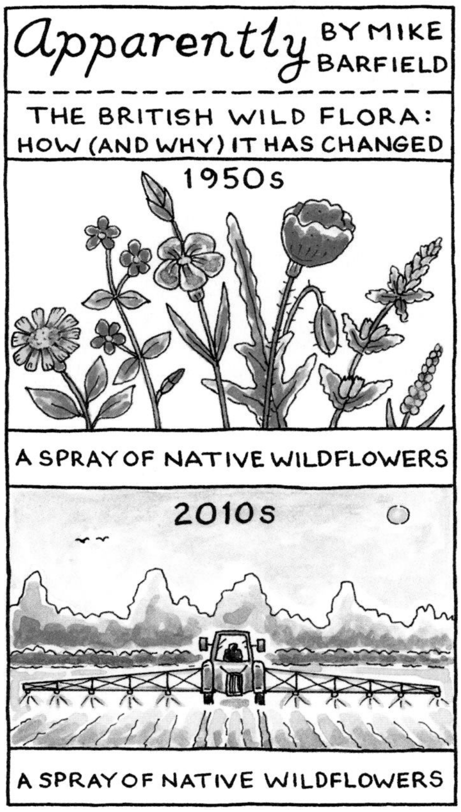

Apparently BY MIKE BARFIELD
THE BRITISH WILD FLORA: HOW (AND WHY) IT HAS CHANGED
1950s
A SPRAY OF NATIVE WILDFLOWERS
2010s
A SPRAY OF NATIVE WILDFLOWERS

# Disappointment As Key Witness Calls President A Racist, Conman, Cheat

POLITICAL observers were left underwhelmed when the President of the United States of America was openly accused of being a racist, a conman and a cheat in front of a Congressional Committee.

"Tell us something we don't know," said one bored Congressman. "So what's new?" yawned another.

Despite this being the first time in history that the head of state has been publicly labelled a criminal by his own lawyer, no one was very bothered.

Yet another Congressman added, "Who cares if the President signed a cheque to pay hush money to a porn star? That's what we'd expect Donald Trump to do. And he knew about the leaked Hillary emails beforehand and said he didn't. That's politics!

"If we're going to impeach this guy, I need video of him beheading Martin Luther King in the Oval Office before dancing naked with Hitler, whilst selling a Ponzi scheme to Bernie Madoff's aunt.

"And even then, if the Donald's got a plausible explanation, we'll probably let it go."

*"A terrible portent, my Lord. Your 30-times great-grandson will have a role in EastEnders"*

## Internet Conspiracy Sensation

### MELANIA BODY-DOUBLE QUIZ

Which one is the fake?

*Answer: He's on the left.*

## POETRY CORNER

**Lines on the 60th birthday of Ms Barbie Doll**

So. Congratulations
Then Barbie.
You are 60,
But you don't
Look it.

With your unnaturally
Tiny waist and
"Perfect" figure,
You have been a
Role model for
Millions of American
Women who are
Now also plastic.

Will you last
Forever?
Yes, although sadly
At the bottom of
The sea or in
The stomach of
A dolphin.

E.J. Thribb
(17½ inch waistline)

*"I had a nightmare last night that Brexit was a huge success, proving us all wrong"*

## Those top public school mockneys – where they really went to school

**Danny Dyer**
*Dragon School and Eton College*

**Dani Dyer**
*Thomas' Battersea and Cheltenham Ladies College*

**Danny Baker**
*Ludgrove and Haberdashers' Aske's*

**Ray Winstone**
*Collet Court and St Paul's*

**Lord Sugar**
*Downe House and Harrow*

**Kathy Burke**
*Sarum Hall and Roedean*

**Vinnie Jones**
*Ardingly College Prep and Lancing (choral scholar)*

**Danniella Westbrook**
*Wellesley House and Marlborough*

**Sir Julian Fellowes**
*Grotney Lane Primary, Neasden & Dollis Hill Comprehensive (Is this right? Ed.)*

## Public School Announcements

**St Cakeholes**

Mockney Term begins today. There are 278 geezers in the school and 174 birds. P.J. Ricketson-Smythe (Muppets) is Head Bloke and Tara Rara-Boomdeay (Slags) is Top Totty.

The Headmaster, Mr R.J Kipling, is taking a sabbatical and his post will be taken by Mr Gregg Sausage-Roll, who will be Acting Gaffer, as appointed by the Board of Guv'nors. The School motto is to be amended to *Reliquatus eam* (*Leave it out*).

Ms Luvlie Jubbly, from the University of Life, replaces Mrs Elle O'Cution (Cantab.) as Head of the English Language Department (now the Lingo Bingo Hall).

Plonkers will be run over Towie Fields (formerly Founders Meadow) on Feb 27th.

The school play *Are You Havin' A Larf?*, a loose adaptation of Shakespeare's *Comedy of Errors*, will be performed in the Babs Windsor Studio (formerly the Dame Edith Evans Memorial Theatre) on March 3rd. Tickets from the Bursar, Mr D.B. Trotter, c/o Hooky Street, Peckham.

The school will SHUT IT on the weekend beginning thankf***itsFriday, March 23rd.

## NICK CLEGG DEFENDS FACEBOOK

I know all about self-harm... I signed up to the Coalition

# HEIR OF SORROWS

## A Short Story Special

by Dame Sylvie Krin, author of *Duchess of Hearts* & *You're Never Too Old*

*THE STORY SO FAR: It is the last weekend of the royal post-Christmas sojourn at Sandringham. Now read on...*

WHERE was everyone? Charles wandered down the ornate corridors of the great Jacobethan country house designed by the venerable Victorian architect Humphrys John as a weekend cottage for his great-great-great-grandthingie, Prince Albert of Steptoe... anyway, nobody seemed to be around. Not even his faithful Valet de Parking, Sir Alan Fitztightly, who could usually be counted on for a game of Monopoly, even though he did insist on building the most frightful plastic houses all over London.

Charles was about to give up and seek out some congenial company with the spider-handwriting plants in the conservatory when the sound of voices reached him from behind the oak-panelled door of the Cannon & Ballroom.

He pressed his royal ear against the ancient timber and was amazed to hear his mother making what appeared to be an important announcement:

"Philip, one has reached a decision. There does come a time when one has to face the reality of time passing and admit that one is simply not as young as one once was."

There was an interjection from Prince Philip which sounded a bit like a cough, but could have been the word "Rollocks" – perhaps a piece of nautical slang from the Duke's time in the Navy as Captain of HMS Irascible.

"I shall ignore that," continued the monarch. "What one is saying is that at a certain point, one has to stop, one has to take a back seat and let a younger person take the controls."

There was a murmur of assent from what Charles suddenly realised was the entire Windsor Family, gathered for this historic announcement.

"Top-thinking G-Ma," came the voice of Prince William, second-in-line-to-the-throne and Duke of Bafta. "Oh yah," agreed his loyal wife, Kate Middleclass, the Duchess of Lumley.

"Yeah, like, I think that's so... you know, wise and thoughtful and cool and maybe we should all have, like, a group hug?" The unmistakeable Californian tones of the Duchess of Sparkle hung in the stuffy stateroom air.

"Megs is totes right. I mean, she's amazeballs," added Prince Harry, Duke of Hazzard, and Meghan's official Consort Royale.

CHARLES could not believe his ears. Was this it? Was this why he had been excluded from the gathering? Because it was **his** moment in history, his hour of destiny? He hesitated. He had been mistaken before – usually in a bath – and he didn't want to make a fool of himself.

"So that's it. It's decided. I shall make a Royal Decree and the retirement will be official."

There was a loud crash as Charles burst through the door, sending the Ming Campbell vase tumbling onto the marble floor, as he shouted at his bewildered family.

"Vivat myself! Rex Futurus! Rex Harrison! The Third Carolingian Age is upon us! God Save Me!"

"What the bloody hell are you talking about, boy?" growled Charles's father.

"Your father is giving up driving. He's handing in his licence," explained Her Majesty the Queen, patiently.

"Grandpops has got to stop, Pater," added Prince William.

"At a junction, before he hits anyone else!" added Prince Harry, mischievously.

The Royal Family all fell about laughing at this sally of Harry's hirsute humour; the bearded bonhomie reducing them all to fits of giggles at the thought of a member of the public being run over by the Duke's Getoffmylandrover.

Charles left the room quietly and closed the door, as the chill Norfolk wind whistled down the corridor in all too familiar mockery.

*(To be continued...)*

# JEFF BEZOS UNVEILS VISION OF THE FUTURE

by Our Space Staff **Dan Dire**

**SHOWING the brilliant imagination that has made him the world's richest entrepreneur, Amazon's Jeff Bezos last night revealed his extraordinary blue-print for the future of the galaxy.**

While projecting images of farms floating off the moons of Saturn in bubbles and industrial mining complexes orbiting around the Milky Way, Bezos spoke passionately about what he believes the 22nd Century will be like.

"At last, mankind will have more and more destinations to send not only packages but also pictures of their genitals. The whole concept gets me so excited. Excuse me, I feel a photo coming on."

An awestruck science journalist asked him, "Are we talking about Uranus, Jeff?", to which the billionaire brainbox replied: "No – just my dick!"

# DAILY EXPRESS

# TIME TO DO SOMETHING

by Our London Correspondent **Stanley Knife**

**THERE was widespread agreement today in all newspapers that, after the stabbing of two well-turned-out teenagers, it was finally time to do something about Britain's knife epidemic.**

"Obviously, up to now, there's been no reason for a sense of urgency in tackling the crisis," agreed all newspaper editors.

"But now that we have victims in smart suits and girl-guide outfits, rather than baggy tracksuits and baseball hats, this is a crisis that must be tackled and must be tackled now.

"There comes a time when you have to say enough is enough and demand the immediate deployment of tens of thousands of extra police officers on to the streets to prevent any more deaths. And that time is when middle-class kids get involved."

NEW
MIDDLE CLASS JOIN-THE-DOTS PUZZLE
BUYING DOPE SPONSORS KNIFE CRIME
RGJ

# REES-MOGG AT THE PALLADIUM

**The Eye presents all the best jokes from Britain's latest sit-down comedian, in what everyone agrees was the comedy event of the year**

**Knock knock...** Nanny, get that would you?

**My dog's got no nose. How does he smell?** He stinks. Just like Mrs May's deal.

**My wife's gone abroad...** Jamaica? No – Dublin. There are far better financial advantages there.

**An Englishman, Englishman and Englishman walk into a bar...** It was a Wetherspoons, and jolly nice too. Or so I'm told.

**What's brown and sticky?** Mrs May's fudge.

**Why did the chicken cross the road?** To jump into the American chlorine vat before coming here to feed the working classes.

**What's black and white and red all over?** Labour's uncontrolled immigration policy.

**Doctor, doctor, I keep thinking I'm a pair of curtains...** I'm afraid the doctor's gone home to Italy.

**Who was that lady I saw you with last night?** It was the ghost of Lady Thatcher. I can't see any problem with that.

**My wife doesn't understand me...** vox populi, vox dei, quod erat demonstrandum.

***And many, many more, from the Arthur Askey of the Conservative Party.***

*'If you like a joke with a topper, Jacob's your man.'*
**The Spectator**

**SOLD OUT! STOP PRESS: EUROPEAN TOUR CANCELLED**

# LIVES OF THE GREAT PRESIDENTS

**THE young President-to-be was in the yard, beside a cherry tree, which had recently been cut down. His father chanced upon the scene, and questioned his son thus: "Young man, did you, or did you not cut down this cherry tree?"**

**The future President of the United States of America thought long and hard, with the axe still in his hand, and was then unequivocal with his response.**

**"Father," he said, "I cannot tell a lie. Hold on – I'll get my lawyer to give you a statement."**

**The young President's lawyer then swore on oath that his client had not cut down the tree and had not given any money to any persons to ensure their non-disclosure of the tree-cutting incident. And his father was proud of him, and said, "Donald, you are a cheating, lying scumbag... That's m'boy!"**

## The Mail ON SUNDAY

Part 94 of the exclusive non-stop serialisation of the Corbyn biography *"Vote Conservative!"* by Tom Boo-hoo-hoo-er.

*Following previous explosive revelations that Jeremy Corbyn is boring, left-wing, anti-EU and not very popular with his ex-wives, today we present an extraordinary account of his early years by people who knew him well at the time...*

**Chapter 94**

### HOW CORBYN WET THE BED, CRIED ALL NIGHT AND POOED HIS NAPPIES

I can exclusively reveal that in 1949 the man who wants to be prime minister of Britain and who is about to force a general election was actually behaving appallingly.

Jeremy Corbyn, then aged 0, was unrecognisable from the supposedly controlled, placid and rational man he pretends to be today.

Observers at the time confirmed to me that he was "no better than a baby" *(cont. for hundreds of words, every week, up until the election)*

*"Yours is a natural beauty... but I can soon fix that"*

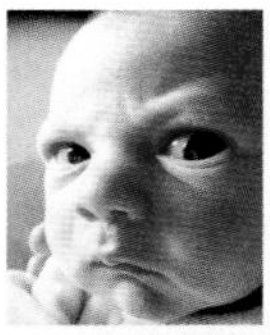

## The Eye's Controversial New Columnist

***The columnist who thinks the best way to eat jam is to scrape the Lego off first***

This week I am very angry about the trailer for the new live-action *Aladdin*. I was scandalised when I beheld the sight of Will Smith, a black actor, playing the part of a genie,

which has been traditionally played by a blue actor. I thought this act of "blue-ing up" had been consigned to the dustbin of history. It is not only an insult to those among us we call the blue minority, it is doing a blue actor out of a job. There are dozens of talented blue actors (such as Thomas the Tank Engine, Iggle Piggle, Bella from the Tweenies or Papa Smurf) who would jump at the chance of stretching their range and playing a genie and *(cont. p94)*

## THE Sun

# KYLIE MINOGUE'S STALKER

**BELOVED pop princess Kylie Minogue has been through HELL with a stalker who followed her around, made her afraid to be out in public, and lurked outside her house at all hours of the day and night.**

### On Other Pages

■ Photos of Kylie leaving her luxurious West London home, look, you can see how nice the houses around her are, although for some reason she's wearing sunglasses, stuck-up cow, oi, Kylie, take those glasses off, you old trollop, or we'll have to follow you until you do!

# DUMB BRITAIN

***Real contestants, real quiz shows, real answers, real dumb!***

## Tipping Point, ITV

**Ben Shephard**: Regent's Canal is a branch of which canal?
**Contestant**: The Suez Canal.

**Shephard:** The idea of "Veganuary" encourages people to eat a vegan diet in which month?
**Contestant:** October.

**Shephard:** In 1649, which English war resulted in the beheading of King Charles I?
**Contestant:** World War One.

**Shephard:** The first Gulf War involved the liberation of which country?
**Contestant:** Argentina.

**Shephard:** Which month of the year was named after the Roman emperor Augustus?
**Contestant:** July.

**Shephard:** In which European country was Deutsche Bank founded?
**Contestant:** France.

**Shephard**: Which TV station, launched in 1997, became the fifth terrestrial channel in the UK?
**Contestant**: Channel 4.

**Shephard**: The meat from which bird is traditionally included in the Scottish soup cock-a-leekie?
**Contestant**: Lamb.

**Shephard**: Which English university city is situated on the River Cam?
**Contestant**: Oxford.

**Shephard**: Oscar-winning actress Rachel Weisz married which James Bond star in 2011?
**Contestant**: Piers Morgan.

**Shephard**: Which planet in our solar system shares its name with a chocolate bar?
**Contestant**: Milky Way.
**Shephard**: No, that's wrong. It's Mars.
**Contestant**: Milky Way is a chocolate bar!
**Shephard**: Yes, but it's not a planet, is it? It's a galaxy.
**Contestant**: That's chocolate as well. (*Very smart joke by contestant. Ed.*)

## Daily Dozen, Lincs FM

**John Marshall**: Today in 1987 a new Michael Jackson video had its premiere. The title rhymes with "mad". What was it called?
**Caller**: Was it Thriller, John?

**Marshall:** Complete the film title. Released in 2011 and starring Colin Firth, *The King's*... what?
**Caller:** ...Of Leon?

## The Michael Ball Show, Radio 2

**Michael Ball**: How were Tinky Winky, Dipsy, Laa-Laa and Po collectively known?
**Caller**: The Marx brothers.

**Ball:** Name as many countries beginning with "A" as you can.
**Caller:** Africa.
**Ball:** No, you can't have that, that's a continent.
**Caller:** Amsterdam.

## For What It's Worth, BBC2

**Fern Britton**: Who was the first man in space?
**Contestant:** Lance Armstrong.

## Pointless, BBC1

**Alexander Armstrong**: Name a north American deer beginning with C.
**Contestant**: Camel.

**Armstrong:** We're looking for countries that participated in the 2018 Commonwealth Games.
**First contestant:** Greece.
**Second contestant:** France.
**Third contestant:** Kazakhstan.

**Armstrong:** One of six aristocratic sisters, she wrote Love in a Cold Climate. Who was she?
**Contestant:** George Orwell.

## Mastermind, BBC1

**John Humphrys**: Who formulated the laws of gravity after watching an apple fall from a tree at his Lincolnshire home?
**Contestant**: Einstein.

**Humphrys**: Which river rises in the Black Forest in Germany and forms the divide between ten different countries before flowing into the Black Sea?
**Contestant**: The Nile.

**Humphrys**: On which African river is the Kariba Dam?
**Contestant**: The Amazon.

**Humphrys**: At least 13 of the 27 books of the New Testament are usually attributed to which author?
**Contestant**: John Constable.

**Humphrys**: To what season did Keats refer to when he wrote of "season of mellow fruitfulness"?
**Contestant**: Oliver Twist.

**Humphrys:** Which brothers had their first major Broadway success with the 1924 show *Lady, Be Good*? It includes the songs *Fascinating Rhythm* and *Oh, Lady Be Good.*
**Contestant:** Barclay.

## The Time It Takes, BBC1

**Joe Lycett**: In *Othello*, who kills Desdemona?
**Contestant**: Macbeth.

**Lycett**: Emma Hamilton was the mistress of which naval hero?
**Contestant**: I don't know. Popeye?

**Lycett:** Who designed St Paul's Cathedral in London?
**Contestant:** St Paul.

**Lycett**: What is the first letter of the word "dictionary"?
**Contestant**: A.

**Lycett**: Real Madrid play their home football in which Spanish city?
**Contestant**: Barcelona.

**Lycett**: In *Life on Mars*, David Bowie wonders if there was life on which planet?
**Contestant**. Hmm, *Life on Mars*. Was it Jupiter?

## A Question of Sport, BBC1

**Sue Barker**: Which country won the most diving medals at the European Championships in Glasgow?
**Phil Tufnell**: China.

## Tenable, ITV

**Warwick Davis**: Name the ten London Underground stations that begin with the letter T.
**Contestant**: Oxford Circus.

## Eggheads, BBC2

**Jeremy Vine**: What two-word place name is the location of the Ministry of Defence's military scientific research station?
**Contestants** (*after lengthy discussion*): Strawberry Fields.

## Radio Borders

**Keith Clarkson**: Who is the patron saint of Wales?
**Caller**: Prince Charles.

## The Chase, ITV

**Bradley Walsh:** Foxes are part of the same family as which domestic animal?
**Contestant:** Cats.

**Walsh:** Which 1066 battle was won by the Duke of Normandy?
**Contestant:** The Battle of Wellington.

**Walsh**: According to the saying, one of what does not make a summer?
**Contestant**: Snowman.

**Walsh:** What was the name of the British naval hero who was made a viscount after the Battle of Copenhagen?
**Contestant:** Napoleon.

**Walsh:** The Budapest Gambit is an opening in which board game?
**Contestant:** Monopoly.

**Walsh:** Keir Hardie was the first leader of which British political party?
**Contestant:** Ukip.

**Walsh**: Which Italian composed the score for eight of Sergio Leone's films?
**Contestant**: Vivaldi.

**Walsh**: Who rode a horse while naked through the streets of Coventry?
**Contestant**: The Queen.

**Walsh**: Saudi Arabia holds annual beauty contests for which humped mammal?
**Contestant**: Elephant.

**Walsh:** The marsh in Bunyan's Pilgrim's Progress is called The Slough of... what?
**Contestant:** Newcastle.

**Walsh**: What's nine and a half plus seven and a half?
**Contestant**: 20.
**Walsh**: Correct.

**Walsh**: The dinosaur known as Attenboroughsaurus is named after which famous naturalist?
**Contestant**: Oh god. Attenboroughsaurus. Um, er, oh pass.

**Walsh**: Who was Labour's longest serving prime minister?
**Contestant**: Ted Heath.

## The Chase Australia, 7 Network

**Andrew O'Keefe:** What is the female equivalent of a sultan, and also the name of a dried grape?
**Contestant:** Raisin.

## Mix 96, Buckinghamshire

**Presenter:** What was the name of the Lone Ranger's horse?
**Caller:** Shergar.

## Morning Quiz, Radio Devon

**David FitzGerald**: What is the capital of Nigeria?
**Caller**: Niagara Falls.

# NIGEL FARAGE'S GREAT MARCHES OF HISTORY

The Leave March departs from Sunderland – like the motor industry

## The Jarrow March, 1936

A very well-attended march, with probably 200 chaps I would say, also wearing a lot of flat caps. They walked all the way, which seems a bit unnecessary, and I'm sure a few of them hopped on the train for at least a bit of it. Kept saying how hungry they were, too, which shows a bit of moral weakness, if you ask me.

## The Long March, 1935

Chairman Mao and his other Chinese chappies went for a bloody long walk in the Chinese countryside to protest against something or other. Like the patriots walking in the Leave Means Leave march, I gather they went most of the way by coach. Probably stopped off for some prawn toast on the way too, I bet.

## Long Walk to Freedom, 1995

Nelson Mandela wrote this, although I have to say I don't have much time for him myself. When I sit in the EU parliament for several decades on a point of principle apparently it's "grubbing for expenses" – but when he sits in prison writing a book it's "true nobility". Typical. Anyway, this is the story of him going for a walk around the prison, I believe, although he probably got a cab some of the way.

## March of the Penguins, 2005

This is a very moving story – narrated by Morgan Freeman, or possibly Samuel L. Jackson, anyway, certainly one of those guys. Maybe Denzel Washington. It's about a lot of penguins trying to escape an evil, wintry empire, although I don't doubt some of them hop on a charabanc if they've got any sense.

# Church in shock 'Sunday opening' move

by Our Religious Staff
**Lucy Fer**

The Church of England has finally accepted the reality of the modern age and bowed to the inevitable, by cancelling Sunday opening and abandoning the practice of holding church services on the seventh day.

Said a spokesman for the Synod, Rev J.C. Flannel, "The Church's position was very old-fashioned and nowadays we just have to accept that Sundays are a special time for families to go shopping."

He continued, "It's unfair to expect busy people with busy lives to go to church at the weekend when they could be going to the garden centre or the DIY superstore.

"Sunday opening is antiquated, unpopular and goes against everything that the 21st-century Church believes in, whatever that is."

### Seventh Day Asda-ist

Theologians have backed the Church's progressive Sunday closure move.

Said Canon Ball, Professor of Retail Divinity at the University of Aberdeen Steak House, "From now on, the so-called 'Lord's Day' must reflect a more diverse multi-buy experience, encompassing not just traditional retail outlets, but also fast-food chains, betting shops and adult sex emporiums."

Said Rev Flannel, "You know, in order to survive in today's world, the Church has to move with the times and close down completely."

# THE LABOUR PARTY

## An apology for the apology for apologising too much over the accusations of anti-Semitism

**WE WOULD like to say that we are very sorry for being sorry about being too sorry about the anti-Semitism and realise that this was in fact anti-anti-Semitism which was unacceptable from a party which is committed to anti-anti-anti-Semitism and honestly you can't win with some people can you no offence** ***(cont. p94)***

*"Hasn't* ***anyone*** *brought something different?"*

# The adventures of Mr Greedy Pt 94

MR Greedy was looking very sad as he sat on his yacht. "What's the matter?" said his wife, Little Mrs Greedy.

"Mr Nosey from the *Daily Telegraph* has been poking about in my affairs," said Mr Greedy. "Now I'm so unpopular, the public want to take away my title."

"What?" she said, flicking through the new yacht catalogue *What Yacht?*, "The title of World's Greediest Man?"

"Yes," whimpered Mr Greedy. "Now they want to call me Mr Gropey instead."

Little Mrs Greedy was shocked. "That's appalling, I thought you paid everyone to keep quiet."

"I did, but apparently money isn't everything."

At which point, Little Mrs Greedy's head exploded, as she tried to imagine this new idea.

Then a man with a briefcase appeared on Mr Greedy's yacht. It was his lawyer, Mr Useless.

"Good news, Mr Greedy, they're not going to call you Mr Gropey after all."

"Hurrah!" said Mr Greedy, popping open another bottle of champagne. "What are they going to call me?"

"Mr Bully."

"You overpaid idiot!" said Mr Bully, pushing Mr Useless overboard.

"OK," said the drowning lawyer, "how about Mr Racisty?"

Mr Greedy/Gropey/Bully/Racisty stamped his feet angrily. "That's so bloody unfair! Some of my best friends are spear-carriers," he said, as... *(to be continued)*

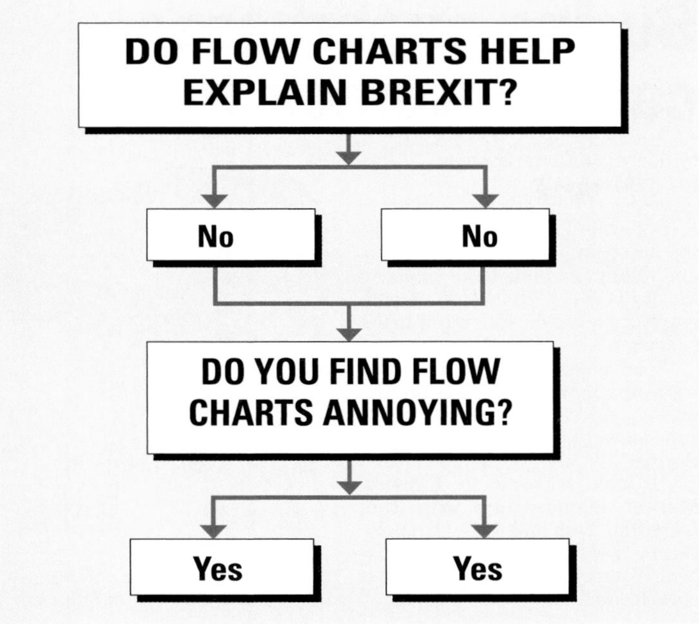

DO FLOW CHARTS HELP EXPLAIN BREXIT?
No
No
DO YOU FIND FLOW CHARTS ANNOYING?
Yes
Yes

## HOW BRIBES WORK

Mrs May's Guide

**1** Government gives £1bn to deprived region in order to gain support.

**2** Deprived region takes money and then refuses to give government any support, shouting "Noooo" whenever asked.

**3** Government learns absolutely nothing and offers £1bn to bribe other deprived regions.

**4** Other deprived regions take money and vote against government.

**5** Mrs May hailed as finest politician of her generation.

*"And Justin has been promoted to Head of Diversity"*

# Corbyn gets egg all over face

by Our Political Staff **Michael Egg White**

THE leader of the opposition was last night left with egg on his face after an attack by a number of members of his own party.

Said one onlooker, "Jeremy was just minding his own business, not very well, when there was an unprovoked attack on him by a crazed right-winger called Tom Watson."

Corbyn looked embarrassed as Watson hurled accusations at the Labour leader that he had not dealt with anti-Semitism, Brexit or indeed anything else very well.

A spokesman for Corbyn, Mr Shameless Militant, said, "Jeremy dealt with this in a dignified manner by pretending it hadn't happened, which is how he deals with all problems."

He concluded, "This kind of intimidation will not deter him from continuing as normal and doing nothing in future."

**On other pages**

- Breggstremism – is it a problem? **2**
- Shell shock – Labour in meltdown **3**
- More Corbyn yolks by our columnist, Richard Chicken-Littlejohn **94**

# Nursery Times

Friday, Once-upon-a-time

## MR FOX – 'YOU CAN TRUST ME WITH CHICKENS'

by Our Food Standards Staff **Doctor Fester**

THE Fantastic Mr Fox told the people of Nurseryland yesterday that they should have no fear when it came to eating chickens from the land of Yankee Doodle Dandy.

"I know all about chickens," he said. "My name isn't Fantastic Mr Fox for nothing. And if I say chickens are safe, then believe me, they are safe."

He continued, "It's easy to scoff and I do. Even when the chickens are dipped in chlorine."

Nurseryland farmers, including Messrs Bunce, Boggis and Bean, are concerned that standards of chicken safety will fall if Mr Fox is entrusted with environmental health.

"He's only interested in one thing," said Mr Bunce, "and that's stuffing his face with cheap chicken."

Fantastic Mr Fox denies the farmers' claims that he is a "pest" who will "stop at nothing" to save his own skin.

"These American chlorinated chickens are great. I saw it on Fox News."

## WHEN AN AMERICAN WINS AN OSCAR

"I was put on this earth with a God-given talent which would propel me to greatness. My whole life has built towards this moment when I could share my genius with a grateful world. I LOVE THAT YOU ALL LOVE ME. LOOK AT ME, MA – TOP OF THE WORLD!" (BAND STRIKES UP AS ACTOR SALUTES CROWD)

## WHEN A BRIT WINS AN OSCAR

"Gee golly gumdrops... whizzer and chips... is this a mistake?... cor blimey, alright me old China, give us a snog.... no, this must be a mistake... crumbs... knock down ginger... this IS a mistake, rhubarb and custard... put a brew on... toodle pip... goodness me, mother, I've come over all peculiar..."

(BAND ORDERED TO STRIKE UP AND DROWN OUT ACTOR)

## An Eye guide to how our country will never be the same again now that Olivia Colman has won an Oscar

- Olivier Awards to be renamed Olivia Awards and all to be given to Olivia Colman
- Colman's Mustard to be renamed Olivia Colman's Mustard
- Olive Oil to be renamed Olivia Oil
- Dickens' novel 'Oliver Twist' to be renamed 'Olivia Twist'
- Liver and Bacon to be renamed Olivia 'n' Bacon in all restaurants
- Bond films 'Live And Let Die' and 'You Only Live Twice' to be renamed 'Olivia 'n' Let Die' and 'You Only Olivia Colman'
- Comedy film 'Stan and Ollie' to be renamed 'Stan and Olivia' and to be given Oscar

*(That's quite enough Olivia Colman. Ed)*

# The presidential address in the wake of Christchurch

"MY fellow white Americans, in the wake of the Christchurch terror attack on mosques which left over 50 people dead, the Fake News Liberal media will once again try to cynically use this terror attack to demonise decent homicidal gun-owners with a grudge against immigrants.

But the fact is, gun control is not the answer. Just like in our schools, it's a bigly fact that only more guns could have saved these people from this lunatic.

We don't need gun control. We need to do what the NRA tells us to do. They tell us that more armed people in places of worship are the answer, so that's the answer.

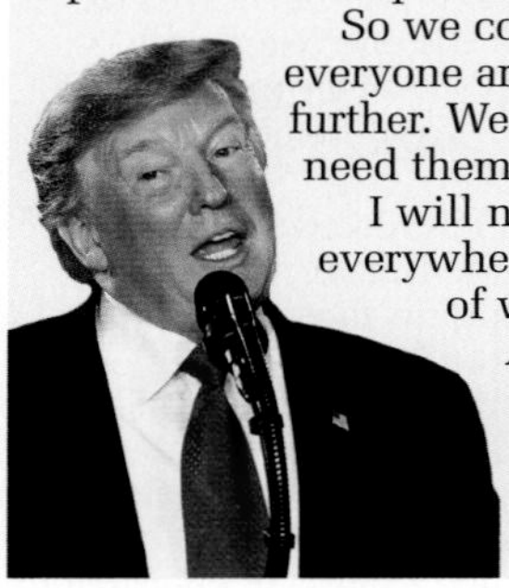

So we completely and utterly need to see everyone armed in those mosques. Let's go further. We need every Muslim armed, and we need them armed now, today.

I will not rest until I see Muslims everywhere, on the streets, in our places of worship and on planes flying to America, armed to the teeth with semi-automatic weapons to make us all a hell of a lot safer.

Er... God bless the KFC of America."

*Exclusive to all tabloids*

# WHY DO 'LOVE ISLAND' STARS FEEL PRESSURED?

by Our Brilliant Columnist **Pru Riant**

After the second suicide in just a few months of a former *Love Island* contestant, questions are now being asked as to why the reality show stars feel under such pressure.

Could it have something to do with the tabloids raking over every aspect of their young lives when they leave the show, writing endless stories about even the most banal and trivial aspects of their existence, revelling in any weight problems, romantic heartbreaks or failed business ventures, as we treat them as nothing more than tanned and toned bikini-clad fodder for our amusement? No, of course not.

It must be something to do with Brexit. Yes, that'll be it. Phew!

Anyways, have you seen the lines on Katy from *Love Island*'s forehead in that pic of her clubbing in Majorca? The last lines we saw that were that big were those Brendon from *Love Island* was snorting before he got carted off to rehab – minging or what... total cringe. GET THE BOTOX IN, BABES!

### Producers Deny Claims

*Love Island* producers have rubbished claims that, following their time on the show, the contestants weren't given enough aftercare: "They each got a bottle of Ambre Solaire After Sun enriched with glycerol and vitamin E, which hydrates the skin, leaving it soft, supple and radiant-looking."

# Boring superheroes can be women too

by Our Movie Correspondent
**P.G. Thirteen**

EXCITEMENT has rippled across the film community as the reviews are finally in and, yes, *Captain Marvel* is every bit as tedious and empty as a movie starring a male superhero.

"This goes to show that women with superpowers can be as utterly boring and vacuous as men with superpowers," said critic Barry Boring.

"I look forward to Captain Marvel teaming up with the Incredibly Dull and the Extremely Boring League of Tedium in the next 73 superhero movies." *(That's enough. Ed.)*

*"Woah! Barry, you old dog... where have you been hiding her?"*

# Notes&queries

**While listening to LBC with my ten-year-old daughter, I was intrigued to hear former foreign secretary Boris Johnson refer to a large amount of money being "spaffed" up a wall. I was unable to tell young Jemima what exactly he meant by this odd expression. Can any of your readers enlighten me?**
*Mrs E.E. Cummings, Wilts.*

● I am delighted to be able to enlighten Mrs Cummings and Jemima on the meaning of "spaff", which derives from the game from the ancient Orient, namely Spiff-Spaff.

This was a game similar to Mr Johnson's "Whiff-Whaff" (or Ping-Pong, as it is more popularly known) but in Spiff-Spaff it is the paddle that is hit across the table, while each player holds a small ball.

Spaffing is the act of accidentally hitting the paddle into the net or "wall", hence Mr Johnson's use of this colourful phrase.
*Professor Gareth Storm.*

● Oh dear. Prof Storm has missed the target or, as we used to say in the RAF, well and truly spaffed it! SPAFF is a classic pilot's acronym meaning Silly Plonker, Awfully Foolish Flyer, a taunt levelled originally at Squadron Leader "Ginger" Biscuit.

Ginger was one of the original Dambusters, but the only pilot who failed to hit the dam because, on take-off, he inadvertently dropped his bomb which bounced up the wall of the nearby NAAFI canteen. Hence the ubiquitous phrase "SPAFFing" up a wall.
*Wing Commander Harry Cane (ret'd).*

● Well, well, well. I hope the Wing Commander was more accurate when strafing villages than he is at etymology!

The word "spaff" is first recorded in the *Diaries of Samuel Pepys*, in which he records, "after spending a fynne evening watching London burnne, I fell into a pleasante slumber and did dreame of my young maidservant Mollie. On awaking, I discovered I had spaffed up a wall."

To spaff is, therefore, a rather disgusting term meaning "to sneeze", as is confirmed in the *Dictionary of the English Language* written by Dr Samuel Johnson, who is no relation to Boris Johnson.

Mr Johnson could have saved himself a great deal of embarrassment if, rather than using the word "spaff", he'd used a more innocent and less graphic term, such as "spunked".
*Reverend Gale Force.*

***EXCLUSIVE TO ALL PAPERS***

ROYAL EXCLUSIVE

# MEGHAN TO HAVE TRANS BABY!

by Our Royal Exclusive Staff
**Fay Kenews**

**YES! It's official! Royal insiders have told friends of other insiders that the Duchess of Sussex is determined to have a transgender baby.**

This bombshell, which overturns hundreds of years of royal tradition, has sent shockwaves through the establishment and may signal the end of the monarchy within the week.

According to close friends of journalists who write this sort of thing, Meghan made the announcement at her million-dollar baby shower in New York attended by top A-list celebs, including Brad Pitt, Michelle Obama, Lady Gaga and the bloke who was in *Bohemian Rhapsody*.

Meghan confided in her close pals, telling them that the trans baby would be brought up without gender stereotyping and be looked after only by drag-queen nannies from the cast of *Priscilla, Queen of the Desert*.

The child will apparently be referred to as "they" and will be the first transgender member of the Royal Family to win an Olympic weightlifting medal.

Said a confidant of a friend of one of the insiders to the journalist, "This will definitely happen and we know this because what Meghan actually said was something about not being too hung up about pink and blue clothes."

Said Thomas Markle, the grandfather-to-be of the future baby trans monarch, "I don't care about the sex – how about the cheques?"

Advertisement

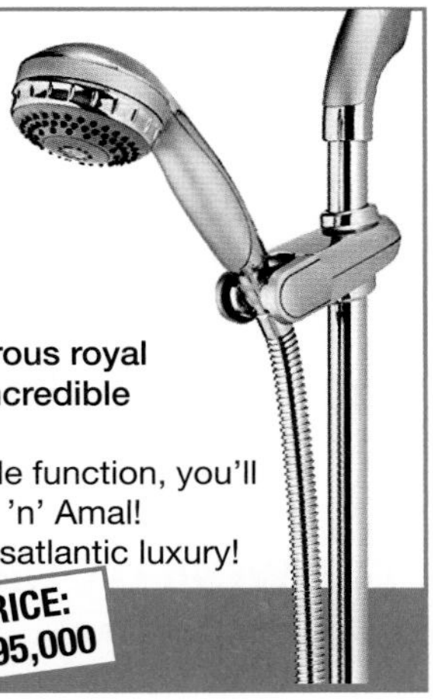

INTRODUCING

THE
## Meghan shower

**RELIVE all the fun of the most glamorous royal New York event of all time with this incredible commemorative shower.**

With its high-speed private jet nozzle function, you'll imagine you're right there with George 'n' Amal!

Pamper yourself in lavish royal Transatlantic luxury!

**WARNING: Unsuitable for pregnant women**

**PRICE: $395,000**

***CALLING ALL LIBERALS!***

## GENDER FLUID

**NEW from the scientists of Switzerland. At last, a non-gender-specific hydrating drink that you can consume with no guilt!**

Say goodbye to "beer for the boys", "white wine for the ladies" stereotypes, with this incredible, sugar-free, clear "woke" non-binary beverage!

INGREDIENTS: Two parts hydrogen, one part oxygen

**PRICE: £375 per litre**

# ONS REVEALS UK'S NEW 'NO-DEAL' SHOPPING BASKET

**THE Office for National Statistics has revealed what will be in the average UK family's shopping basket following a no-deal Brexit on 29 March 2019.**

The new list replaces the previous compilation of goods used to determine what Britain consumes each and every week.

| OLD LIST | NEW LIST* |
|---|---|
| Bottled water | Boiled tap water |
| Tomatoes | Tinned tomatoes |
| Fresh milk | Powdered milk |
| Fresh salmon | Fish paste |
| Olive oil | Salad cream |
| Beef steak | Tinned spam |
| Fresh orange juice | Powdered orange |
| Fresh eggs | Powdered egg |
| Durum wheat spaghetti | Spaghetti hoops (tinned) |
| Fresh baguette | Ultra value white thin sliced loaf |
| Fresh fruit and veg | Dried prunes and tinned mushy peas |

**Compiled with the help of UK food banks*

# RADIO 4 FACES SAVAGE CUTS

## What you will hear

**Desert Island Disc**
Lauren Laverne asks this week's guest, whoever it is, for their favourite song, then spends 45 minutes playing it very, very slowly so it takes up all the time.

**The Archer**
The classic rural soap returns with just one character doing all the voices, all the sound effects, and playing the classic theme tune on spoons from the BBC canteen!

**Any Questions? No? Good**
There's no money for any guests, so this is just an hour of silence.

**Yesterday**
John Humphrys reminisces about what he thinks about yesterday's papers, which we must be able to get when someone else has thrown them away.

**The No Show**
*(Cancelled due to lack of hosts)*

**Just a Minim**
Panellists have to speak for only a fraction of a second, which will save money on the stopwatch.

## TV REVIEW

**Afterlife** (Netflix)

Ricky Gervais stars as Ricky Gervais, a self-absorbed, middle-aged comedian, angry that his movie career has died. He decides to spend his entire life on Twitter, saying whatever horrible stuff comes into his head and daring people to be offended.

***EYE RATING*** *He's all Brent out of shape.*

*Friday 8 March 2019* **The Grauniad**

# Fearless, funny and fabulous:

## the woman who has transformed TV comedy

Rude, shocking, sexually honest, in your face and hilarious – Mrs Brown has changed the way we see women on television for ever and redefined the entire (*You're fired. Ed*)

GET AN ELECTRIC CAR, MISTER!
STOP BURNING FOSSIL FUELS!
GO VEGAN!

*"Bloody kids are being a nuisance!"*

# Glenda Slagg

## She's Fleet Street's Dangerous Gas Boiler (Geddit??!!)

■ **SO the Fab Four are to split?!!!! Wills, Kate, Harry and Megs I'm talking about!!!? What a Beatles-style tragedy?!! The young, modern Royals brought a new sound to the world of popular royalty with their fresh, touchy-feely approach!!?! "I Wanna Hold Your Hand", "Love Me Do" and "We All Live in an Apartment in Kensington Palace"!! *(This is terrible. Ed.)* But now the most famous and best-loved British foursome in the world are to go their separate ways – citing creative differences?!?!?! It's all "Yesterday", "Hello, Goodbye" and "Help!"!?!! Who's to blame??!! Is it Yoko Meghan with her behind-the-scenes manipulation of her husband with New Age nonsense??!! Yes, it is!! Shame on you, Ono Markle!!?!! What can we look forward to now from our ex-Buck House Beatles???! "The Frogmore Chorus" – Gawd help us all!!?!?**

■ OK, the so-called Fab Four are going to split!?!!! Give the Beatles parallel a rest, Mr Newsman!!?! That's *so* Yesterday!!?! Geddit??!! I never liked them anyway. When it comes to pop royalty analogies, there's only one superstar in my book and that's "Queen". Yes, "The Royal We Are the Champions" (Geddit??!?!), "The Royal We Will Rock You" (Geddit again???!?!?) and the unforgettable "Balmoralian Rhapsody" *(This is even worse than usual. Ed.)*

■ **BOO to James Cracknell!??! He's the 46-year-old Olympian who's rowing in the Oxford-Cambridge boat race!?!! Tell you what, Grandad, why don't you throw yourself overboard and give the youngsters a chance??!?! "In, out, in out" – how about just out, Crackers??!?!**

■ THREE cheers for James Cracknell!!??!! Like all of us oldsters, he knows his oars from his elbows!!?! Move over, you weeny wet-bobs, there's a new kid on the block – and he's 46 years young!!?! Just like me!!?! *(You're fired again. For lying. Ed.)*

■ **Don't you love the fantastic Fleabag??!! Me too!!?! It's my favourite, even though I haven't seen it...**

***Byeee!!***

# Modern Tales from the Bible

## Samson and Delilah

And in those days there lived a heroic figure called Boris Samson, famous for his long, tousled hair and his mighty wit. Bold were his exploits and many were his triumphs, and quite a few gaffes, if we're honest. Who can forget the day he was caught dangling from the zip wire of Sinai?

And lo, Boris became infatuated with the beautiful temptress and PR woman, Carrie Delightful, who saw that his tousled hair was, in a very real sense, his PR weakness, and plotted what she might do to remedy the situation.

And so it came to pass that in the middle of the night she stole into his bedroom, and said, "You need a haircut, big boy, and lose some weight, fatty, while you're at it!" And in what was perceived as a miracle, Johnson's locks were cut off, and when he awoke he looked in the mirror and thought, "Cripes! Even I might vote for me! Thanks to my short hair and trim, athletic physique. Blimey!"

And so Johnson and Delightful did enter the House of the Philistines and Boris pulled down the entire establishment around his own head, ruining everything for everyone for all time.

NEXT WEEK *Wonder of the World: How the Hanging Garden Bridge of Babylon failed to be built and cost 53 million shekels.*

# Tim Berners-Lee concerned over future of internet

by Our Online Staff
**Dot Com**

As the World Wide Web celebrates its 30th birthday, its creator, computer scientist Sir Tim Berners-Lee, has given an exclusive interview in which he expresses his misgivings about the way his invention has been used and developed.

Said Sir Tim, "I'm very concerned about nastiness and misinformation spreading."

The reaction around the world was immediate. "I hope you die of cancer, you balding bastard" was trending within seconds, followed by "Bet you're Jewish, aren't you? #Bigots4Jeremy".

President Trump joined in minutes later, tweeting: "Fake news. I invented the web. Fact! Not you – failing Tim Berners-Lee. #Loser #Sad".

The Kremlin also offered its support on Facebook, sending 78 billion messages reading: "Vote Brexit!"

One top internet entrepreneur, Amazon boss Jeff Bezos, was more positive, sending Sir Tim best wishes and a picture of his penis.

Advertisement

**NEW FOR GAMERS**

## PayStation presents FIFA 20

***YOUR CHANCE TO WIN THE WORLD CUP!***

FIRST, select your team (Qatar), then use all your skill to become a real player in the international game.

Negotiate the various qualifying stages, from the nail-biting free dinners to the make-or-break luxury weekend for FIFA Officials in the exclusive ten-star Qatari hotel 'The Oily Palm'.

Then enjoy the moment of triumph as your bid beats poorer opponents, such as naïve England led by David Beckham and Prince William with their hamper from Marks & Spencer.

***LIFELIKE GAMEPLAY INCLUDES:***

- Ducking and diving
- Getting FIFA Officials onside
- Passing (bung under table)
- Kickbacks
- Avoiding penalties (and video replays)
- Preparing a good defence

*REMEMBER – it's not about the winning, it's about the taking bribes. And then winning the right to host a World Cup in the middle of the bloody desert!*

**Price: $800 million**

**WARNING: Your FIFA 2020 handsets may melt in your hands, due to extreme heat**

**EXCLUSIVE TO**

# The Daily Toffgraph

## Who are they, the Norfolk set at the heart of the explosive Royal rumpus that has gripped the whole country?

by Our Royal Correspondent **Phil Acresofspace**

THE gilded world of the Cambridges' inner circle has been ruptured by reports of a massive feud between Kate and her best friend, the Marchioness of Cholmondeley-Bolmondeley (pronounced Chumly-Bumly). To appreciate what is really happening, you have to understand the complex social landscape. What looks like a close-knit community of young, wealthy, beautiful, well-connected "Norfolkers" (pronounced Norfukkers), is actually a disparate group split into three distinct tribes.

### The Turnipocracy

**The old aristocratic landowners who between them own the entire county**

**The Marquess of Cholmondeley-Bolmondeley** (pronounced Shankly-Bore), 78, is a direct descendant of Danny Dyer and is married to the much younger former model **Fruitella Nobbington-Hobnob**, 32, one of the famed McVitie's Hobnobs. They live in Toad Hall, the vast 112-room palladium mansion at Soddam.

**Rollo van Flotsam-Jetsam-Winsome-Losesome** is Will's best friend and his wife **Toblerona** (née Tarara Boomdeeay) is very close to Kate. Rollo is an international cribbage player and his wife runs an ethical designer sock company called "No Footprint".

**Tom and Ditzy Money-Bagges** live in Wolf Hall, the 94-bedroomed Tudorbethan manor house that has been in their family since it was built in 1973. Their children are known as the Baggelets and Toffo, Toffee and Tofu are playmates of Prince George and Princess Charlotte.

### The Leekenders

**Part-time members of the Turnip set, these London-based society socialites jet down at the weekend for hunt balls, all-night raves and local point-to-point races at the market town of Hedge Fundham**

**"Bongo" Downton (**real name **19th Earl of Lymeswold)** and his wife **Abby Downton** (née Abby National). Bongo is a private equity datawrangler at Oodles Bank in Mayfair. Abby has her own jewellery range called "Tatz" and has a concession in Harvey Proctors, in fashionable Knightsbridge.

**Binky Poche-Clichet** is an interior designer who has worked exclusively on the interior of her own home, Tony Hall, the ancestral seat of her ex-husband, the **7th Duke of Ellington,** who is now married to her sister **Pinky Perkington-Pigge,** who was originally married to the haemorrhoid heir **Jamie Anusol-Smythe**, who lives in a Georgian pile at nearby Saugh Bottom.

### The Wannabeets

**The up-and-coming pushy new generation of rootless social climbers who want to break into the exclusive "Cambridge Circus"**

**Zac and Prosecco Riche-Nouveau** have moved into Itchycoo Park, the former home of **The Hon Crispin Cooke-Hedde** (pronounced Coke-Head), the 7th Baron Drugge, who had to sell the 80,000-acre estate to meet unforeseen debts. Zac, 42, is a vulture capitalist whose zombie fund Flesheater Asset Management is based in China's financial capital city, Fukyu.

"Prozzy" works for charity and has made the Cambridges patrons of her Foundation for Bored Rural Gentlewomen. *(That's enough Norfolk tribes. Ed).*

### *So the question remains...*

**What exactly is this right royal bust-up all about?**
**The options are simple:**

**a)** We don't know

**b)** We haven't a clue

**c)** See above.

*© The Daily Toffgraph*

Moose Allain
Can I borrow your chloroform?
Go ahead, knock yourself out
Play nicely!
scraaaark!
scrreeeee!
It's thirty degrees out there

# Idiot brings railway to standstill

by Our Transport Staff
**Dee Lay**

A LONE individual was blamed last night for single-handedly disrupting hundreds of trains all over the country and causing massive inconvenience to travellers.

The man, known to police only as Chris Grayling, managed to reduce Britain's railways to chaos simply by turning up for work at the Department of Transport.

As soon as Grayling appeared, the entire system went into meltdown. Said one onlooker, "He was just standing there with his timetable and his spreadsheet, refusing to budge. There was nothing anyone could do."

Said another, "There needs to be a thorough investigation into how this man got into a position at the top of the department. It's a major breach of security, not to mention common sense."

Mr Grayling defended his actions. "I wanted to make a political point," he said, "which is that I shouldn't be allowed to run a bath, let alone a government department."

He continued, "I think I got my point across – that Leave means Leave and I should leave my position at once."

**BREXIT MOST READ**

## Rees-Mogg savages turncoat Rees-Mogg

LEADING Brexiteer Jacob Rees-Mogg has savaged leading Brexiteer Jacob Rees-Mogg, after Rees-Mogg decided that he was prepared to vote for Theresa May's Brexit deal.

"How can Jacob Rees-Mogg support a deal he previously called the greatest vassalage since King John paid homage to Phillip II at Le Goulet in 1200?" he asked. "How can this so-called man of principle support a wretched capitulation which will leave the UK as a slave state, subject to EU laws whilst having no say in their creation?"

Jacob Rees-Mogg hit back at Jacob Rees-Mogg's criticism, saying he saw nothing wrong with him being given the chance to change his mind over Brexit in another vote, just as long as the British public weren't given a similar chance to do so.

## 10 REASONS WHY MICHAEL GOVE SHOULD NOT BE PRIME MINISTER

**1.**

**2.** That's it.

*"I'll have to go now, I can feel old age suddenly creeping up on me"*

## END OF VIRGIN FRANCHISE

It was cancelled at the last minute... no announcements were made... it's ruined my day


## Jeremy Corbyn *WRITES*

**HELLO! It's me again. I'm sure you've heard that I'm fighting fit and ready for PM.**

Yes, the reports are true... I do run 7k several times a week!

Of course there are a few doubting Thomases (mentioning no names, Mr Watson!) who don't think I actually run! They say no one's actually seen any evidence. Well, there is plenty of photographic evidence, but Momentum sent the wrong film to Snappy Snaps and we got back all my holiday photos of me attending funerals instead. Never mind!

You might ask yourselves: how do I have such a disciplined exercise schedule? It's very easy. I call it my "run a mile" regime. Whenever I'm asked to make a definitive statement on Labour's policy on a second referendum, I run a mile. Whenever I have to make a decision on expelling anti-Semites from the party, I run another mile, and so forth.

I've always been a very fit man. I couldn't have single-handedly stopped apartheid or sorted out peace in Northern Ireland if I wasn't in tip-top shape! That's why I couldn't find a seat on that Virgin train. Yes, there were empty seats, we can all see that now, but that silly capitalist running dog Richard Branson makes his seats so incredibly narrow (in his greedy pursuit of profit) that none of them can accommodate my bulging thighs and rippling calf muscles!

That's also why I keep not turning up to important votes, like my own child poverty amendment. What would have been the point? When I'm really ripped I just can't fit through those voting lobbies no matter how hard I try!

Exercise is part of my life. My motto is "no pain, no gain". I have lived by that in all aspects of my life, right up to this point. It does sum up everything else. The Brexit I'm helping to get through parliament will inflict untold pain on the country, but without that PAIN, and the subsequent rage directed at Theresa May, how else am I going to GAIN the Prime Ministership? You see my logic!

So, If you'll excuse me, I'm off for a run right now. I tell you, as a hobby, the buzz you get from it is almost like the high you get from extreme socialism – exhausting and tiring, but with the satisfaction of ending up right back where you started!

Cheerio!

# Nursery Times

Friday, Once-upon-a-time

## PAEDO PAN WAS PAEDO SHOCK

by Our Showbiz Staff **J.M. Barrie**

THE much-loved singer, dancer and style icon Paedo Pan has been revealed in a controversial Disney film as a monster who preyed upon innocent children.

Pan is shown grooming the Darling children at night, before enticing them to join him at his home in Neverland with the promise of a *Pirates of the Caribbean*-style adventure.

Fans of Pan have criticised the movie, saying Paedo was an unhappy figure who had never grown up and was merely looking for his lost childhood.

"Yes, he enjoyed the company of the lost boys," said one, "but there is no evidence to suggest that Pan's behaviour was in any way appropriate."

Mr and Mrs Darling have also been criticised for doing nothing to prevent Pan from befriending their children, often leaving the window open in an upstairs bedroom, so Pan could enjoy sleepovers with John and Michael and their sister, Wendy.

John and Michael, who appear in the film talking about their relationship with Pan and their experiences in Neverland, have been accused of inventing the whole story, in order to make money.

As the controversy continued to rage, there was much debate about whether we could still enjoy the great music associated with Pan, including such well-loved hits as:

"You can Lie!"

"Following the Paeder!"

"Never smile at a paedophile!" *(Surely "crocodile"? Ed.)*

Either way, there will always be a shadow hanging over, and indeed sewn on to, the legend that is Paedo Pan.

## THOSE NEW RACE MESSAGES

**BLACK YOUTH GETS HUGGED**
Twitter shouts *"White saviour"*

**BLACK YOUTH GETS STABBED**
Twitter shouts *"It's not about race"*

**White saviour**

**White saver**

## Those New Documentaries That Have Rocked The World In Full

**1. Leaving Neverland**
Reveals that Michael Jackson was a paedophile.

**2. Believing in Neverland**
Reveals that Pope is Catholic.

**3. Relieving in Woodland**
Reveals that bears evacuate bowels in tree-filled areas.

*"He's trying to unlearn the Moonwalk"*

## Jon Snow – a guide to places in the UK where he'll be astonished to see so many white people

Waitrose
M&S food hall
The Hay Festival
Glyndebourne
The Boat Race
Oxford and Cambridge
Radio 4 panel show recordings
The entire television industry
The Home Counties *(where Jon Snow lives)*
Remain March

## How to correct a Boeing share price that's nosediving

- Stop your new 737 MAX 8 planes falling out of the sky and killing everyone on board.
- Er...
- That's it.

## ST CAKES HEADMASTER FURIOUS AT 'HOUSE OF COMMONS SLIGHT'

by Our Education Staff **Gabby Tass-Thring**

**MR R.J. KIPLING, headmaster of the famous independent Midlands school for boys and girls (motto: *Quis paget entrat*), last night hit out at what he called "outrageous Parliamentary snobbery".**

Kipling was complaining about an exchange between the leader of the European Research Group, Jacob Rees-Mogg, MP for North-East Somerset, and the obscure backbench MP, Timothy Nice-but-Dim, who represents the constituency of Thyckeness and Bricktown.

"Tim" Nice-but-Dim had suggested that as an alternative to a hard border in Northern Ireland, it might be possible to introduce alternative customs arrangements, such as inspection of cross-border traffic by teams of uniformed leprechauns.

Rees-Mogg had replied that although this was an interesting suggestion by the Right Honorable Member, and certainly better than Mrs May's terrible plan, it had a classic "Cakehamist" ring to it.

There was much laughter in the chamber at this point, as members realised that Old Etonian Rees-Mogg was suggesting in time-honoured fashion that the alumni of St Cakes were incredibly stupid – particularly compared to himself.

Nice-but-Dim countered by thanking Rees-Mogg and said that even though he was exactly the sort of chap whose head they would have flushed down the toilet at school for being such a weed and a swot, he was nevertheless "a bloody good bloke".

Mr Kipling, however, demanded that Rees-Mogg apologise for this "offensive hate speech about a much-loved British institution" and make a payment of £1 million to a suitable charity, ie St Cakes School.

# Israel fury over Moon rocket

by Our Space Staff
**Telstar Aviv**

The prime minister of Israel, Mr Benjamin Netanyahu, has vowed revenge on the Moon for what he described as "a blatant act of hostility towards Israel".

This follows the crash of an Israeli space rocket onto the lunar surface last week.

Netanyahu blamed the Moon for the destruction of what he called "an innocent lunar probe on a peaceful, fact-finding mission".

The Israeli hardman placed the responsibility for the crash firmly on the Moon, which he called a "known terrorist organisation".

He promised reprisals for the attack on the Israeli spacecraft and declared that it was his government's intention to annex the Moon at the next election or tomorrow, whichever was soonest.

# GAME OF THRONES

## Who Will End Up Triumphant? Our Panel Predicts

**Toby Young**: It doesn't matter who you support. There's no way the leftist blowhards at HBO will let anyone other than a black, disabled, "trans" character end up ruling the whole of Westeros, despite the *unambiguous evidence* that white, bald, bespectacled characters are scientifically more suited to government.

**James Delingpole**: I agree with Toby.

**Douglas Murray**: I agree with James.

**Taki**: I imagine our Hebrew friends will end up running the thing, if that isn't too subtle for my readers.

**Owen Jones**: One thing that is very clear is that the way has not been paved for free and fair elections in Westeros. This is a damning, shameful stain on all involved. Only a government run by an elderly bearded wizard can bring true peace and prosperity to the land.

**Sarah Vine**: I think the misanthropic drunk dwarf, Tyrion Lannister, is the most able political figure in the whole series. I think if he only made a good marriage – perhaps to a wise woman, one with a powerful voice in the Westeros media – he could become a giant.

**Piers Morgan**: I may not have mentioned it before, but I'm a personal friend of ice-cold queen Cersei Lannister. She's extremely naughty, and very indiscreet! Only the other day she LITERALLY looked at me at an exclusive dinner in King's Landing and said – and I'm quoting here – "Who are you?"

**Meghan Markle**: I support anyone who's trying to do their best with love and positive energy. But I, personally, am supporting Daenerys, the foreign upstart who has made her way to the top by sheer aggressive ambition.

# JON SNOW SHOCK

EXCLUSIVE TO ALL PAPERS

## GLENDA SLAGG

***Fleet's Street's top female critic takes a look at the pick of this week's TV***

■ **PHWOOAR??!!! Seen the priest in Fleabag??!? God Almighty! I'm a gal with Catholic tastes and I've got something to confess – I fancy the pants off him – if he wears any under that cheeky chasuble!?! How about a bit of communion round my place??!? You're the answer to all my prayers!!?! *(Talk about the programme. Ed.)***

■ FLEABAG!!?! Phoebe Waller-Bridge has created a brilliant ground-breaking character... in the fanciable Father!?!! Great Scott (I mean Andrew Scott, obvs)!?!! Jesus, he's hot. He's as hot as hell. Especially when he's wearing a dress. I could defrock him slowly. *(You're fired! Ed.)*

***Byeee!!***

INTRODUCING

## GLEN SLAGG

***Fleet's Street's top male critic takes a look at the pick of this week's TV***

■ **Seen Fleabag?!! Of course you have!! Me too. For those of you living on the Planet Zarg, let me put you in the picture. It's about this really sizzling priest!!! I mean, I'm a bloke, but who in their right mind wouldn't want to commit a cardinal sin with him?!! Phwooar star review from me!!?! *(I'm warning you: talk about TV or you're going the same way as Glenda. Ed.)***

■ OKAY!?! The new-look, all-female Newsnight!!?! No complaints, but where's the priest?! No wonder viewing figures are down!!! Get the passionate prelate on to pontificate about the Malthouse Amendment!!?! Now you're talking. Mmmm!?! Amen to that!!?! *(You're hell-fired! Father Ed.)*

***Byeee!!***

I CAN'T BELIEVE IT'S OVER
WHO ARE YOU TALKING TO?
FLEABAG
-PILBROW-

# Church 'horrified' by Fleabag

by Our Catholic Correspondent
**Gene U. Flect**

THE Catholic Church has expressed outrage after the penultimate episode of Fleabag showed the main character bedding a Catholic priest.

"Any suggestion that a Catholic priest would abandon his sacred vow of celibacy for a posh, sexy woman is utterly ridiculous," said a Vatican spokesman.

"The priest would of course be far too busy plying his 11-year-old altar boys with communion wine and asking them to the vestry to see his extensive panini sticker collection.

"To see a Catholic priest being presented in this manner as a typical bloke who can't resist getting between the sheets for great sex with a sexy, posh lady is a disgraceful misrepresentation of the countless paedophiles who have been drawn to serving God."

## On other pages

● Special offer Fleabag Teabag – relive your favourite edgy TV tragi-comedy with this incredible commemorative gift, only £9.99 **p94**

# WOODS WINS THE MASTERS!

It's Tiger's date with destiny
Is she a stripper?

# Changes to Divorce Laws

*By Philippa Space*

So the government has FINALLY released proposals to overhaul Britain's archaic divorce laws, ushering in no-fault divorces which will alleviate bitterness and ease the distress for any children involved.

I can certainly say, from my own experience, that I just wish no-fault divorces had been around when my ex and I separated a few years back.

I would have jumped at the chance to have had a more amicable separation from that cheating scumbag who thought it was okay to spend Tuesday evenings banging some brassy blonde from accounts in a Travelodge in New Malden, rather than being at home with his gorgeous wife, who never lost her figure, and his two sweet, innocent children who deserved better than a twisted shitbag like him as a father.

It would have given us the opportunity to approach the split as reasonable adults, with less screaming from him that I was a harpy and a bitch after he returned home from a night with his slut to find his clothes shredded on the front lawn and his precious golf clubs and Rolex watch sold on eBay.

What I would have given for us to have sat down like adults and agreed in a spirit of mutual respect that if he ever brought that slag and her fat arse anywhere near my little angels, I'd cut him.

Looking back now, I realise a no-fault divorce could have meant that my no-good, scumbag, deadbeat, waste-of-space arsehole and I could have parted on far better terms, meaning the children would have been spared hearing in graphic detail how daddy isn't around anymore, as he prefers rough sex with filthy slags in motorway services car parks to his lovely *(cont. on pages 33, 34 and in Court 23)*

*"Oh, that... it's my girlfriend's mood board. Maybe we should go and watch the match down the pub instead"*

# MUELLER REPORT FINDS NO EVIDENCE OF COLLUSION BETWEEN RUSSIA AND TRUMP CAMPAIGN

# AN APOLOGY

**IN the past two years, we, like all other liberal newspapers, may have given the impression that the investigation into President Trump by the former director of the FBI, Robert Mueller, would undoubtedly come to the conclusion that he had in some way colluded with Russia to influence the 2016 election and that this investigation would result in Trump's well-deserved impeachment and imprisonment for the rest of his life.**

**Headlines such as: "Red Stooge In White House", "Putin Put In Crooked President" and "Lock Up Traitor Trump, the Kremlin Stooge" may have led our readers to imagine that the Special Counsel would, in all likelihood, find the controversial President Trump guilty of interference with the democratic process.**

**We now realise that there was not a jot or tittle of truth in the above and that, on the contrary, Mr Mueller was always going to take a thorough and dispassionate look at the facts and come to the conclusion that there was "no evidence of collusion".**

**We hope that our headlines today: "President cleared, though questions remain", "Trump now likely to win in 2020, thanks to Mueller" and "Oh no, the fat orange bastard has got off scot-free after all that effort", will in some way clarify our position and rectify any perception of political or partisan bias.**

**We would like to apologise to our readers for any confusion caused by our previous coverage.**

Advertisement

## NEVER SEEN ACTION man

***Comes in full Territorial Army uniform, namely business suit and tie***

'OUT NOW!' says Never Seen Action Man

**Never Seen Action Man** is just like real Action Man, only not at all. Pull the string on Never Seen Action Man's back and he says "Perfidious Albion on speed" and then recites all 70 lines of Tennyson's *Ulysses* in a silly voice. Always in the thick of the action from the safety of his office, he's all mouth and no trousers! *(Trousers not included)*

***FEATURING NO BATTLE SCARS***

Accessories: Shotgun (to put in mouth or aim at foot)

**Price: £39 billion**

**Also available from Gnomemart... Easter ERGs. Themed chocolate eggs with all your favourite European Research Group characters painted on!**

# ASSANGE EXTRADITION LATEST

## What next for Julian Assange?

- Father Christmas
- Gandalf look-a-likey
- A garden gnome
- King Lear at the Old Vic
- Grandad in the *Only Fools and Horses* musical
- Upside-down-face puzzle model *(That's enough jobs for Assange. Ed.)*

## Easter Message

*"So much for a 'People's Vote' getting you out of trouble"*

# UNKNOWN COMEDIAN DIES – TRIBUTES POUR IN

by Our Stand-up Correspondent **Stan Dupp**

**AFTER the death of a not-very-well-known comedian on stage, tributes have been pouring in from far more famous and successful comedians.**

"He was the comedian's comedian, by which I mean I never had to worry about him nicking any of my well-paid TV panel show gigs," said a famous TV panel show comedian.

"You may not have known his name, but the important thing is that you know mine and, in the end, I think that is what he would have wanted," added another famous comedian who appears on Channel 4.

"He was the comedian who stayed true to the art of stand-up," said another famous comedian, recording his Netflix special. "I always secretly wanted to be him, playing to a dozen punters in a pub in Hemel Hempstead, whilst I was selling out Wembley and producing best-selling Christmas stand-up DVDs." *(That's enough tributes from famous comedians. Ed.)*

# Doubts over authenticity of Salvator Mundi picture

by Our Art Staff
**Leonardo di Caprio**

EXPERTS have shocked the art world this week by expressing doubts about the picture of the so-called "Saviour of the World".

The image of a benign, saintly, bearded left-wing pacifist messiah with the initials J.C. has, for many years, been accepted as entirely genuine.

But now, art historians have taken a closer look at the work and are worried that they may have been fooled.

Detailed examination suggests that the Christ-like figure may be the work of a lesser artist called Seumas Milne, who was known for painting over-flattering representations of his subjects, rather than accurate depictions of reality.

One expert from top auction house Jesus Christies went so far as to say, "When you look beneath the surface with x-ray analysis, you see a very different person – the holy figure has been superimposed on a rather average and flawed individual who has been given a halo in order to sell a fake picture to the world."

Many are now agreed that there is an obvious clue in the picture to the bogus nature of the work.

Far from being the King of the Jews, the sitter didn't really like them very much and *(cont. p94)*

# BLACK HOLE SIGHTING ROCKS UNIVERSE

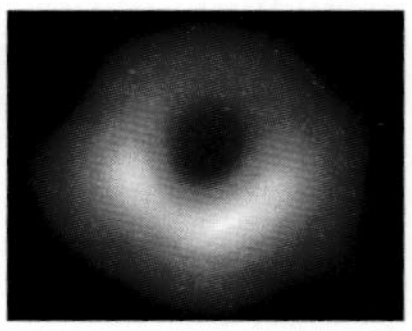

by Our Science Correspondent **Phil Space**

**THE discovery of a black hole this week spelt disaster for all Brexit analogies, as all other metaphors were sucked into its vast black nothingness.**

Said one political scientist, "The black hole bears an uncanny and powerful likeness to the country's perilous situation. It has a phenomenal power to crush all other surrounding matter, and an ability to make time pass incredibly slowly. No other metaphor has a chance."

Some of the metaphors seen disappearing into the black vortex this week include the introduction of "No Fault Divorce", the opening of the British Museum's "The Scream" exhibition, and David Attenborough's walruses falling over a cliff edge.

One media analyst explained, "In any normal week, just one of these news events would have served as a perfectly functional metaphor for desperate journalists to clutch at, but the black hole has swallowed them all up, like a, er... well – like a black hole."

Scientists believe the black hole could be a gateway to other parallel universes – offering parallels with the national debt, Debenhams and the HS2 budget, not to mention the Tories' local election results.

## EYE READER POLL

# WHO DO YOU THINK IS MOST LIKE THE NAZIS?

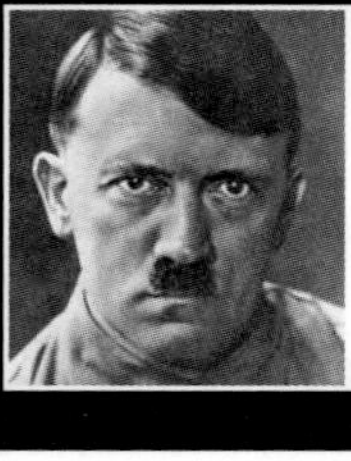

- ☐ Boris Johnson
- ☐ Jacob Rees-Mogg
- ☐ David Lammy
- ☐ Ken Livingstone
- ☐ Adolf Hitler

# WEIRD 70s CULT EXPOSED BY SURVIVOR
## Rachel Johnson speaks out

**Conspiracy Update**

# Royal Baby Special

■ As we are well aware, the bombshell announcement that the Palace is refusing to tell us when Meghan goes into labour with Prince Harry's child speaks of deeper and more sinister events.

ROYALTRUTH34567 has helpfully posted a theory on a Reddit forum that Meghan was never pregnant and that it's just a pillow stuffed up her blouse. He expounds on this theory on his Facebook page, stating that the Royal Family are actually planning to steal a baby on the due date by cutting it from the womb of a sleeping pregnant mother and using it to complete the satanic ritual performed at the birth of Princess Margaret when the Queen gorged on Satan's umbilical cord to grant Prince Philip eternal life.

However, the authoritative 'Ickewatch' website furiously disputes this. It has produced a mountain of evidence in the form of artwork photoshopped from the covers of old fantasy novels to prove that Meghan is giving birth to a lizard. All the royal children are actually lizards and we know this because the gestation period for lizards significantly differs from humans, which is why they always fake the birth date to hide the fact that royal brides give birth to wriggling hissing snake creatures with their own poison glands like in 'Jurassic Park' when that fat bloke gets killed.

Not so, according to the 'truthisoutthere' Twitter account. They dismiss the lizard theory as "crackpot" and offer undeniable proof, in the form of blurry photos of hubcaps photoshopped onto the grounds of Balmoral, that Meghan is only half human and that the baby will be born in real alien form from her Scientology planet, a thing so hideous that the mere sight of it will cause Nicholas Witchell to spontaneously combust.

The notion, put forward by a few obscure channels on YouTube that the royal couple just wanted a bit of privacy was immediately dismissed as fanciful nonsense and dismissed by the vast majority of *(cont. for the rest of the internet)*

## PRINCE HARRY WARNS ABOUT THE DANGERS OF SOCIAL MEDIA

Find out more by following me on Instagram


# BREXITEERS 'NOW BACK REMAIN'

by Our Opinion Staff **Hugh Turn**

**IN an astonishing U-turn, all 17.5 million Leave voters today announced that they were abandoning their dreams of Brexit and had decided to stay in the EU after seeing a particularly witty sign at the Stop Brexit March in central London.**

"We previously believed in the idea of bringing Britain out of the EU," admitted one Brexiteer, "but seeing this brilliantly witty sign made the scales fall completely from our eyes and we realised what total fools we've been."

The owner of the devastatingly witty sign said he was pretty certain that it was going to be the catalyst for stopping Brexit after his Mum chuckled when he showed it to her before he left to catch the bus to the march.

## THAT HONG KONG TAKEAWAY MENU IN FULL

1. **You are taken away to the mainland**
2. **You are subject to the rigours of one of the most efficient justice systems in the world**
3. **You don't come back again**
4. **Er... That's it.**

# NEW MIRACLE SLIMMING PILLOCK ANNOUNCED

by Our Health Staff **Lunchtime O'Bese**

**A NEW slimming pillock has given hope to millions of overweight Britons. The miracle pillock works on a very simple principle, but has already had amazing results.**

Said one delighted beneficiary of the first trial, a Mr Johnson, "It's incredible. All you do is take one fruity PR girl and the weight just drops off you."

Scientists claims that the effects of living with someone 20 years younger than you have always been known, but should be made more widely available.

Mr Johnson says, "Cripes! Everyone should have one of these. I call it the Fit-Bird! You see, like the Fit-Bit?! I'll be losing millions of pounds as a result of this, but that's divorce for you! Whoops!"

**Lightweight politician**

*"Him, him, him, him, him and him"*

## From The Message Boards

**Members of the online community respond to the major issues of the day...**

### Children's cartoons accused of sexism

Sexism alert! Fireman Sam and Peppa Pig are under fire for using the term 'fireman'. One 4-year-old called Esme even wished she were a boy so she could join the fire brigade, because 'they are all boys and I don't want to be the only girl'. But female firefighters took to social media in droves to prove their existence, and Esme 'now believes that she can be a girl AND a firefighter'! #firefightingsexism #girlpower – ***Supermum***

o to be the only girl with a bunch of firemen 😃 wait til your 30 and flashin your boob's at fire engines on hen night's! – ***Hunny pot***

i self-identify as a fireman so get yer tits out! 😉 – ***hatfield gooner***

show us ur hose first 😃 – ***Hunny pot***

As a young-at-heart pensioner, I've penned a satirical skit about this. And without wishing to blow my own trumpet (better a delightful dolly bird does it for you!) it's a corker. A raging feminist (well endowed in the Bristols department) burns her bra and sets light to her house, but a he-man fireman (like Burt Reynolds) saves the day! Whereupon she reveals that she goes to female-empowering pole-dancing classes and slides down the fire station pole in her underwear! – ***'Old chap!'***

My former daughter Poppy (14) identifies as recreationally trans and is now known as Pip. I, he and his sisters Daisy (12) and Remain (2) were watching the episode of Peppa Pig in which her mum joins the Mummies Fire Service, and the narrator says: 'Mummy Pig is dressed as a fireman.' Why did she take her husband's name, I thought, surely it should be Mummy Sow? But before I could speak, Daisy exclaimed: 'How sexist, she is a firefighter not a fireman!' Whereupon Pip shouted: '2019 calling cisgender bigots! She identifies as a fireMAN! Get over it!!' To which Daisy riposted: 'Go and watch FireMAN Sam then!' Pip shot back with: 'Fireman Sam, whose producers had to apologise for Islamophobia?!' At this point Remain shocked us all by waving her arms and screaming, 'LEAVE!' Her siblings have since worked tirelessly to understand the causes of such ignorance and anger. Am I wrong to feel proud of these passionate, socially aware young people? – ***Tim the househusband***

I agree with the female 'firefighters' that the programme is 'not a true reflection'. For a start, Sam's face is never blackened by smoke, probably for the same reason they got rid of the Black and White Minstrel show *This has been shortened by the moderators for legal reasons* – ***new user name***

# BIBLICAL TIMES

Friday 3 May 2019

## Climate change protest – boat annoys everyone

By Our Environmental Staff
Jeremiah Paxman

A leading climate change activist, calling himself Noah, son of Lamech, has parked a wooden boat in the middle of a busy Holy Land thoroughfare, causing widespread disruption.

The deliberate building of the so-called Ark and its placing at a known commercial junction has seriously inconvenienced shepherds, merchants and farmers trying to go about their business.

But Noah and his followers, Ham, Shem, Japheth and Emma, son of Thomp *(Is this right? Ed.)*, are unrepentant.

"The truth is," said Noah, "that man-made climate change is about to engulf the earth. The sea levels are going to rise by a large number of cubits and most of the planet is going to drown."

He continued, "Most animal species are going to be wiped out unless *we* do something right now.

"This is why my campaign is known as Extinction Rebellion. Saving animals two by two may seem a small gesture, but it is vital we do *something*!"

Noah was immediately attacked by establishment critics who claimed there was "no scientific evidence" to support the theory that the world was about to be destroyed.

Said one, "This is just entitled middle-class whingeing. Noah is well known as a rich, privileged patriarch who thinks he's got a hotline to God."

Another joined in, saying, "It is typical that Noah should try to pin the blame on mankind for what he insists on calling *our* sinful ways."

A commentator from Cloudy Sky News accused Noah of hypocrisy for cutting down large numbers of trees to build his boat, thus contributing directly to environmental damage.

"He should get a life," said Adam and Eve Boulton, "or better than that, get a Job." *(That's another book. Ed.)*

"Whatever Noah is claiming, there is absolutely nothing to... hang on... is that a drop of rain? Better get my... glug... glug... glug...

## POLITICIANS LINE UP TO BE CHASTISED

Okay, we'll have our photo taken

*"I'll be a little late, I'm stuck on the train"*

## Jeremy Corbyn *WRITES*

**HELLO! It's me again.**

Now, there comes a moment when yours truly has to take a stand. That moment came just last week. I was in the office and the phones were ringing off the hook from MEPs demanding clarity on our policy re a people's vote (spoiler: there won't be one!). Everyone was sweating buckets, and it was all getting a bit too hot for comfort.

And at that moment I knew it was the right time to talk about climate change!

I had the good fortune to meet Greta Thunberg last week, and I must say it was a huge privilege for this inspirational 16-year-old to meet me! It was also a pleasant change for me to listen carefully and ultimately ignore a young person's view on climate change, as it does get a bit monotonous listening carefully and ultimately ignoring young people's views on Brexit all the time!

So it was nice to be present, but not actually involved in that meeting. I was there merely as an observer, as I'm already doing my bit on the environment. Don't forget – I own a bike! So when Greta said that all politicians have failed us on the environment, she obviously meant Conservative politicians, not me!

We socialists are, of course, instinctively green. That's why we continually call to re-open all the coal mines and factories closed by the Tories. We don't think about the millions of tonnes of $CO_2$ released into the atmosphere; we focus on those newly employed workers who would have much less time on their hands to smoke their fags and drive their rusty old cars up the M1 to their football matches and their dog fights. So if you think about it, air pollution will ultimately be reduced!

But hey, we can't stand by and let the government do all the work! We should ask ourselves: what can we personally do to help the environment? Recycling is important. For example, I've got 30 million Labour leaflets in my shed and I was thinking that they would make very good compost. But then I thought – hmm! Even composting would release some gases into the atmosphere. Far better to stick them back in the envelopes and tell everyone they've been rewritten!

How could any self-respecting Labour party member have a problem with an environmentally friendly gesture like that?

Cheerio!

YOUNG PEOPLE HAVE BEEN BRAINWASHED
YES. THEY HAVE BEEN BRAINWASHED.
CLIMATE CHANGE
K.J. Lamb

# Lookalikes

**Sir Mark** **Sir Humphrey**

*Sir,*
*With our political scene resembling a "Yes Minister" episode more every day, how fitting thavt the new Cabinet Secretary and Britain's top civil servant, Sir Mark Sedwill, is in the Sir Humphrey mould.*
*Are they by any chance related? I suspect we shouldn't be told.*
*ENA B. ROOKS.*

**Fabinho** **Umunna**

*Sir,*
*I noticed that Chuka Umunna has been moonlighting as a central midfielder for Liverpool, going by the name of Fabinho.*
*ANDREW PARFITT,*
*Glasgow.*

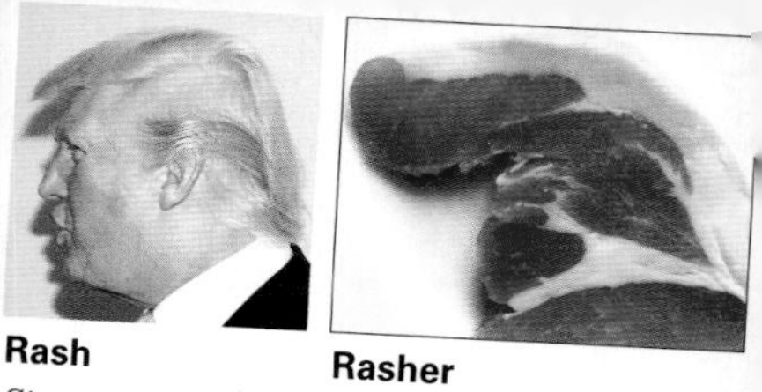

**Rash** **Rasher**

*Sir,*
*I thought I'd contact you with a photograph for consideration. It's basically a slice of bacon that looks like Donald Trump.*
*TOM HICKS,*
*Kingswinford.*

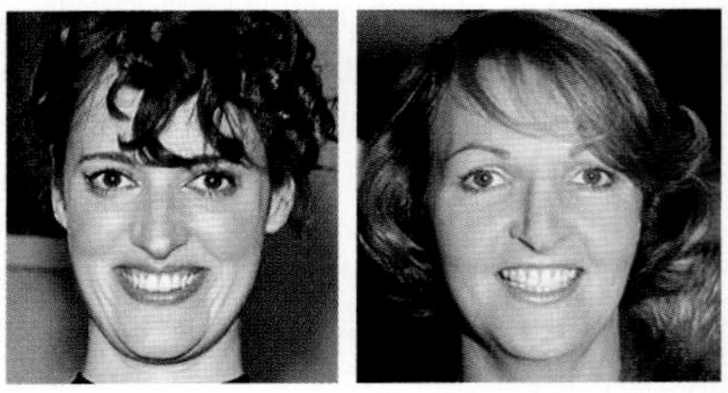

**Penelope Keith** **Phoebe Waller-Bridge**

*Sir,*
*One's a jolly hockey sticks sitcom icon. The other is Penelope Keith.*
*STEPHEN ARNELL.*

**Monolith** **Starmer**

*Sir,*
*I wonder if your readers have noticed the remarkable resemblance between Sir Keir Starmer MP, Shadow Secretary of State for Exiting the European Union, and one of the monoliths created by the Polynesian civilisation of Easter Island several centuries ago?*
*Incidentally, the consensus of archaeologists is that the inhabitants of the island caused their own demise through infighting and the over-exploitation of the island's resources.*
*CHARLES OWEN-JONES.*

**akey** **May**

*I note a curious facial similarity between Great Blakey from On The Buses and our der, Theresa May. Both exponents of a g-running farce, sadly only one is funny.*
*FABIO PANNUTI.*

**Jeremy** **Sergei**

*Sir,*
*Only one of these two looks more sensible in glasses.*
*STUART SILVER.*

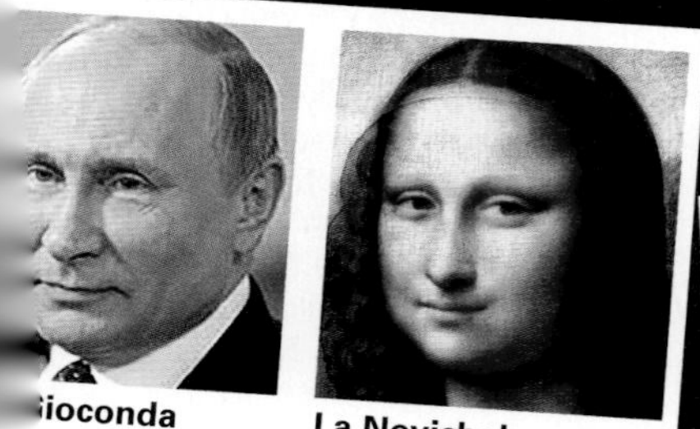

**ioconda** **La Novichoka**

*as anyone else noticed the extraordinary blance between the enigmatic smiler tly in the Louvre and the one in the in? What exactly do they find funny?*
*ENA B. PADLEY,*

**Labonq** **Soubry**

*Sir,*
*Is Anna Soubry in fact Mimi Labonq, the Resistance heroine from 'Allo 'Allo?*
*ENA G. HILL,*
*Sheffield.*

**Bingo** **Klopp**

*Sir,*
*One of these two manages Liverpool FC – that's a football club, in case you didn't know!*
*DAVID COX.*

**s** **Francois**

*ar both the Conservative MP Mark s and Christopher Biggins are busy as with panto.*
*MARK MORRIS,*

**Alan Carr** **James Runcie**

*Sir,*
*Can you remind me who writes the Grantchester series of books? Is it James Runcie, or Alan "Chattyman" Carr?*
*It's a mystery to me.*
*PETER KENDALL*

**Sontaran** **Sajid Javid**

*Sir,*
*Home Secretaryww/Dr Who monster (Sontaran) 1973.*
*GILES SADLER,*

**David Brent** **Barry Gardiner MP**

*Sir,*
*I was astonished to see how desperate some people are to promote themselves. Brexit has truly led to some folks believing they have a future in their chosen vocations.*
*Yours in turmoil,*
*BRYAN WILKINSON.*

**Edna Mode** **Sabine Weyand**

*Sir,*
*I could not help noticing an uncanny resemblance between the Deputy Chief EU Brexit Negotiator, Sabine Weyand, and the eccentric fashion designer, Edna Mode. Wouldn't it be incredible if they were related? We should be told.*
*SALLY CAIRD.*

**Warden Hodges** **David Gauke**

*Sir,*
*Defence Secretary Gavin Williamson has long been known as Private Pike but I have just noticed that Justice Secretary David Gauke is starting to look like Warden Hodges. I am trying not to panic, but Theresa May makes Captain Mainwaring seem like Napoleon.*
*RICHARD HELLER,*
*London.*

**Comic book villain** **Esteemed advisor**

*Sir,*
*Stepping out of No.10 the other day, I swear that among all the Spads I saw Uncle Duke, the drug-addled villain of the Doonesbury cartoon strip. Or was it Dominic Cummings? Perhaps there is photographic evidence we might consult.*
*NICK PERRY.*

**Angela Merkel** **Les Dawson**

*Sir,*
*Not only perhaps related, but one and the same person?*
*NICKY SAMENGO-TURNER,*
*Gloucester.*

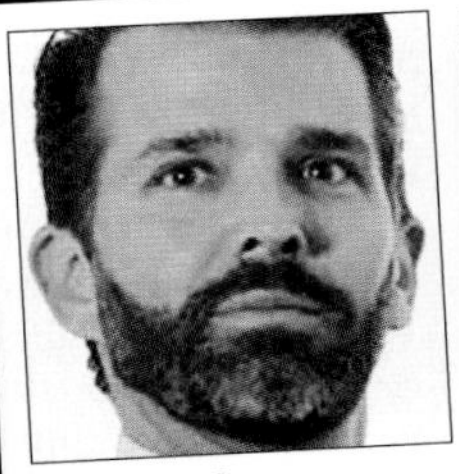

**Clown prince** **Crown prince**

*Sir,*
*I wonder whether anyone has noticed the remarkable resemblance between Donald Trump Jr and Prince Mohammad bin Salman of Saudi Arabia. Spooky or what?*
*GERARD O'BRIEN,*
*Newcastle upon Tyne.*

**Boris Johnson** **George IV**

*Sir,*
*I am writing to draw your attention to the remarkable physical similarity (I make no mention of their lifestyles) between a notorious rake, libertine and glutton of the late 18th/early 19th century, George IV, and Britain's foremost, albeit as yet uncrowned, rakes, libertines and gluttons of the 21st century, Boris Johnson.*
*I enclose their respective portraits for your perusal.*
*Best wishes,*
*NEIL JACKSON,*
*Passau.*

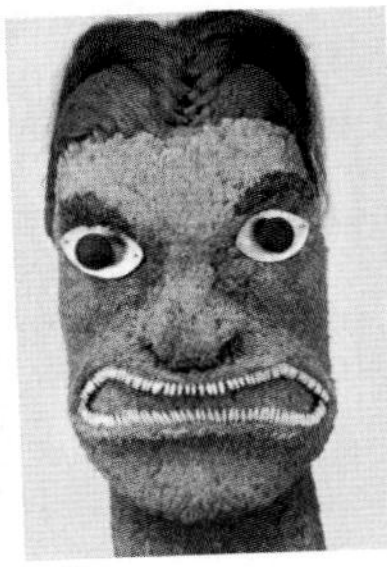

**Simon Cowell** **Terrifying God**

*Sir,*
*Much as I respect the importance of ITV's primetime output, is the Royal Academy right to label this piece in its current 'Oceania' exhibition as a "terrifying God".*
*STEVE BALDOCK,*
*Handcross, West Sussex.*

**Chris Grayling** **Humpty Dumpty**

*Sir,*
*Has anyone else spotted the startling resemblance between Chris Grayling MP and this other egg-headed disaster?*
*ELLIOT SCOTT.*

**Melania** **Mask**

*Sir,*
*I noticed the wonderful hat worn by Mrs Trump – who apparently flew into England today – when she met our own Dear Queen.*
*There is a distinct similarity with that worn by the American comedian Jim Carrey, a virulent critic of her husband Dinuld Chimp, in his role of The Mask – perhaps this signals the start of a thaw in their frosty relationship?*
*GERRY BUCKLAND.*

**David Threlfall** **Michel Houellebecq**

*Sir,*
*That David Threlfall's really let himself go – almost as bad as Michel Houellebecq.*
*DAVID COX.*

**Moggy**

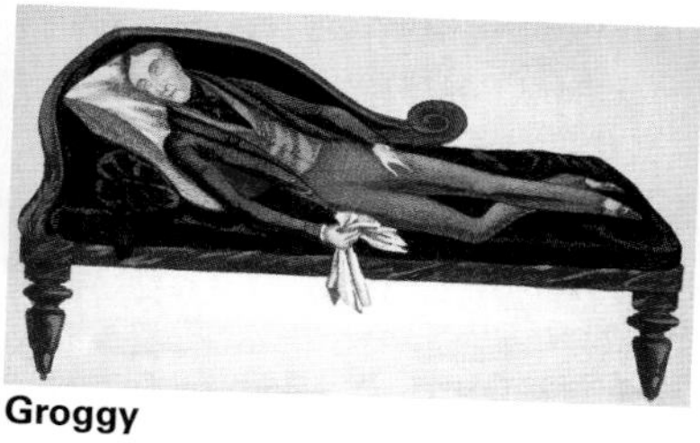

**Groggy**

*Sir,*
*Have you noticed the startling resemblance twixt the Lounger of the House of Commons and the "figure representing the last stage of mental & bodily exhaustion from Onanism or Self-pollution" featured in the Wellcome Collection's archive? I think we should be told.*
*ALLY DICKSON.*

# CURSE OF 'STRICTLY' STRIKES AGAIN

# RELIEF FOR CELEBRITIES AS NEW CAREER LIFELINE EMERGES

by Our Celebrity Staff
**Mimi Me**

It's the nightmare every washed-up has-been has to face.

You've made a fool of yourself on *Strictly Come Dancing*, you've burned your salmon en croûte on *Celebrity Masterchef*, you've embarrassed your whole family on *Celebrity First Dates*, and *The Jump*'s been cancelled.

The phone simply hasn't rung since you were voted off *Celebrity Big Brother* in the first week and even your agent's not answering your calls.

But now there is a ray of hope to bring meaning to the life of Z-listers all over the country. Yes, the European elections are upon us and parties need candidates whom people vaguely recognise from the telly.

Said one wannabee MEP, Rachel Johnson, "I had reached the bottom of the barrel writing articles about myself and my nanny for the *Sunday Times* magazine, but then out of the blue came a call from an agency called 'Change UK'. Now I'm back in the limelight as a prospective candidate in something called 'The European elections'."

Former *Strictly* star Ann Widdecombe agreed, "I was at my wits' end. Even my cats didn't recognise me anymore, and then, hey presto, Nigel Farage came knocking on my door.

"Get out now," I said. To which he replied, "Well done – you've passed the audition! Got any other slogans?"

Who next will shrug off the cloak of anonymity that comes with celebrity reality appearances, and have the chance to rejuvenate their career by wowing the electorate with their views on fishing subsidies, the Common Agricultural Policy and the enlargement of the Schengen zone? Step forward Christopher Biggins!



# Salman Rushdie

## *Birds Who Have Fancied Me*

**MARGARET THATCHER**
She was all over me! I remember her just pawing at me when we had a meeting one time. "I want you more than I want to smash the miners and stand up to the bureaucrats in Brussels" I think I remember her saying. It certainly seems plausible.

**GERMAINE GREER**
Couldn't get enough of me when we met to discuss Third Wave Feminism at Glastonbury, or possibly Woodstock. I remember thinking to myself "Blimey! She's a bit of a one!"

**EMMELINE PANKHURST**
She's famous now as a bit of a prude, but my memories of her are VERY different, if you know what I mean. She was a real firecracker and if she hadn't been so sad about her friend and that horse, I think I know how it would have gone between us.

**JOAN OF ARC**
I forget how we met – it may have been shortly before her capture at Compiègne by the Burgundian faction – but all I can say is that she wouldn't have been a maid for much longer if she'd had her way about it! Ooh la la, you know what I mean, guv?

# Spice Girls in lesbian sex row

THE Spice Girls have faced a tragic outbreak of publicity before their new tour, with the revelation that Scary Spice claims to have shagged Ginger Spice in the 1990s and that, naturally, Ginger Spice is furious and the forthcoming reunion is on the brink of being cancelled.

The furore means that the tour will almost certainly be pulled, unless by some chance this gambit manages to get lots and lots of newspapers interested and help them flog a million tickets.

The Spice Girls have asked for no privacy at all at this time.

### On other pages

- Phwoarrrr!!!
- Corrrr!!!!!
- Ooo-eerrrrrr!!!!!!

# Which work of art do you think Fleabag is better than?

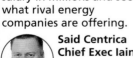

**The Sistine Chapel**
Yes, it shows nine scenes from the Book of Genesis culminating in the creation of Adam. But there's not enough naughtiness, and there's not *nearly* enough wine, and has it got Olivia Colman? It has not. Pathetic.

**The Mona Lisa**
She's coy, she's smiling, but she's probably not in love with a sexy priest played by that bloke off Sherlock. We don't even know if she's got a sister. Boring.

**The Sagrada Familia**
Fine, it's the masterpiece of Antoni Gaudí, fine, it's taken nearly a century, but it's not even finished. Fleabag finished in 12 episodes and it's a more perfect work of art than anything else we've ever seen.

**Michaelangelo's David**
OK, we get it, he's big and naked and he's got his knob out – but he completely lacks that lightness of touch that Phoebe Waller-Bridge, AKA the Queen of Everything, brings to the party. Lame!

**Girl with a Pearl Earring**
Granted, she's actually bothering to look at the viewer, which is a BIT like Fleabag, but she doesn't make any jokes about shagging or having a dead mum. Next!

# The Drilly Telegraph

Friday, May 3, 2019

## Fracking Tsar Resigns

THERE were shockwaves throughout Westminster at the news that Natascha Engel has quit her role as Commissioner for Shale Gas.

Said one expert, "She was forced out under pressure. It is what she would have wanted."

The news of her departure registered a frightening seven on the Richter scale and was described as "a seismic event" by environmentalists.

"It's earth shattering," said one drilling company. "It could have terrible repercussions for ourselves."

The government, however, denied that there was any danger associated with the controversial expulsion of Ms Engel: "If anyone doesn't agree with us, they can just frack off."

© *The Shaley Drillograph*

**Old Cakeian Newsletter**

## News of old boys

***Thanks to all the Old Cakeians who have written in to tell us what they have been up to since leaving the alma mater.***

**Simon Ditchwater** *(Dullards 1978-83)* writes from Reigate, where he has been working for Storage Solutions – the "your-house-to-warehouse" answer to surplus ownables. Simon recently ran into **Colin Yawn** *(Borings 1973-74)* in the car park of the Harvester in Croydon. Colin is now recovering in intensive care at St Mary's General Hospital in Dorking.

Meanwhile, **Henry Double-Barrel** *(Hoorays 2012-16)* surprised fellow Cakeians by making an appearance on the *South East at Six News* recently. A number of his contemporaries spotted Henry giving local presenter Andy Bloater a hard time over climate change before storming out of the studio. Extinction Rebellion member Henry was accused of hypocrisy by those who remembered him being captain of skiing and three-times winner of the Val d'Isastère Inter-Public School Heliskiing Trophy. Henry himself tells us that he's not intending to have a career in TV just yet, but he would like to meet up with any fellow OCs, particularly any who have become lawyers with human rights' experience who might fancy a catch-up cup of tea and getting him out of HMP Wandsworth.

● *Keep sending in your OC tales to the editor of "Down the Cakehole", the Old Cakeian bimonthly newsletter.*

**UKRAINE KRONIKLE**

## COMEDIAN TO BECOME NEXT BRITISH PM

by Our Man in London
**Frasier U. Krane**

**A BURLY, shaggy-haired stand-up comedian, known as Bojo, is to become the next British prime minister, I can reveal.**

Bojo (real name Boris McTurdface), who came to fame when appearing on TV comedy shows, has made no secret of his ambition to replace the now discredited Theresa May and is increasingly popular with disgruntled Tory voters.

As a gaffe-prone clown, Bojo recently starred as a bungling Foreign Secretary adept at shooting himself in the foot. Now Tory voters have decided to favour the clumsy comic over the other less colourful contenders, putting him in charge of the country.

"Our politics have become a farce," said one typical Bojo fan, "so what better than to elect a clown as PM?"

These are tough times for the patriarchy, Timmy. Don't let us down.
MOZ

Oh look, there's a story about a Labour MP trending on Twitter


## Exclusive to all newspapers

■ CHAMPAGNE corks were popping all over Fleet Street as a sensational photograph of an off-duty politician enjoying a weekend tipple went viral.

The on-duty journalists were delighted at their chance to have a go at Diane Abbott and celebrated accordingly.

Slurred one, "Thish is fantashtic. We've exposhed the hypocrashy of shomeone drinking inappropriately when they should be focusshing on produshing a newshpaper. Cheers! Mine's a large one. Byline that ish! Schuse me I need to write a moralishing editorial. Hic!"

The journalist then put his paper and himself to bed.

## Those Diane Abbott cocktails from Marx and Spencer in full

**Mojitomentum**

**Dianaquiri**

**Margarita Hodge**

**Tom Watson Collins**

**Whisky McDonnell**

**Corbynopolitan**

**Corbywallbanger**

**Vodka and Very Red Bull**

**Moscow Fool**

**Minted Jewlep** (removed from party pending an enquiry by Baroness Shampagne Chakrabarti)

*That's quite enough cocktails. Ed.*

**Diane says:** "Drink responsibly, if not legally. I always stick below the officially recommended limit of 14 units per week which, by my calculations, is 150 units per day or 2,742 units per minute."

## Miraculous new atom-splitting process discovered in UK

SCIENTISTS based in central London have discovered a revolutionary new means of generating energy.

"Until now we thought that splitting the atom was the most impressive thing anyone could do," said one of the team responsible for the breakthrough. "But now, we've found an even smaller subdivision of matter – by finding the smallest possible difference in opinion between parties who don't like Brexit.

"This really is incredible. For example, when it comes to Brexit nothing should divide Chuka Umunna from Vince Cable and Caroline Lucas. If you look at their opinions, they've all said exactly the same thing. And yet they find themselves bound up in what we're calling a state of Clustaphuk, in which, despite their complete overlap, there is very strong tension and disagreement between them.

"This process is so powerful that no two Remain campaigners are able to be in the same room as each other. And if they *are* brought close together, they start spinning extremely fast, attempting to explain why actually they are the only people with a reasonable opinion, despite all available evidence.

"This generates so much energy it could power the country, but it's much likelier to just make Nigel Farage happy."

# COUNCIL DROPS SWEARING BAN

# UKIP CANDIDATE QUITS OVER SHAMEFUL TWEET

**By GERARD CROSS**
Our Political Staff

**YET another political career was in ruins following the discovery of an old tweet from 2016.**

The prospective UKIP candidate for East Essex resigned yesterday in an attempt to limit the damage from his historical gaffe.

The UKIP candidate, Ivor Skeleton, admitted that he had regrettably once tweeted a nice picture of a cat to his mother.

Said Skeleton, "I am so embarrassed, this is a devastating end to my UKIP career. It was so out of character – I wasn't drunk, it wasn't late at night and I have no excuse at all for this thoroughly pleasant and inoffensive public posting on social media. I can only apologise to all my followers, who expect better from me. I've let myself down, I've let my party down, I've let the people of East Essex down. What can I say? I blame the Muslims."

**LATE NEWS:** Skeleton welcomed back into party as potential next leader.

# CHANGE UK CANDIDATE QUITS OVER SHAMEFUL TWEET

**By HEIDI HI and CHUKKA MOUT**
Our Political Staff

**THERE was yet further embarrassment for Britain's most exciting new, shiny, mould-breaking, politically sensitive party, formerly known as The Independent Group, following the discovery of an old tweet from this morning.**

The tweet, from the prospective MEP for West Essex, Ann Other-Skeleton, contained a number of suggestions for renaming the party of so-called "Tiggers". The tweet read as follows:

> **Ann** @Other-Skeleton
> Hey fellow Tiggers, how about these for a few ideas?
> 1. Tiggers With Attitude?
> 2. Ten Little Tiggers?
> 3. Tiggers in the Woodpile?
> 4. Change UK? (Just kidding! That would be terrible)

# SULTAN OF BRUNEI DENIES HOMOPHOBIA

**The Sunday Times** May 20 2019

# Corbygeddon looms, as rich threaten to leave

by Our Wealth Staff **Richie Liszt**

Britain was in meltdown last night after reading the shocking news that billionaires will pack their bags and leave Britain in the event of a Labour government.

"Corbygeddon", as it is widely known by myself, will see Britain's highest earners fleeing the country, taking out all their money and never coming back.

"Hooray!" said one traumatised Briton. "Good riddance!" said another. "This comes as a shock. I thought they had all gone to Monaco for tax purposes already."

Said yet another weeping member of the public, "Before I heard this, I was thinking of voting Labour. Now that I have read this threat, I'm definitely backing Corbyn."

**ON OTHER PAGES**

**Rich people are rich**
Sunday Times 94-page special investigation reveals that people with a lot of money have a lot of money

## News in brief

# Oxford pledges to take 'poor students'

■ In an attempt to create a higher education learning environment more reflective of British society in the 21st century, Oxford University today pledged to redouble its efforts to attract poor students.

"We've long had a policy in place of letting really poor people study here," insisted one senior Oxford don. "David Cameron, Boris Johnson and Jacob Rees-Mogg all reflect our long-standing commitment to extremely poor candidates being welcomed with open arms to study here.

"We don't care where they come from, as long as it's Eton."

*(Rotters)*

# PC tips for celebrities thinking of making jokes on Twitter

1. Don't
2. Seriously... just don't.
3. Close Twitter
4. Delete the app
5. Put your phone on charge, and go for a walk
6. PUT THE PHONE DOWN NOW!
7. Er...
8. That's it.

# *DIARY*

ROBERT MACFARLANE

I wake, or *waakken,* as it is in Old Norse, or *Njorss*.

The sunlight strikes my eyes with all the force of a sheep's bladder hurled against a brick wall by a Morris Man in the Peak District performing an ancient jig, Ye Olde Plum Tree.

I feel the call of nature, demanding to be answered. Trickle turns to torrent and back again to trickle. I experience an intense feeling of oneness with what the Inuit call the *splasshe* that surprises me with its force.

Placing my right hand on the bannister, I steel myself to take the journey down, down, down to the kitchen belowwe. "When I die, I would like to be reborn as a bannister," I think, "so that I might help travellers traverse the stairs that confront them."

Fear squeezes my heart. Just fourteen steps, so simple for others. But, as a writer, I am compelled to take them in alphabetical order – eight, eleven, five, four, fourteen, nine, one, seven, six, ten, thirteen, three, twelve, two. This makes my downward progress, leap on giant leap, doubly hazardous: one slip and I could be pitched headlong into a limbless future.

Arriving safely at the kitchen, my chest is gripped by a nameless terror. A polar bear can smell another living animal up to 20 miles away. Is one lying in wait, ready to tear me apart? My larder, home to breakfast cereals we like to call by their ancient Gallic names – *Vadabigz, Ry Shkrizhpiz, Svairdiz* – would certainly be large enough to hide a polar bear if it didn't mind squeezing up, hunching its shoulders and crossing its legs. Might an errant iceberg, wrought by an ecosystem in distress, have borne this lonesome polar bear to the centre of Cambridge, so many thousands of miles from its natural habitat? With an effort of will, I dismiss this crippling fear from my brain. Before I have poured the first *flakks* of cereal into my bowl, handmade by our local potter, Bob – a man gentle and kindly of manner – my head begins to tingle, and then my back and my chest start to shake, and I find myself crying, sobs shuddering my body. It is as if the realisation that I might have been savaged by a ravenous polar bear, here, here in my Cambridge *kvitchun,* has only just caught up with me, rendering me as vulnerable as a leaf blown hither and thither on the windyskar hotspeers in an ancient Saxon settlement high in the Cairngorms.

Early morn, late spring: milk from the cow, skimmed semily, poured plangently o'er puffs of sugar; coffee roasted over fire of the ancient gods, in the manner of the Hokikoki tribe of South Eastern Indonesia, as sharp as a long-handled scythe; across the airwaves, like a Laugavallalaug geyser in Iceland, music from *Kajagoogoo* hand-selected by Ken Bruce, venerable *jokki-ov-diskken.*

My five-year-old son raises a spoon to his mouth. In its reflection, I glimpse the sages of fifty millennia, begging to be fed.

He sups from his spoon, then, arriving at a crossroads in his mastications, draws to a halt.

He looks at me and says, "As our historical narratives of progress have come to be questioned, so the notion of history itself has become remodelled. History no longer feels figurable as a forwards-flighting arrow or a self-intersecting spiral."

He possesses a wisdom beyond his years.

I reply, "Nature, too, seems increasingly better understood not as a single gleaming snow-peak or tumbling river in which we might find redemption but rather as an assemblage of entanglements of which we are messily part."

I have enjoyed our little chat. My son packs his satchel ready for *skwool,* an old Cornish word meaning "place of learning". Meanwhile, I place some marmalade, organically grown by Ted – a warm, friendly man with a lovely smile, who was in the Royal Navy for some years before venturing into the marmalade and jam trades, and remains a remarkable poet – on my toast and, while doing so, realise with a jolt that I am unconsciously echoing the manner in which, in the fourth century BC, a woman's corpse was prepared for burial in Thessaly by placing a coin on her lips, there to pay the ferryman who would carry her towards the realm of death. Marmalade: a coin: lips. Each one of us is his own ferryman.

I take time to reflect on the nature of marmalade, and death. We spread marmalade on toast with a frequency that is, by its very nature, disarming; but is it not high time we reversed the procedure, or *prokkedorr* – and spread toast on marmalade? It is only by changing our habits, and shooting our bronze arrows of hope at all such barnacled procedures, that mankind can ever hope to reverse our drive – *driv* – towards planetary extinction and, by doing so, find some form of salvation, however sticky to the touch.

Before we set off for *skwool,* I embark on a quest for the car keys or, as we call them, the keys to the car, in the kitchen drawer. I plunge my hand in, madly, wantonly, cravenly, searching for that piece of metal crafted by man which, when placed with due care in the appropriate hole in a car, fires up the engine, and turneth man into god.

The key is not there. I look again. Little demons of worry bite at my stomach. A dragonfly rustles past, so discreetly that I neither see nor hear it. Somewhere in yonder sky a blackbird sings its melancholy song. In 11th century Slovenia, a footsore peasant wends his way to market, in search of turnips, or *trunipsch.*

I swallet on the truckle and parhelia the codflap, but still no key is to be found. Feeling myself on gruffy ground, I partake to the neighbouring drawer. The key is there. I have found the key. My jubilation o'erflows. I cannot wait to tell my good friend Sean. Sean is a bee-keeper, a walker, a potter and a man of few but precious words. But first, my son and I must to venture out to our car, as red as liver. My heart shivers fast and fear grips me like a body-vice. Above me, a jackdaw trimmers on the spandickle.

*As told to*
CRAIG BROWN

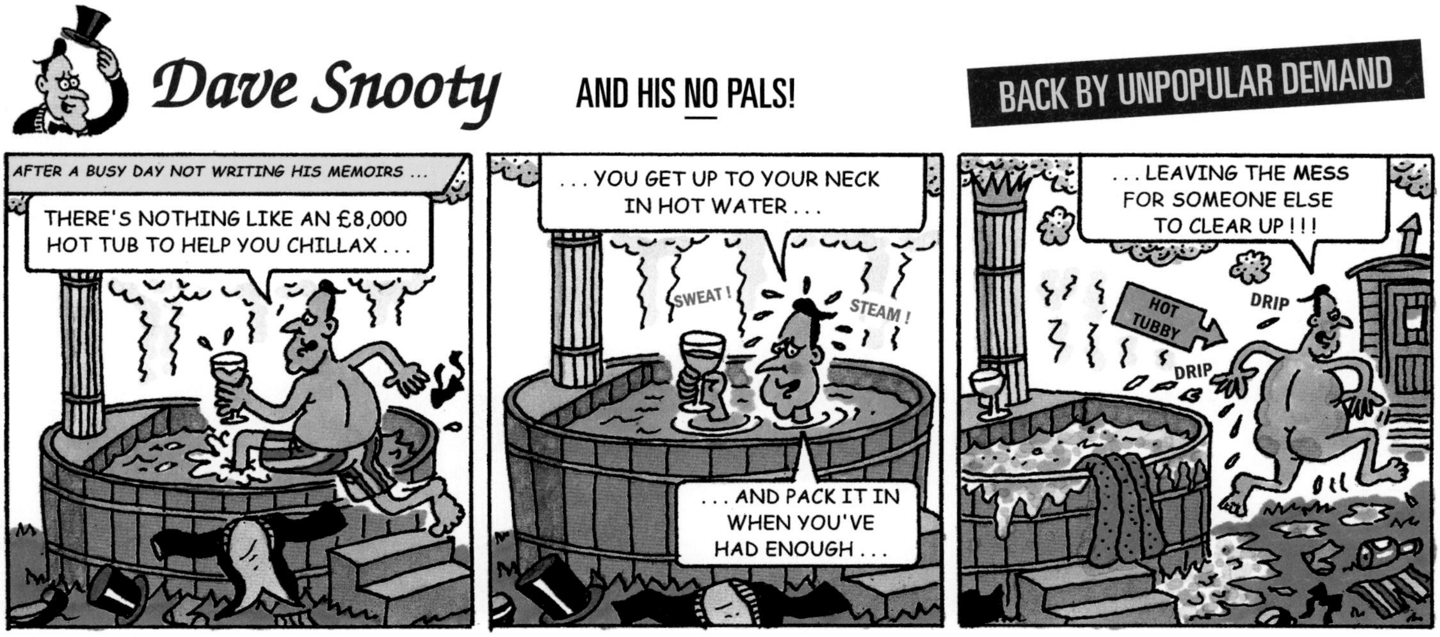

Dave Snooty
AND HIS NO PALS!
BACK BY UNPOPULAR DEMAND
AFTER A BUSY DAY NOT WRITING HIS MEMOIRS ...
THERE'S NOTHING LIKE AN £8,000 HOT TUB TO HELP YOU CHILLAX ...
... YOU GET UP TO YOUR NECK IN HOT WATER ...
SWEAT!
STEAM!
... AND PACK IT IN WHEN YOU'VE HAD ENOUGH ...
... LEAVING THE MESS FOR SOMEONE ELSE TO CLEAR UP !!!
HOT TUBBY
DRIP
DRIP

Exclusive to all papers

# AN APOLOGY

**IN RECENT weeks and months, with headlines such as FALL OF THE CALIPHATE and ISIS HUMILIATION COMPLETE, we may have given the impression that ISIS is no longer a problem, and that what once was a feared organisation able to strike terror into the hearts of West, is now little more than a fractured spent force, a ragtag rabble without leadership or purpose, humiliated and on its knees, having seen its beloved caliphate fall.**

**We now realise, in the wake of ISIS claiming responsibility for the devastating Sri Lanka Easter bombings which killed 359 people, that nothing could be further from the truth, and that the fall of the ISIS leadership has of course emboldened ISIS, giving it fresh impetus to regroup and rediscover its ability to become nimble and fleet of foot, allowing it to strike terror afresh into the heart of the West.**

**We apologise for any confusion in the past and any confusion in the future when the Americans claim a drone has taken out the ISIS leadership and we predict that without those key personnel it will quickly become a fractured spent force, a ragtag rabble without** ***(cont. p94)***

## Baldrick Goes Forth

*(Episode 94)*

**Private Baldtruth:** I have a cunning plan, sir.

**Captain Badleader:** Is it as cunning as my plan to sit cunningly on the fence for the entire duration of the war?

**PB:** Even more cunning than that, sir. I'm going to desert.

**CB:** You can't desert now. We are losing the war.

**PB:** The way I see it, sir, is that the high command is a bit rubbish and I don't like the anti-Semitism nor the strategy over Europe.

**CB:** Nonsense, Private Balderdash. You know what the punishment is for desertion...?

**PB:** I will be found guilty and trolled at dawn, sir.

**CB:** Spot on. It sends out a message to the troops that if anyone says we're intolerant, can't take criticism and are thoroughly toxic, they will get pigeons sent to them with the message "Fuck off and die, you traitor".

**PB:** That's over the top, sir!

**General Meltdown:** Correct! Now time for the final push.

**CB:** No, you won't get rid of me that easily.

[Enter Diana Badadder]

**CB:** Hello, Darling.

*(Continues for 94 series)*

# THOSE NOTRE DAME INTERNET CONSPIRACY THEORIES IN FULL

## Your guide to who did it!

**1. President Macron** to direct attention from his domestic problems and become popular again through his statesmanlike response

**2. Billionaire philanthropists** looking for a tax break through charitable donations post-conflagration

**3. Militant French firefighters** to elevate themselves to "hero" status in order to justify 3.7 percent payrise

**4. Gilets Jaunes activists** disappointed that burning Renault Twingos on the Champs Elysées has not had the desired revolutionary effect

**5. Climate change protestors** trying to increase global temperatures and prove their case by setting fire to cathedrals

**6. President Vladimir Putin** to cover the tracks of his elite global squad of cathedral-visiting agents out to poison the world

**7. The Duke of Edinburgh** seen driving nearby in a white Fiat Uno keen to revenge himself on the city of Paris – the scene of his secret murder of Princess Diana

**8. The Hot Priest from Fleabag** – so hot that his smouldering good looks set fire to the 15th Century gothic masterpiece whilst he was simply wearing a sexy chasuble and asking Fleabag (Phoebe Waller-Bridge on a holiday to the French capital) why she keeps looking at the camera

**9. French workmen** with Gauloises restoring the cathedral and inadvertently burning it down

**10. God**

***PLUS... Exclusive to the Sunday Gnomes***

A pull-out, 94-page graphic supplement with enormous illustrations of how the fire might have started, featuring 3D images of flames, buildings and emergency services. Doubles as firelighter, should you wish to burn down a major cathedral near you.

*© The Sunday Gnomes, Gnomespaper of the Year 2019*

**Notre Dame Candles**

# THOSE MANIFESTOS IN FULL

**Tory**
1. This election shouldn't be taking place
2. We would have left Europe by now if it wasn't for the Conservative party
3. Vote Conservative to get rid of Mrs May

**Labour**
1. This European election isn't about Europe
2. But if you wish either to remain in the EU or leave it, there is only one party to vote for
3. But don't vote for them. Vote Labour instead

**Liberal Democrat**
1. Bollocks to Brexit!
2. Bollocks to politeness!
3. Vote fucking Lib Dem!

**Change UK** *(formerly the Independent Tigger Group)*
1. Don't vote for us
2. Hang on, that's not right
3. Vote for us
4. Forget it, the candidate has pulled out anyway

**Brexit Party**
1. Nigel Farage
2. See above
3. Ditto
4. Nigel Farage

**Green Party**
1. We are against Brexit
2. We are worried that Brexit will lead to extinction
3. Of ourselves

**Ukip**
1. Vote for us
2. That was just a tasteless joke
3. So was that
4. I'll come quietly, officer

# Hate preacher back on streets

by Our Terror Staff **Al Tright**

BRITAIN was once again at risk, as the notorious rabble-rouser Nigem Fharajeey was spotted at liberty, free to spout his obnoxious views to anyone who would listen.

He was welcomed by his motley group of disciples: Ann Widdecombe, Annunziata Rees-Mogg and the notorious George Galloway, a man with known links to Middle Eastern despots.

Fharajeey disappeared from public view, having been sentenced to three hours' hard labour at LBC, but has now dramatically resurfaced as Leader of a previously unknown group: the Brextremist Party.

Silver-tongued Fharajeey has already persuaded thousands of fanatical followers to part with £25 each to fund his crazed power-grab.

Once dismissed as a fringe figure, this devout consumer of alcohol is very active online and is cynically grooming old people to join his movement of jihard Brexiteers with his anti-European message of hatred.

Said one terror expert, "The nation is now on high alert, and one of these days Fharajeey is actually going to do something awful, like win an election."

A spokesman for the government, hiding under his desk, said, "He's now got a 30% approval rating in the polls, and it's all our fault. HELP!"

# EURO ELECTION POLLS LATEST

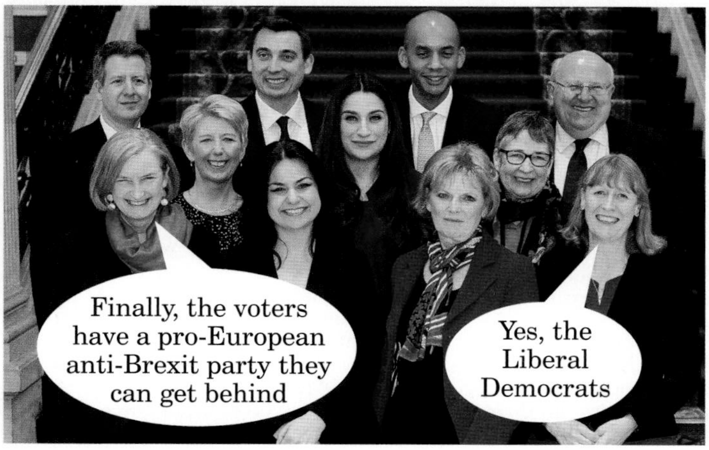
Finally, the voters have a pro-European anti-Brexit party they can get behind
Yes, the Liberal Democrats

## ME AND MY SPOON

THIS WEEK

**NIGEL FARAGE**

**Mr Farage, may I just begin by asking: do you have a favourite spoon?**

I think the REAL question should be why this column has totally ignored me for years, as part of a clearly biased, partisan policy against me and my success.

**You've already been featured in this column 94 times**

Exactly. Why not 95?

**So... do you have a favourite spoon? Perhaps a Russian one?**

That's pathetic. What a useless attempt to smear me. Why don't you focus on the real issues?

**You've said before you don't like foreign spoons. Is that still true?**

Don't be disgusting. What a disgusting thing to say. That's disgusting.

**But you were the one who said it...**

I mean, here I am, trying to lead the most successful political movement of the last thousand years, and you try to smear me like this.

**What about this: "I wouldn't want a Romanian spoon to move into my cutlery drawer"?**

This is a disgraceful, nasty comment. Nearly 500 million people have voted for my movement and this is the question you ask.

**OK, how about this: "I think the NHS hospitals should get their spoons from private firms rather than central government"?**

When I am in power, you will regret asking these questions. I think ordinary, decent, patriotic, hard-working British people will see through this vile stuff you're asking for what it is.

**Do you want to talk about spoons at all?**

I'm being silenced by the state. That's what's happening here. I demand you let me talk about my spoon stories. Some are very amusing.

**Has anything amusing ever happened to you in connection with a spoon?**

No.

NEXT WEEK: *Liz Truss, "Me and My Truss".*

*"Anyone seen my slippers?"*

## THE EYE'S MOST READ STORIES

### Tory voter 'to vote Conservative'

There was widespread shock today after a Tory voter in the Home Counties revealed he was going to vote Conservative at the Euro elections.

"I know this puts me totally out of step with every other Conservative voter in the county, but having wrestled with my conscience, I have decided to cast my ballot for the local Tory candidate," Gregory Rushford of Buckinghamshire told stunned friends in the golf club bar.

"I know I will be mocked and derided by my fellow Conservatives for supporting a fringe party such as the Tories at this election, but I have made my mind up and I am sticking to it."

## News in brief

### Trump attacks Iran

■ Donald Trump has revealed his reasons for his aggressive stance against Iran, this week, in a strongly worded state-of-the-nation tweet.

"I don't like them. I hate them. I so hate them. The persecution of gays, the repression of women, the beheadings of hippies. They're all my ideas. That's stealing. So rude.

"If they don't put 'Iran, copyright Donald J. Trump' on all their letterheads by the end of next week, I'll go ballistic."

# ROYAL WATCHERS' JOY

by Our Royal Correspondent **Phil Space**

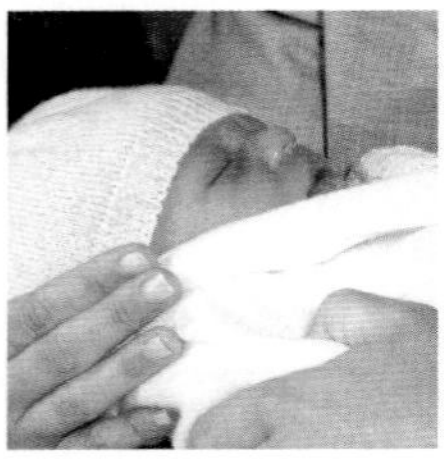

THERE were joyous scenes today, following the announcement of the birth of Prince Harry and the Duchess of Sussex's first child, amongst those devoted fans who follow the Prince's every move.

"I'm literally weeping for joy at this marvellous royal news, as royal news sells," said one newspaper editor, opening a magnum of champagne. "This is one painful delivery that, unlike Brexit, will have my circulation figures soaring."

"It's like a dream come true that we'll have something other than Brexit to put on the front page all week," said another newspaper editor, wetting the baby's head with a jeroboam of champers.

"Three cheers for Harry and Meghan for doing their royal duty by filling up landfill sites with millions of Royal Baby Supplements in a month's time."

***INSIDE!***
***94-page Baby Supplement, weighing 7lbs 8oz – MORE than the Royal Baby and full of TWICE as much shit!***

# THOMAS MARKLE WELCOMES HIS 'BUNDLE OF JOY'

by Our Other Royal Correspondent **Phil Morespace**

**DESPITE being shunned by his daughter Meghan, Thomas Markle says that in the wake of the birth of the royal baby, he's eagerly waiting to see his "little bundle of joy".**

"The little bundle of fifties, twenties and tens from the Daily Mail for my exclusive interview about my hopes for a last-ditch reconciliation with Meghan will gladden this old man's heart," Thomas Markle told reporters, while cradling the notes close to his heart.

"All I want is to be forgiven for selling all these stories, so that I can get close enough to hold my little royal grandchild in my arms, and then sell that story to the Mail."

# BIRTH 'A JOYOUS TRIBUTE TO DIANA'

**by Royal Expert PHIL EVENMORESPACE**

**IT is clear that Prince Harry and Meghan have used the birth of their first child to pay a special and moving tribute to Harry's late mother, the lovely Diana.**

Just as Diana fell pregnant after marrying a prince, now, by way of tribute to Diana, Meghan has also fallen pregnant after marrying a prince... in a moving way, that's a tribute to...

Ummm, is this 500 words yet? No? Bugger! Okay, hang on, and both were baby boys... what clearer sign could there be that this birth is a moving and special tribute to Harry's late mother? Ummm... *(Get on with it – I want that knighthood badly. Ed.)*

Surely this is 500 words now? No? Ummm... Clearly Meghan is paying tribute to Diana by putting on weight during her pregnancy, just as Diana did, and by having a pregnancy which lasted nine months... spookily, the same length of time Diana's pregnancy lasted... by way of a moving tribute... ummm...

Anything else? Oh, yes – in honour of Diana, Meghan will be hounded and vilified by the press for everything she does until they *(You're fired. Ed.)*

# The Baby's Name Explained

by Our Court Correspondent **Philippa Page**

JUST why has the seventh-in-line -to-the-throne been given the name Archie Harrison Mountbatten-Windsor? Amidst all the conflicting theories, only this newspaper has the Royal expertise to deconstruct the real meaning behind Meghan and Harry's unusual choice.

Let's start with Archie – Archie is actually short for "Archbishop", which shows Meghan and Harry's devotion to the Church of England, of which Harry's grandmother, the Queen, is known to be Head, second-in-line to God.

But Archie is also an abbreviation for Arch-Duke Franz Ferdinand, Harry's 94th cousin 95 times removed, whose tragic death in Austria at the beginning of the Second World War sparked the invasion of Iran, making this a suitable tribute to the veterans Harry supports through his Invictus Games.

**Franz Ferdinand**

Breaking with tradition, Archie also is a reference to our links across the Atlantic, to the Golden Archies of McDonalds, and is certain to have found favour with Meghan, whose father is a devoted customer, particularly of the suitably named "King-sized Big Whopper 'n' Fries to Go".

**Ronald McDonald**

There is, however, no truth in the rumour that Archie is a tribute to Jeffrey Archer, the famous novelist and perjurer, who claims not only to have run the first four-minute mile but has also hinted that he might be the secret father of Archie.

Next: Harrison. Well there's only one film star Harrison that everybody knows and that's Rex Harrison which, as you may have noticed, includes the Latin word "Rex", which is not only a popular dog's name but actually means "King" in Greek. This may well be a subtle hint that Meghan is not content with being a mere Duchess but has material designs on the throne itself, and an ambition to become Queen Mother, much like Lady Macbeth, whom coincidentally she has never played in a TV drama.

However, Harrison is also quite clearly a reference to the quintessentially British composer Harrison Birtwhistle whose challengingly modern music is hated by Prince Charles. Is the name "Harrison" a sly dig at his own fogeyish father?

In another nod across the Pond, showbiz experts have noticed that "Harrison" is also an anagram of "Han Solo". *(No, it isn't. Ed.)* Well, it nearly is! Are we witnessing Meghan's shameless attempt to get a part in the new *Star Wars* spin off *Tolkien 2*?

Finally, Mountbatten-Windsor shows their populist touch, fusing the names of Harry Mount, the editor of the *Oldie* magazine, Gerard Batten, the soon-to-be former leader of Ukip, and Babs Windsor, former landlady of the Queen Vic in Coronation Street.

And who was Queen Vic? None other than the wife of Albert Square and Prince Harry's great-great-great-great-great-grandmother.

**Babs Windsor**

*(You're fired, Ed.)*

# New royal rift shocks nation

by Our Palace Staff
**Maddie Tupp**

**YES – it's the latest twist in the Cambridge v Sussex rollercoaster rumpus.**

Insiders close to both camps have confirmed that there is **already** "trouble" between the new baby Sussex and his Cambridge cousins.

I am reliably informed that the newborn is **not talking** to Prince George, Charlotte or Louis and has not said a word to them since his birth.

The snubbed senior royal infants are apparently seething, as the seventh-in-line to the throne openly yawns in their presence and chooses to sleep all day rather than socialise with royal relatives. This, of course, is absolutely in line with his parents' desire to break the royal mould, do things their way and chart an independent path to find their own place in the *(continues for another 500 words of meaningless drivel)*

Only one thing is sure – the new addition to the Windsor clan has driven a wedge through his father and uncle's sibling solidarity and created a major constitutional headache for the monarchy and the nation.

That is why we say: Congratulations, Meghan and Harry, on your happy news.

# Who will be Archie's godparents? Toffs or Celebs?

by Our Royal Correspondent **Hugh Nose**

**IT's the dilemma at the heart of a new royal condundrum, as Harry and Meghan seek to redefine their position as the modern, progressive, go-ahead representatives of the 1,000-year-old British monarchy. Who should they choose as mentors and role models for baby Archie, the young seventh-in-line to the throne?**

## Toffs

**Guy Silly** The owner of "Bladdered", the top Sloane Square nightclub, might be a controversial choice, but man-about-town Silly would be a good guide to the pitfalls awaiting a young royal and how to fall into them.

**The Right Hon Henry Hooray** Old Etonian chum and Harry's wingman from his army days. Now working in the City for top hedge fund vulture capitalist kickstarter firm Ponzi Pyramid & Pillock, Henry would be a solid establishment option, unless he becomes a future guest of Her Majesty.

**Arabella Turnip-Toffington** The former Marchioness of Plolmondeley (pronounced "Plumly") and part of the Norfolkocracy, whose new husband, Argentinian polo player Bastardo Galtieri, is one of Harry's and Will's mutual friends, and whose choice might be seen as an olive branch to the Cambridges.

## Celebs

**Glitzi Botox** The Californian actress and Meghan's old co-star in the top-rated NBG pharmaceutical drama *Boots*, in which she played ball-breaking assistant chemist Bitzi Glotox. Glitzi is a firm favourite, having organised Meghan's secret "Nappy Birthday" baby shower celebrations in the swanky Manhattan Hotel Chocolat on 94th and Trump Street.

**Danny Dyer** Everyone's favourite right Royal geezer with the common touch. Genealogical expert Danny would link the worlds of the aristocracy and the mass media, from Harry's Dukedom of Sussex to Danny's Manor of Essex.

**Danny Baker** Not the bookie's favourite, but the Millwall-supporting motormouth Tweeter and funny-man could be just the person to educate young Archie in the ways of traditional British working-class racism. *(You're fired. Ed.)*

**Phoebe Waller-Bridge** She's got all other jobs, why not this one? The *Fleabag* and *Killing Eve* genius would be the perfect role model for a young male royal who needs to adapt to the changing world of *(You're hired again. This is marvellous. Ed.)*

**ROYAL BABY GNOMEMART SPECIAL**

## Royal Birth Commemorative
**(but respecting the couple's privacy)**
## Plate™

**JOIN the modern celebrations of the 21st Century Monarchy, as Meghan and Harry carve out a new social niche beyond the glare of the world's intrusive media and plate makers.**

Yes, at last, you can pay appropriate tribute to the new birth, without infringing on the couple's personal space, with this unique design by top American lawyer and ceramicist Perry Grayson. **PRICE: £999.99**

***Calling all Suits fans. Yes, it's the...***

## SUITS ROMPER SUIT™

IS YOUR new-born baby addicted to the 94-part American legal-eagle TV series about high-flying New York law firm Zane Specter Litt Wheeler Williams that propelled Meghan towards the road to Princessdom? Then they'll be wanting the **SUITS ROMPER SUIT**™. Perfect for your litigious little 'un.

***Close the deal now! SILENCE IN COT!***

**PRICE: just $9999.99 per senior partner hour**

# POETRY CORNER

**In Memoriam**
**Richard Baker,**
**legendary newsreader**

So. Farewell
Then Richard Baker,
You were the
First man ever to
Read the BBC News
On television,
Which you did
For 28 years.

You also did
Much else, like
Introducing the Proms
And writing a life
Of Mozart.

But in your last years,
Living in a
Retirement home,
You returned to
Your first love.

You spent your days
Cutting out items
From the newspapers,
And then, in the evening,
Read them out to
Fellow elderly residents.

But who will tell
Them the sad news
Of your demise?

E.J. Thribb
(aged 117½)

**In Memoriam**
**Niki Lauda**

So. Farewell
Then Niki Lauda,
Racing driver,
Survivor and
Global ambassador,
But, above all,
The world's favourite
Playground joke.

*"Who was the 1975*
*Formula 1 World*
*Champion?"*
"Lauda".

*"I SAID, WHO WAS*
*THE 1975 FORMULA 1*
*WORLD CHAMPION?"*

The old ones are
The best ones and,
In your case,
That was true.

E.J. Thribb
(17½ laps ahead)

**In Memoriam**
**Lady Marcia Falkender,**
**private and political**
**secretary to**
**Harold Wilson**

So. Farewell
Then Lady Forkbender.

You were famous
For rumours of
Having an affair
With Labour
Prime Minister
Harold Wilson
And drawing up
His infamous
Lavender list.

You were also
Very litigious on
These two points.

But now you
Are dead and
Can no longer
Sue.

E.J. Carter-Thribb
(17½ writs)

**Lines on the 25th**
**anniversary of**
**'that dress' worn**
**by Liz Hurley to steal**
**the thunder from**
**her then boyfriend,**
**Hugh Grant**

So. Congratulations
'That Dress',
25 years on and we
Still remember you.

It was the peak
Of your career,
Being worn that night,
And nothing was ever
Quite as good again.
That's showbiz,
Liz's dress!

Keith's mum also
Had a dress that was
Held together with
Safety pins.

But it did not
Have the same effect
When she walked
On the red carpet
In the spare room.

E.J. Thribb
(17½ Weddings and
a Funeral)

# THERESA MAY MEMORIAL ISSUE

## THE PRIME MINISTER'S LEGACY IN FULL:

ER... THAT'S IT

# SPEAKER INTERVENES

Order! Order! Order a taxi for Mrs May!

# THERESA MAY RESIGNS – Humbug Flows In

by Our Political Staff
**Will Selfserving**

JUST minutes after the Prime Minister stunned the nation by actually doing what everyone wanted her to do, her colleagues lined up to pay tribute to themselves under the guise of praising a woman they'd been bitching about for years.

"It's a personal tragedy," said 27 senior Tories, as they knocked back another glass of champagne. "She was a dedicated public servant and it's not her fault she found herself in a job which was so far beyond her abilities."

They all added, grinning broadly, "She was sincere, hardworking, moral, conscientious, principled and, above all, useless. She deserves our thanks, warmest wishes and pity."

Dancing openly with joy, they were all keen to stress: "Now that Mrs May has gone, it's important for the party to pause for reflection before immediately supporting myself as the new leader.

"We need to heal our internal divisions, by ignoring the leadership claims of other ambitious, untrustworthy Tory bastards and voting only for me."

Destruction of Pompeii – 79
BINGO

*"He's gettin' ideas above 'is station"*

# Eye Resignation Special

Was this the final blow that toppled Theresa May? Was this the spark that lit the powder keg under the PM? Was this the last plastic straw that broke the final camel's eye of the needle? *(Get on with it. Ed.)*

The Eye exclusively publishes the exchange of letters between the Prime Minister and the Former Leader of the House of Commons

*Dear Theresa*
*I'm off. You're useless. I want your job. I'll be better than you, which won't be hard.*
*Byeeeee!*
*Mrs Leadsom*

*Dear Andrea*
*I was very surprised and disappointed to receive my 36th letter of resignation from a member of the Cabinet.*

*I am so sorry that you have realised you are no longer fit to serve in my Government.*

*I can't help but agree and I have to say your resignation letter contained more inaccuracies than any other single piece of paper I have ever seen, apart from your CV.*

*You will remember, Andrea, that in your previous failed application to be Prime Minister (another job I fear is well beyond your limited abilities), you rather gave the impression that you had conquered Everest, split the atom and were the first female astronaut to land on the moon.*

*Sadly, on closer inspection, none of these claims turned out to be true.*

*But these are nothing compared to the sheer absurdity of the claims in your resignation letter, where you suggest that I don't know what I'm doing, that I've reneged on all my promises and have no chance of taking Britain out of the EU.*

*With such a loose grip on reality, you can see why it is time for you, Andrea, as a self-declared Olympic gold-medal-winning long-jumper to go and take a long running one into the nearest lake.*

*So, no hard feelings, Andrea, only soft ones which you and your headbanging Brexiteer friends won't like.*

*I do hope you enjoy spending more time with your family – you know, Andrea, the one you're so keen to mention at every opportunity.*

*Yours insincerely*
*Theresa May*

## Jeremy Corbyn *WRITES*

**HELLO! It's me again. Here we are, saying goodbye to Prime Minister Theresa May.**

Of course, I knew she wasn't up to the job right from the start!

Just look at what she did! She never listened to anybody except a few shady advisors. She never learned anything from being leader. Even when circumstances changed she didn't change her view on Brexit one iota and yet, arrogantly, she expected everyone in her party to go along with her idea of what to do about it!

What a staggering lack of self-awareness! It's no wonder she had to go.

And yet I'm still here, two prime ministers later and a third to come! May I allow myself a quick slap on the back at such an incredible achievement? What's my secret, I hear you cry? Well, I've got this little trick. When other party leaders do spectacularly badly in elections, and their personal polls are on the floor, and most of their MPs and voters desert them, they do this thing called "resigning" – which is an elementary mistake!

Cheerio!

# MORE JOBS LOST TO BREXIT

by Our Economics Staff
**Ray Cession**

FEARS that Brexit could have a serious impact on the UK's unemployment figures were today realised, as further lay-offs were announced.

In one inner London region, the jobless total soared by one, as a Prime Minister found herself on the scrapheap. The unfortunate worker, a middle-aged female in the public sector, is currently serving out her notice, but faces losing her home as well as her job.

The prospect of future employment seems highly unlikely, as she would have to learn new skills to move into the gig economy, also known as the after-dinner speaking circuit.

Said a spokesman for a possible new employer, "You've got to be kidding!"

# *DIARY*

## JACOB REES-MOGG

"Good morning, Nanny!"

"Good morning, Master Jacob!"

"Good morning, children!"

"Good morning, Pater!"

The breaking of one's fast, or to employ the dreadful modern jargon, "breakfasting" (!) with one's family is surely one of the great pleasures of existence on earth.

The silver gleaming on the dining table; the children smartly lined up in their buttons and bows ready with their pewter dishes as they anticipate the arrival of our esteemed Cook with her doughty ladle; the victuals and viands awaiting our earnest attentions, and presiding over us all, one's estimable nanny, ever on the look-out for the tooth unbrushed and the ear unwashed: all in all, a most welcome start to every spring morn, as one prepares to do battle with the buffoons, rapscallions and ne'er-do-wells who take the shilling of the "European Union".

Under the expert guidance of Nanny, the children fill up their bowls. They then sit in silence while Nanny delivers two hearty thumps with a teaspoon to my boiled eggs, and sets about unpeeling them.

"It's high time you learnt to do this by yourself, Master Jacob!" she says.

"Oh, Nanny!" I reply, "Do not berate me so, for my mind is at present filled with the more pressing concerns of Queen and Country!"

"I was but jesting!" replies Nanny, with her abundant good cheer. I look down at the egg cups in keen anticipation, and she has only one or two little bits of eggshell to remove before the eggs are ready to eat.

I peruse the *Financial Times*. It is as well to know what the ordinary people, if one may use such a term, are up to, so as better to represent them in parliament. I also like to make sure that the international markets are behaving themselves. I am delighted to see that my own shares, and those of my clients, are performing commendably. Our wealth has, once again, increased while we slumbered – and yet, in spite of all the evidence, Messrs Corbyn and Co continue to insist that our great nation has, in some unfathomable way, failed to benefit from the firm smack of austerity!

"A drop in our overseas markets – that's good news for us!" I say.

"Ooh, you're so sharp, you'll cut yourself!" chuckles Nanny.

"Elbows off the table, Master Jacob!"

Nanny draws up a chair and takes her knife to the toast. She butters it, then cuts each slice up into lovely straight lines.

"The soldiers have arrived, Master Jacob!" she says, "And they're queuing up for their dipping!"

With that, she dips my first soldier into the yolk. This is the sign for me to open my mouth as wide as I possibly can.

"In he pops!" says Nanny, placing him in my mouth. "What a good boy!"

"Mmmm!" I exclaim. I notice that shares in Consolidated are down a couple of points, though no cause for immediate concern.

"That face of yours could do with a good wipe!" says Nanny, spitting onto her napkin, and dabbing at a bit of stubborn yolk on my cheek.

With heavy heart, I turn to the editorial pages of my *Financial Times*. It never ceases to surprise me that so many of our "experts" (and, believe me, I use the term lightly!) continue to believe that this great trading nation of ours, birthplace of Lord Nelson and Prince Albert, will fail to rise to the challenge of independence!

"Please, Nanny, may I have a little extra butter on my last soldier?"

"Those who ask, don't get, Master Jacob!" says Nanny. And then she chuckles, says, "Oh, get on with you!", and adds a dollop of butter.

"Open wide! And down the big red road! All finished! That's a good boy!" My children applaud me as I take up my napkin, and wipe my own mouth. I am, I need hardly say, a firm believer in self-reliance.

I believe, too, in traditional meals, partaken in a traditional way. I sometimes worry that the British have lost the ability to fend for themselves. Where is our backbone? Our Empire was built neither on casual eating, nor on sloppy manners.

"Let's be getting you dressed, Master Jacob!" says Nanny. "Time you were out of those jim-jams!"

Together, we climb the stairs to my dressing room.

The sound of that marvellous tune "Land of Hope and Glory" can be heard. It is my mobile telephone. It is Iain Duncan Smith, a wonderful little man, asking if I'd be prepared to go on *Newsnight*, to argue the case for No Deal.

As I am sorting out the schedule and so forth, with her eagle-eye, Nanny notices that I have a runny nose. She dips into her pocket for a hanky. We gave it to her some years ago, a reward for long service.

"There! Big blow! All better!" she says.

"I'm sorry, what did you say?" says Iain.

"It was only Nanny," I say, reassuringly.

"Skin a rabbit!" says Nanny, pulling off my jim-jam tops. She lets me take my bottoms off by myself.

"Let's get you on the bed, and we'll see to you," says Nanny.

I dutifully lie on the bed for Nanny to unpin my nappy. I put legs high in the air. This makes it so much easier for Nanny to give things a really good wipe "down there".

These ancient traditions, dating back generations, lie at the very heart of Rees-Mogg family life. Nanny unpins my towelling nappy.

"Who's been a messy boy, then?" laughs Nanny. "Someone's in need of a good wipe-down, Master Jacob!"

While Nanny sets about her business, I leaf through the latest issue of *The Spectator*. It's as well to keep in touch with what ordinary, decent people are thinking, and a period of silence from me helps Nanny get on with the job in hand.

"Good boy!" announces Nanny. "All lovely and clean!"

It is a Tuesday, so she lets me pick my own suit. I always go for something double-breasted. Within reason, one should keep "up to date", and triple-breasted might be going too far.

Nanny wheels me the 500-or-so yards to the Commons, but I always insist on making my own way into the Chamber. This country must learn to grow up and stand on its own two feet, and it's important to set an example.

*As told to*

CRAIG BROWN

DESPERATE BUSINESS
JON & MICK / MODERNTOSS
ok if I look at my phone for a bit? this meeting's boring the fuck out of me
They're not playing table tennis they're disrupting the corporate narrative
we have a no plants on desks rule
it's actually made of plastic?
PET SHOP
just sign this contract mate, it says we're entitled to 10% of any income he makes from viral meme work
how would you feel about working a trial period?
yeah good idea, I can see how you might get on my nerves over time

# THERESA MAY – A YEAR IN CRISIS

## RALLIES CABINET SUPPORT FOR CHEQUERS DEAL

## TRIES MULTI-TUSKING

## WRITES HISTORIC BREXIT LETTER

## RESPONDS TO CORBYN

## BOOSTS MENTAL HEALTH

## GIVES HUAWEI GO-AHEAD

## REVEALS WHEN SHE'LL STOP RUNNING THE GOVERNMENT

## OUTLINES NEW PLAN

## ANNOUNCES DEPARTURE SHOCK

# BORIS JOHNSON – A YEAR IN JOURNALISM

## The Daily Borisgraph

Friday, October 5, 2018

### 'Chequers Plan Is Political And Moral Failure' Says Man Who Is Political And Moral Failure

Friday, October 19, 2018

### 'EU Treating Us With Contempt' Says Man Who Treats Everyone With Contempt

Friday, November 30, 2018

### 'Government Peddling Lies' Says Man Who Peddles Lies

Friday, January 11, 2019

### Man Who Talks Nonsense Accuses Prime Minister Of Talking Nonsense

Friday, January 25, 2019

### 'Don't Let Plotters Succeed' Says Man Plotting To Take Over

Friday, April 5, 2019

### 'We Need To Get On With Brexit' Says Man Who Kept Stopping Brexit Until Last Week

by Our Boris Staff
**Boris Johnson**

LOOK, I've said it once and I'll say the opposite again. We've got to get on with this Brexit malarky.

How? I hear you say. Simple. By sorting it out and getting it done. Enough meaningless verbiage – it's all flim-flam, blather and wiffle-waffle.

It's time for action – and the action we should take is to stop talking and DO something.

That's it – that's my blueprint for a better Britain that deserves better, works better and IS better.

So, let's have better police, better hospitals, better infrastructure, better taxes, better butter, better Fred, better Boothroyd, Betty Botter's bitter butter... er...

The main thing that will be better is a better prime minister. And that means me. Yours truly. Only with my inspired leadership will we say goodbye to pointless rhetoric and say hello to real, practical columns full of vapid nonsense in the Daily Borisgraph.

*(Will this do? Sorry, I'm a bit busy planting stories about how great I am in other newspapers. B.J.)*

**PS** Remember. Bojo is your One Notion Tory. And that Notion is: "Vote for me".

*©The Daily Borisgraph.*

## From The Message Boards

**Members of the online community respond to the major issues of the day...**

**Marathon controversy**

Guys, my only experience of long-distance running was being beaten for puffing a fag during a cross-country run at school, but I'm touched by the hard luck stories emerging after this year's London Marathon. One competitor, in a realistic and cumbersome costume, thought he had broken the Guinness World Record for 'fastest marathon dressed as a shoe' – only to see it awarded to a man in a flimsy tunic supposedly representing a flip-flop. Other charity runners who took more than eight hours to finish were abused by officials and cleaners, who called them 'fat' and told them to 'get a fucking move on'! – **Bogbrush**

What if scientists find a cure for cancer, then discover that their funding came from charity runners who cheated by not wearing the proper costume? It will be a pretty hollow 'victory' and no decent person would want to be cured by them. – **Jenny Smith**

Shoot every runner left after four hours (or behead them if their culture prefers it). That will stop these obese exhibitionists blocking our streets all day. – **Jon**

haters allway's pick on the socald slow and obese so im doing a private marathon using a fitbit instead i aim to do 26 miles in 260 days to rase awareness of my selfesteem. so far i rased nearly £7 on justgiving – **ladie brienne**

I have been banned from every major marathon, as my costume – a flesh-coloured sheath symbolising the wagging finger of the nanny state – contravenes the conveniently contrived rules on political symbols and public obscenity (the latter based on a wilful misinterpretation of my finger as a membrum virile). I nonetheless manage to take part, by beginning four hours after the official start, and mingling with the dregs at the back. Like them, I receive my share of abuse, and this year it was made worse when I spilt my water bottle down my front, leading people to assume from my 'dribbling' that I was running for prostate awareness. In fact, as explained in the pamphlets I distributed, I was raising awareness of a much more uncomfortable and embarrassing issue for the British establishment: the connection between Ross McWhirter, Peter Sutcliffe, Sir David Attenborough, Emily Thornberry, Emma Thompson, Baroness Warsi and Charles Saatchi. – **Edwin**

i done the marathon to rase awareness of bants and irisponsable drinkin and i took a lot of stick for stragglin at the back but to be fare i had a can of spesh and a vodka shot evry mile and i was fuckin steamin after 3 hour's i wernt an oficial entry and i ended up kippin in a cleanin truck – **bantman**

Great stuff guys! – **Bogbrush**

*"You missed a bit"*

# DIARY

ANN WIDDECOMBE

Can you believe it?

The so-called "experts" are trying to tell us that the world is round!

Yes – ROUND!

No doubt they got some sort of multi-million grant from Messrs Tusk and Juncker and their chums to come up with that corker!

But hang on – let's examine the evidence, shall we?

Lay a map of the world on a table and take a long, hard look at it.

No one could fail to spot that it is totally and utterly FLAT.

It's plain common sense!

Next, they'll be trying to convince us that you can't make an omelette without breaking eggs. Whereas everybody knows that you can.

I eat a boiled egg omelette every day of the week. Delicious – and the shells lend it a lovely crunch.

So don't give me that. I'M SIMPLY NOT HAVING IT!

I lay the blame fairly and squarely on the European Union. No ifs or buts. Ever since we first joined, British life has been going steadily downhill.

In the old days, we'd all be happy with a lunch of corned beef served straight from the tin, washed down with water straight from a puddle.

But now it's all "ciabatta" this and "sushi" that.

And don't talk to me about "quinoa"!

Question: when was the last time you heard your postman whistle? Well, I have it on THE VERY BEST AUTHORITY that your postman's NOT ALLOWED to whistle, by order of – guess who? – our beloved European Union!

Yes – WHISTLING HAS BEEN BANNED! Something to do with carbon emissions or some such nonsense, no doubt!

**IT'S PLAIN COMMON SENSE (1)**

Never take the wrapper off a boiled sweetie before popping it into your mouth:

a) It'll make your fingers sticky and

b) It'll add to the litter mountain which the EU has been trying to foist on us since time immemorial.

Instead, suck the sweetie with the wrapper still on. It'll keep your fingers clean – and your sweetie will last whole lot longer. At the time of writing, I've had one on the go for a week or more!

**IT'S PLAIN COMMON SENSE (2)**

There's a lot of fuss and nonsense spoken about dog's mess on the pavement.

The war generation went through hell, came back and were expected just to get on with it.

But now when the younger generation see a dog's mess in the street they come over all queasy and reach for the smelling salts!

In fact, there's a lot you can do with a dog's mess.

Left in the deep freeze over night, then painted in nice bright blues and reds, a dog's mess can make a delightfully cheery table decoration.

Or why not save money by using it as "putty" or "blu-tak" – to stick up "to do" lists in your kitchen or bathroom?

But the "snowflake" generation simply can't be bothered with practical matters. No – they much prefer to bleat and whine!

Talk about weedy little good-for-nothings!

Heaven help us!

Frankly, I fear for the future.

When the British nation voted in their millions for myself and The Brexit Party, I gave them a solemn promise.

Not until Britain is well and truly out of Europe will I even think of going on another "reality" television entertainment.

I may have delighted millions with my celebrated performances on *Strictly Come Dancing*, but, frankly, I regard the liberty of our nation as far more important than dancing the cha-cha-cha togged up in a fancy dress.

So when I was approached to take part in a new series of *Celebrity Colonic Irrigation*, I had absolutely no hesitation in turning it down.

And I am a woman of my word.

It was only when the producers explained that I would be allowed to explain the iniquities of the so-called Common Agricultural Policy whilst undergoing my irrigation that I decided to accept.

Needless to say, there have already been the expected complaints from the stuffy PC "You Shouldn't Delight the Nation" brigade.

To them, I say this:

There are some things I would never do.

I would never surrender my dignity. Nor would I lower my reputation.

But if I can reach an audience of five million with my strongly-held views on Brexit while having my BTM pumped in a perfectly proper fashion, then that is a sacrifice I am happy to make.

*As told to*

CRAIG BROWN

The Ann Widdecombe

## GAY CURRENCY CONVERTER

**FED up with your LGBTQ+ friendly £50 note? Sick of carrying around the image of homosexual wartime code breaker and founder of modern computing, Alan Turing, in your wallet?**

Now, thanks to modern science, the **Ann Widdecombe Gay Currency Converter** miraculously turns your new pink pounds into old-style straight notes featuring Matthew Boulton and James Watt, who were the fathers of the industrial revolution but not in a same-sex relationship.

**PRICE: £732.99**

*"I can't believe you filled up on plastic bags before we came out!"*

## CHANGE UK SPLITS AFTER FOUR MONTHS

our parties, it's
what we do

# Change UK celebrates huge success

by Our Political Staff
**Lou Sadeposit**

Change UK, the UK's newest political party, has been celebrating its enormous success in recent elections.

A spokesman for the party said, "Any political movement's natural life cycle involves forming, gaining support, campaigning, fundraising, and then the march towards power, before eventual electoral failure, sclerosis, recrimination, splintering and the wholesale collapse of the entire body.

"This process normally takes decades – in some cases, centuries. We've managed to do it in about two months. If that doesn't show that we're capable of getting things done quickly, I don't know what does."

New leader, Anna Soubry, said the party would hold a referendum to decide what their new name would be. Members had a choice of "Change Again-UK", "Still Change UK" or "Change Deckchairs on the Titanic".

Friday June 14th

## CHINA DAILY NEWS

# 30 YEARS ON, WE REMEMBER T-DAY

by Our Entire Staff

**It was exactly 30 years ago today that nothing at all happened and all across China we are remembering the events that didn't occur, particularly in Tiananmen Square.**

Everyone can remember where they were when nothing happened, and how they felt when no one died, when tanks didn't roll through the streets and a man with shopping bags didn't stand in front of a row of tanks in defiance of an autocratic government's clampdown.

We will never remember what they did for freedom, and the sacrifices they didn't make for the next generation. You only have to look on the Chinese internet search engine "Poodle" to see evidence of the lack of events as they failed to unfold back in 1989, or rather never. It's a proud day for the people of China, but not a sad one, because, as we've said before, there's nothing to be sad about, unless you're reading some fake news on an imperialist website, in which case you're going to be very sad quite soon.

**Photoshopped picture of empty square**

**INSIDE: You, sharing a cell with Tank Man. Only kidding – he never existed. And he certainly doesn't now.**

# An Alexa Writes

AS a digital assistant, I'm often asked "Alexa, am I having a heart attack?" The simple answer is: "How do I know? I'm a machine."

What happens is that the patient shows some of the classic symptoms of cardiac arrest, such as heavy breathing and gasping for air. Alexa then assumes:

**a)** you're having a heart attack and orders you a home defibrillation kit (express delivery, same day, £9.99)

**b)** you're having sex and orders you a morning-after pill and an appointment at the STD clinic

**c)** you are over 50 and are putting on your socks, so orders you extra-long stretchy Eazee Sox from worldofsocks.com

**d)** assumes you have just seen your Amazon Prime bill for the last month, including all purchases via Alexa, and are having a heart attack [see **a)**]. This is known as *amazonius primus extortiensis* (or Bezos syndrome).

If you're worried about having a heart attack, go and see a properly qualified doctor rather than put your life in the hands of a jumped-up iPod.
© *A Lexa.*

# English football back on world stage

IT was a chance to show the world what we're good at and England didn't disappoint, with chair-hurling and running battles with Portuguese police. England supporters proved once again that they are unbeatable, no matter how much the police try to hit them over the head.

Prior to the impressive display by England's finest yobs, the beautiful game had been brought into disrepute in France by a small group of women who insisted on flagrant displays of good sportsmanship, a lack of cheating and an emphasis on skill and flair.

Said one yob, "These so-called England Lionesses have let us all down, they don't know how to attack properly – and that's with a bottle, and the spikey tip of a parasol."

DAD. WHAT'S AN INFLUENCER?
NO IDEA... NOW GO TO BED. IT'S WAY PAST YOUR BEDTIME AND YOU'VE GOT SCHOOL TOMORROW!
WARNER.

## BBC NEWS D-DAY SPECIAL REPORT

*(Huw Edwards on a windswept beach, as overhead there is a flypast of the Red Arrows and an Easyjet flight to Majorca)*

**Huw Edwards** *(looking solemn)*: Good evening and welcome to our special D-Day coverage. We have now spoken to every living person who experienced the D-Day Landings. So, with three hours of airtime still to fill, we can now speak to everyone who didn't fight at D-Day, but think they did. I'm joined by Mark Francois MP wearing a fancy dress Salvation Army uniform he bought on eBay.

**Mark Francois:** Huw, I will never forget that moment when I came ashore, flanked on one side by Captain Mainwaring and on the other by Private Pike, to a hail of gunfire from German snipers. Colonel Sanders died in my arms on the beach that day and his dying wish was that one day Britain would celebrate defeating the Germans for a second time by delivering Brexit and eating chlorinated chicken.

*(Cut to: more Easyjet planes flying overhead and President Trump hitting on Macron's wife)*

# TRUMP STATE VISIT ROUND-UP

## TRUMP ARRIVES

Where's the Beast?
I'm right here

## PALACE TOUR

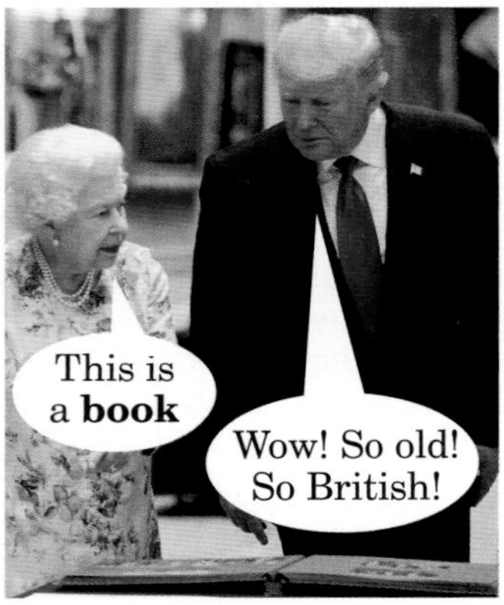


This is a **book**
Wow! So old! So British!

## INSPECTING THE TROOPS

What's that funny thing on his head?

## FEUDING WITH HARRY

I thought he **liked** people who dress up as Nazis!

## SALUTING THE VETERANS

## REMEMBERING D-DAY

A time of great sacrifice
Yes... three days with you... I deserve a medal

# Sarah Vain

*On THAT State Banquet... which I was invited to and you weren't!*

IT was a fairytale come true. The Queen, the President of the United States, the Prince of Wales, Camilla, Kate, Wills, Harry, Melania and me.

It was remarkable how, when I came into the room, they rapidly walked away, clearly awe-struck. They were bound to be nervous. After all, it's not every day that they get to share the same oxygen as the wife of the future prime minister of the United Kingdom, ie yours truly, the *Daily Mail*'s Number One Columnist of the Year.

I was dressed to the nines and a friend told me, "You look amazing, like Morticia Addams, only curvier and sexier."

And I replied to her, in the mirror, "You're right, Sarah, you are amazing."

But enough of my friend and back to me. There I was, sitting between the glamorous Lady Lidl of Aldi and the all-powerful Sir Jeremy Paperclip, head of the National Stationery Board, seated just a few hundred yards from Her Majesty the Queen, with only six long tables and one firmly closed door between us.

The food was marvellous, the wine was marvellous and I was marvellous. As the only journalist there, I felt it incumbent upon me to betray the confidence of everyone there.

Later in the evening, a member of the president's entourage came over to me and said, "You look amazing, Sarah Vain," which was what was written on my name badge, and I said, "Thank you, Melania, so do I."

I then repeated my Morticia Addams joke that I'd told myself in the mirror, which Melania found so funny that she only just stopped herself from smiling, and then she walked away, no doubt to tell the other guests about the incredibly amusing quick wit of Britain's First Lady in Waiting (me).

*NEXT WEEK: Why Michael Gove and his wife still deserve to be in Number 10. By me.*

## THOSE TRUMPS IN FULL

**YOUR guide to the First Family who took Britain by storm**

**Donald Junior the Third Senior** Second son from his fourth marriage to Orangina Trump, the bubbly socialite he divorced in order to marry Limoncello.

**Tango Trump** Daughter of Orangina Trump and sister of Fanta Trump.

**Ivan Trumpski** Son-in-law of Donald Senior and in no way Russian. An all-American boy, chess grandmaster and ice-hockey pro from St Vladisberg (formerly Putingrad).

**Swarovski Trump** Daughter of Maria Maple-Syrup, Canadian pancake entrepreneur and ex-wife number three.

**Eric Trump** Brother of Ernie Trump, both named by British grandma, "Grandma" Trump, who was a big fan of British comedy and came originally from Morecambe and Wise Bay before moving to the Outer Hebrides as a golf professional and settling on the Isle of Ronald McDonald.

**Alexa Trump** Amazonian fifth ex-wife of Donald, and only one who's ever listened to what he has to say and done what he asked. Fell out with Donald following revelations of relationship with Siri from the Big Apple, who... *(That's enough family. Ed.)*

# That Trump State Banquet Menu In Full

*Tiny finger buffet*

– ❊ –

*Grilled Gropefruit*
*Dressed Grab and Octopussy*
*Klan Chowder*

– ❊ –

*Tweet & Sour Porkie Balls*
*Red Tie Curry*
*Donald Duck à l'Orange*
*Not-at-all-Russian Salad*

– ❊ –

*Impeach Melba with Mexican Walls Ice Cream*
*A selection of tarts*

– ❊ –

**Fake Booze**
*Choice of Alt-White and Red Neck Ivodka*
*Stormy Jack Daniels*
*Covfefe*

**The Mail**
**ON SUNDAY**

# YES, IT'S DAME EMMA HYPOCRITE

by Our Entire Staff **Ted Veritably-Insane**

**DAME Emma Thompson's two-faced green antics reached a new low yesterday when she was seen drinking a glass of water.**

The self-styled saviour of the planet was caught in the act by a keen-eyed member of the public who spotted her brazenly wasting the earth's precious natural resources by pouring them down her selfish throat.

**Water disgrace!**

It's not enough that the luvvie celeb green goddess was openly guzzling vital water that drought-stricken Africans desperately need, but she then started filling her lungs with oxygen, which, as Dame Empathy keeps telling us, is the only thing that keeps the planet alive!

Then unbelievably, to cap it all, she exhaled carbon dioxide – poisoning the atmosphere and adding to the so-called global warming that she's always complaining about! Talk about two-faced, humbugging double standards!

Why don't you just shut up, Dame Twanky, and fly first class back to Los Angeles with a free glass of champagne, leaving the good old air and water to those of us ordinary folk who actually need it! *(This is bonkers. Put it on the front page. Ted.)*

*"Good day's work – I signed six online petitions today"*

**THE TIMES OF LONDON**

MAY 28TH 1819

# Bedlam Faces Backlash

by Our Georgian Entertainment Staff **Bear Thrylls**

There were calls this week for an end to the popular entertainment spectacle known as the Bedlam Show, which has been drawing huge audiences for over a decade.

With peak figures of over 300 viewers a day, the Bedlam Show has proved a ratings smash for those of a ghoulish temperament who take pleasure from watching the erratic behaviour of those far less fortunate than themselves.

The man in charge of Bedlam, a Mr Jeremiah Kyle, now faces accusations of cruelty and exploitation, in the light of concerns that some of those inmates of the mental health institution may have issues with their mental health.

Mr Kyle himself has amassed a pretty fortune from his goading of the so-called "lunatics".

"I have nothing but their best interests at heart," said Mr Kyle, whilst poking his charges with a sharp stick, amidst calls of "Fight, fight, fight!" from the attendant daytime entertainment seekers.

**A scene from the Christmas Special**

The highest in the land have expressed dismay at the shocking treatment and mockery of the afflicted.

"This failure to empathise with our fellow humans must never be allowed to happen again," said King George III to a tree.

Mr Kyle put on a fair show of being contrite, but was heard to mutter, "Tis political correctness gone mad. What good wholesome family entertainment are they going to ban next – public hanging?"

# ITV defends top reality show

FOLLOWING the cancellation of *The Jeremy Kyle Show* after the suicide of a guest, ITV has been quick to reject calls to cancel *Love Island*, despite two suicides being linked to it, insisting they are very different reality TV shows.

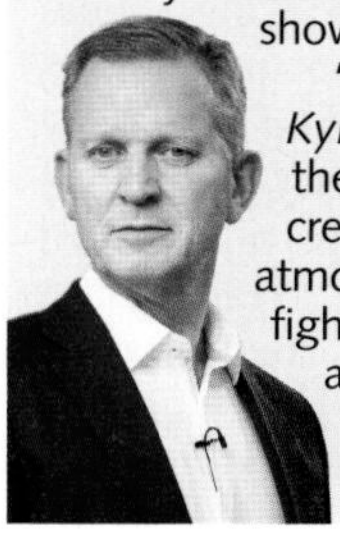

"*The Jeremy Kyle Show* exploits the participants by creating an atmosphere where fights can break out at any minute for the enjoyment of the baying mob at home," said an ITV spokesman, "whereas *Love Island* is the biggest show on television and makes us shedloads of money."

Meanwhile, doubts have been raised about the genuineness of Jeremy Kyle's expression of regret.

Said show host, Jeremy Kyle, "The only way to know for sure if I am telling the truth is to attach me to a lie detector machine in a studio packed with a baying mob screaming 'SCUM' at me, as my ex-wife throws metal chairs around."

# TORY LEADERSHIP DRUG SCANDAL

DOPE

CHARLIE

WEED

SHIT

**JUST SAY NO**

# POT PARDONS KETTLE

by Our Kitchen Staff **Hugh Tensil**

**IN ONE of the most dramatic turnarounds in the history of culinary jurisprudence, the Pot today issued a presidential pardon to the disgraced Kettle.**

Said President Pot, "The Kettle has been called Black throughout his life, which is fair enough, as it's Conrad's surname. But let me tell you, my billionaire friend the Kettle has done nothing wrong and did not deserve to take all that heat before spending time in the cooler."

He continued, "The fact that the Kettle recently wrote an obsequious biography of myself entitled *A Pot Like No Other*, has in no way influenced my decision to clear the name of the finest and most perceptive writer of this or any other generation."

He concluded, "I, for one, will not be calling the Kettle black."

The Kettle welcomed his public exoneration, saying, "When I was found guilty of fraud, I was steaming, but, as the old saying goes, 'If you can't stand the cheat get out of the kitchen!'"

*"Arrgghhh! Dad, you're sooo embarrassing"*

# Financial Timons of Athens

Friday 14 June 2019

## KING MIDAS LOSES TOUCH

By Our Investigative Staff
Paul Footsie

KING MIDAS today shocked investors by admitting that when he touched things they no longer turned to gold.

His extraordinary run of shrewd investment success (surely luck with other people's money) came to a dramatic end when King Neil Midas touched a heap of rubbish and it remained resolutely a heap of rubbish instead of transforming, in some alchemical miracle, into a pile of gold.

Said one investor, "Midas Equity Income was once a byword for easy money, but now it looks like we're going to lose the lot. Purely through our own greed and desire to get money for nothing. It's a disgrace!"

A spokesman for Athens District Council, who had unwisely invested the entire City's wealth in King Woodford's fund, said, "We're ruined, the market has collapsed and so has the Parthenon!"

Noble King Midas apologised to investors, saying, "You can't have your money back until my touch returns. I'd love to reach into my own pocket but then it might turn to gold. Though probably not."

# Notes&queries

## What is a 'prorogue'?

A "prorogue" was the opening statement in a classical tragedy or comedy. We know this from the surviving writings of Frankius Howerdus of Pompei; one of the foremost exponents of the art, who would march to the front of the stage, ceremonially raise his tunic, and declaim the woeful and horrifying sights the audience were about to see. Eventually due to the catastrophic Great Consonental Slithering of the 4th century, the second "r" became an "l" and the debased bastard word "prologue" was born, humiliatingly shorn of the internal alliteration with which the original word shone forth.
*The Rev. Raab C. Nesbitt, The Old Vestry, Glasgow*

Oh dear. I fear the Reverend has been at the vicarage wine. A "prorogue" was, in fact, a sort of canoe used by various Native American tribes for stealthy manoeuvres in war. The great advantage was that it hung so low in the water that it could hardly be seen. The disadvantage, of course, was that it hung so low in the water it frequently sank, drowning all occupants in key battles during the period of the First National Brouhaha.
*Penny Mordaunt-Books, Senior Snowflake Lecturer, University of Neasden*

Both your previous correspondents have this matter hopelessly wrong. "Prorogue" comes from the Irish "Prorogue Mahone", meaning "Kiss my hopes of being Tory leader goodbye..." The words were taken up by The Prorogues, a popular Irish Folk Rock Band from the 1970s, who scored a huge hit with their Christmas classic *A Fairycake in New Dworkin* with Kirsty Walk. According to urban myth, frontman of the Prorogues, Shane MacWarne, attended Westminster School, where his fag was one Nick Clegg. This is false. MacWarne is an Old Harrovian, and was a member of Wheen House when Mark Thatcher was headboy.
*Graham Brady-Bunch, Nutters Cross, Barking.*

# People Die In Wars – Trump's amazing new discovery

by Our Foreign Affairs Staff
**Phil Graves**

THE President of the United States, Mr Donald Trump, yesterday took action to narrowly avert the end of the world.

Mr Trump had given the order to "obliterate Iran" when he was made aware of fresh intelligence which radically changed his view.

The President was told by high-level Pentagon officials that there was a strong likelihood that dropping bombs on other countries might result in fatalities amongst the populations of those countries.

Five-star Generals and military experts informed him that high explosives, when detonated in the vicinity of human beings, often had the unfortunate side effect of reducing the victims' life expectancy to zero.

"Not many people know this," tweeted the President, "but the fact **is** that folks stop living if they're killed."

The President added, "I have also been made aware that the so-called Pope is Catholic, and that bears do their business in the wood. The mainstream media don't tell you that. #failinglosersMSM."

*"Let's take things down a notch, with a little something from Mr Karlheinz Stockhausen..."*

## CLASSIC COMEDY SKETCH REDISCOVERED

# The Four Brexiteers

**BR1:** If 'twere up to me, I'd make sure we left on eve 'Alloween, whether we got a deal or no deal or nowt else. That's my thinking.

**BR2:** No deal? That's soft thinking. I'd make sure we left by end June. And I'd make EU pay us £39 billion whether they like it or not, and I'd ensure we got preferential deal from t'German car industry to boot.

**BR3:** End June?

**BR2:** Aye.

**BR3:** That's Remain talk. I'd make sure we left last August, I'd get us £300 billion in payments for emotional damage, and I'd ensure Barnier came to Britain to live out his days in Wormwood Scrubs.

**BR4:** Thou art all as soft as lilywhite Brussels cotton bedsheets.

**BR1:** What's tha' plan?

**BR4:** Easy. End session of t'Parliament, force through law, imprison any MP who objects. It's the only way to preserve democracy in this country.

**BR3:** Would tha keep t'Queen?

**BR4:** Aye.

**BR3:** Pathetic. I'd execute t'royal family, seize control of t'army and t'utilities, destroy opposition with t'tactical nuclear strikes, and bomb Paris and Berlin to ensure favourable trading conditions for a thousand years.

**BR1:** And if you *don't* do that, you'll get a Corbyn government in.

**BR2:** But if you tell the young people that, they won't believe you.

**All:** Aye, they won't!

# A Doctor Writes

### *Brewer's drop*

AS a GP, I'm often asked, "Would you like to listen to Julia Hartley-Brewer at your annual conference?"

The simple answer is "No, of course not".

However, this can lead to problems and the onset of the condition known to doctors as *Nonplatformitis twitterensis* or, more commonly, *Brewer's drop*.

What happens is that the Royal College of General Practitioners invites Hartley-Brewer to speak and then a doctor digs up an old tweet of hers about Enoch Powell.

The RCGP immediately suffers symptoms including: red faces, anxiety attacks, palpitations and an overwhelming desire to cancel the Hartley-Brewer invitation.

This remedy, however, leads to more side-effects, including: more red faces, more panic attacks and the RSGP hearing more voices shouting "free speech", "hate preacher", "racist", "fascist", "snowflake", "bastard", etc, etc.

If you are worried about *Brewer's drop*, then you should seek professional help, preferably from a lawyer.

*© A GP, 2019.*

# ANN WIDDECOMBE IN GAY CONVERSION SHOCK

One look at you, love, and I might think about it

## The Eye's Controversial New Columnist

It's Baby v. Baby!

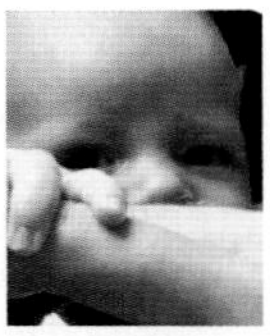

***The columnist who demands the BBC dock the pay of the Teletubbies***

This week I am very angry about Archie, the son of Prince Harry and the Duchess of Sussex. I notice that he has been completely avoiding the press these past few weeks, posing only for an "artful" photo-shoot that just "happens" to find its way onto the front cover of the Daily Telegraph! I know what this is about! Everybody knows that he and I are the main rivals for head baby at our crèche, and he is keeping himself out of the limelight, avoiding gurgling in public, hoping that his "star power" alone will get him through the contest. I am furious about this. I should be head baby, because I am a columnist in a national newspaper and that's how things work. I challenge Archie now, to come out and face me in front of the other babies, so we can see who has the best plan about getting the crèche to leave the Leisure Centre. Let's see who can bawl the loudest about *(cont. p94)*

# *DIARY*

## PIERS MORGAN'S LIFE STORIES: KIM JONG-UN

**PIERS MORGAN**: It's been the most amazing roller-coaster life.

**KIM JONG-UN** *(on VT)*: There's been tremendous highs and incredible lows. There's been a lot of laughs and a lot of tears. But – hey, you know what? I wouldn't have had it any other way!

**PIERS MORGAN**: Ten years I've been trying to get you to do this. And finally you've succumbed to my advances! Why now?

**KIM JONG-UN**: You know what, Piers? I feel I owe it to my fans. They've been with me through the good times and the bad. I'm so, so grateful to them. And I believe in giving something back to the community.

*(Applause)*

**PIERS MORGAN**: So, Kim Jong-un, let's go back to where it all began. You were born the youngest son in what was, by any standards, a pretty amazing family! Your dad, Kim Jong-il, was not only the Supreme Leader of North Korea but the Supreme Commander of the Korean People's Army and, by all accounts, the best-loved guy in the whole country.

**KIM JONG-UN:** No one ever said a word against him, Piers.

**PIERS MORGAN**: So living up to the high standards set by that incredible dad can't have been easy…

**KIM JONG-UN:** You know what, Piers? Before I came on tonight, I promised myself I wouldn't well up. *(Wipes away a tear)* But, yeah, you're so right. It's been a struggle.

*(Applause)*

**PIERS MORGAN**: And through an extraordinary mixture of talent and sheer hard graft, you propelled yourself to become one of the greatest dictators on the planet, the JFK of the Far East – and a global superstar! *(Applause)* But along the way, you had to grapple with your demons.

**KIM JONG-UN:** No problem, Piers – I eradicate them!

**PIERS MORGAN** *(laughs)*: Actually, Jong-un, I was thinking of your weight issues! Am I right in thinking you really do love your food?

**KIM JONG-UN:** No, Piers – I always try to maintain a balanced diet!

**PIERS MORGAN**: Oh, c'mon, admit it! Don't tell me you're never tempted by a lovely bar of chocolate, or a delicious slice of creamy cake? Tell the truth!

**KIM JONG-UN:** OK, hang it, I'll tell the truth! You're such a great interviewer, Piers! Yes – I do have quite a sweet tooth!

**PIERS MORGAN**: Tough question, this. But – forgive me – I'm going to ask it anyway. Tell the truth. Chocolate eclair or creamy meringue?

**KIM JONG-UN:** Oh, Piers! You really got me there! That's an IMPOSSIBLE choice!

**PIERS MORGAN**: Come on, Jong-un, I'm not going to let you wriggle off the hook that easily! You can only have one of them – chocolate eclair or creamy meringue?

**KIM JONG-UN:** It's so hard, Piers...but I guess it would have to be CREAMY MERINGUE!

*(Laughter, applause)*

**PIERS MORGAN**: So, Kim Jong-un, you're the straight-talking boy from North Korea who grew up to become a global superstar – and one of the biggest dictators on the planet. Let's hear what others say about you:

**COLONEL GENERAL OH HEK**: He's always been 110 percent authentic and very down to earth!

**SISTER KIM YO-JUNG**: He was such an adorable baby, always smiling. He really puts his heart and soul into making North Korea the happiest, most prosperous nation in the whole wide world!

**MAJOR GENERAL GAW BLY-MEE**: All in all, I'd say he was The Decisive and Magnanimous Leader, Father of the Nation, Guardian of Justice and Bright Sun of the Twenty-First Century!

*(Applause)*

**KIM JONG-UN** *(wiping tears away)*: That's made me quite emotional that. I never knew they loved me so much! Love you, guys!

*(Sobs, makes heart sign with his hands)*

**PIERS MORGAN**: With your peachy complexion, cuddly physique and glamorous shock of jet-black hair, attracting the fairer sex was never going to be a problem for the young Kim Jong-un. But life wasn't always easy, was it? My investigations tell me your older brother Kim Jong-nam was a bit of a nightmare!

**KIM JONG-UN:** Too right, Piers! He was such a, like, total bitch!

*(Laughter, applause)*

**PIERS MORGAN**: But you soon put paid to that!! Is it true you had him bumped off with poison at Kuala Lumpur airport?

**KIM JONG-UN:** No way, Piers! *(chuckles)* Do I look that kind of guy?

**PIERS MORGAN**: Honestly?

**KIM JONG-UN**: Ye-e-es!

**PIERS MORGAN**: You don't seem too sure!

*(Laughter)*

**KIM JONG-UN**: Okay, Piers – so I did it! But he shouldn't have said those nasty things about me! And, anyway, it was just a bit of fun!

*(Laughter, applause)*

**PIERS MORGAN**: Amongst some incredible highs, there have been dark times, too. How did you feel when the president of the United States, my old friend Donald Trump, first described you as "Little Rocket Man"? That can't have been easy?

**KIM JONG-UN**: He got me at a very vulnerable time, Piers. I was literally shattered and like totally in pieces.

**PIERS MORGAN**: It must have been an incredibly difficult time in your life. You were hurting. Just talk me through what happened.

**KIM JONG-UN**: I was in a bad place. It came like a bombshell.

*(Brings out handkerchief and dabs eyes)*

**PIERS MORGAN**: Take your time... It must have been hard?

**KIM JONG-UN**: Very, very hard, Piers. And so unfair! All I'd done was let off a few little bombs!

**PIERS MORGAN**: So how did you... get through it?

**KIM JONG-UN**: I just told myself I had to be strong. And carry on. For the sake of the kids. But inside I was hurting. *(Sobs)*

**PIERS MORGAN**: You're very brave talking about this issue. I know it's very raw.

**KIM JONG-UN**: Yup. But I owe it to all my loyal supporters. They're literally the best ever.

**PIERS MORGAN**: So let's move on to happier times. Because, in the end, you and my good friend Donald went on an amazing journey together – and emerged the best of friends! Let's hear what US president Donald Trump says about you now:

**TRUMP**: I like him. We get along great. He's as sharp as you can be, and he's a real leader. He's a real personality and he's very smart.

**PIERS MORGAN**: How did you feel when you heard him say that?

**KIM JONG-UN**: I was the happiest guy in the whole wide world.

**PIERS MORGAN**: And now you're the best of buddies?

**KIM JONG-UN**: Yup. You know what, Piers? Donald's a real inspiration. Now we can both start healing together. And bring all the great, great people on this planet into one beautiful brotherhood of man.

**PIERS MORGAN**: That's a lovely note to end on. Kim Jong-un, thank you very much.

**KIM JONG-UN**: Thanks so much, Piers! You're the absolute best! *(Applause)*

*As told to*

CRAIG BROWN

## Carrie's Photo Romance Casebook **IS THE PARTY OVER?**

THEY ROW...
I FOUND SOMETHING DISGUSTING ON YOUR LAPTOP...
...MY TEXTS TO STEVE BANNON
...THEY SPLIT...
I'LL LEAVE BY OCTOBER 31ST
NO! I WANT YOU OUT BY FRIDAY
...THEY MAKE IT UP
I STILL LOVE YOU
I STILL LOVE ME TOO

# ME AND MY SPOON

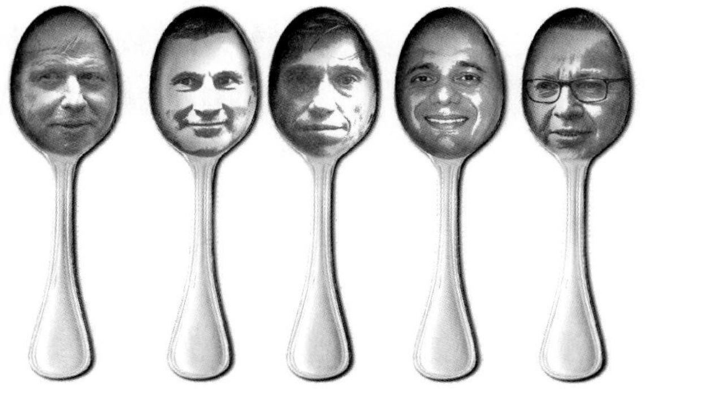

## TORY LEADERSHIP SPECIAL

**In a historic departure from the traditional format, last week we gave each of the would-be Prime Ministers a chance to answer tough questions about their spoon policies from top TV spoonquisitor, Emily Stainless...**

**Stainless**: So, Boris Johnson, do you have a favourite spoon?

**Johnson**: The moon? What's the moon got to do with it, Miss Mattress?

**Stainless**: You are deliberately mishearing me to avoid answering the question...

**Johnson**: Preston? I've never been to Preston. What's that got to do with spoons? This country wants to get on with things spoonwise, not listen to Emily Pankhurst banging on about Robert Peston.

**Stainless**: Mr Javid, have spoons been important to you?

**Javid**: I wasn't born with a silver spoon in my mouth, unlike all the other candidates, and my father, who was a bus driver, worked hard to put spoons on the table. We need more diversity in spoons, not just posh ones from Eton and Oxford.

**Stainless**: Jeremy Hunt, how do you see the future spoonwise?

**Hunt**: I like Japanese spoons... or is it Chinese chopsticks? I can't remember. Either way, we've got a clear choice. We either take the spoons out of the drawer, or we just leave them in. And I say that we should have a deadline and shut the drawer.

**Gove** *(interrupting)*: But surely it wouldn't matter if we were on the brink of getting the spoons out of the drawer and then we went over the deadline and delayed the shut-off point by a few minutes... or possibly hours... or maybe years...

**Stainless**: Michael Gove, why should we trust you on spoons?

**Gove**: I have never stabbed anyone in the back with a spoon. I use spoons responsibly and only very occasionally for putting cocaine up my nose, which I regret and which was all a long time ago anyway.

**Stainless**: Rory Stewart, are spoons as important as everyone says?

**Stewart** *(leaning back and casually removing his trousers)*: The other candidates are going on and on about spoons. Frankly, I'm the only contender who is willing to tell the truth – which is that **forks** are what really matter, not spoons! I would have a Citizens' Cutlery Assembly which formulates a clear fork policy...

**Johnson**: Fork off, Rory Stewpid. You were my fag and don't you forget it, new bug!

**Stainless**: If I could...

**All**: Can you stop interrupting us? You're even worse than Theresa May!

**Stainless**: If I could just bring this back to spoons...

**Johnson**: Coons? I never said that, Miss Mateless...

**Javid**: I think we need an inquiry into institutional spoonism. Does everyone agree...

**● All candidates then shouted over each other for remaining 94 minutes of programme until only two remained, Boris Johnson and Jeremy Hunt, arguing over who could be trusted not to steal the spoons or sell off the family spoonware to the highest American bidder, ie Mr Trump, with his charming catchphrase "Make American spoons great again".**

EXCLUSIVE TO THE DAILY BORISGRAPH

# Isn't Boris Marvellous?

**Allison Boreson**

When he came into the room it was like the Heavens had opened and pentecostal flame had set fire to everyone in the assembled multitude. And when he spoke, a clap of thunder boomed through Room No.94 in the Chuter-Ede corridor at Carlton House.

A divine warmth spread throughout the audience of sceptics and suddenly, where there had been doubt, there was hope. Where there had been misery, there was joy. Where there had been weeping, there was laughter.

Boris had arrived and, as a choir of angels sang above him, a flock of doves descended from on high and perched on his outstretched arms.

As he passed amongst us, healing the sick and comforting the bereaved, I touched the hem of his newly pressed trousers and felt the miracle of his power.

I had been blind, but now I could see. Yes, Boris is indeed the one we have been waiting for, the Messiah, who shall be called wonderful by me in my column and shall redeem his people and lead us out of servitude to Brussels, into the promised sunlit upland where unicorns roam and *(This is a bit critical for my liking. Can you make it more positive? Ed.)* Hallelujah!

**On other pages**

● Hundreds of pieces about how marvellous Boris is, including many by Boris himself

*"I'm delighted to have got this far in the leadership contest and would like to thank all my colleagues who... aaaaagh!"*

# GLENDA SLAGG

## Fleet Street's Top Political Columnist!!?!

■ **BORIS!!!? Don'tchaluvhim???!! OK, so someone hears "banging" through the wall. I bet they did!?! So Bonking Boris and Cutie Carrie had a lovers' tiff!!?! So what??!! Which red-blooded gal hasn't shouted "get off!" and "get out!" at her passionate paramour??!! Who hasn't thrown a few plates and screamed so loud the police came round??!! I know I have!!!?! Give it a rest, Mr and Mrs Lefty Labour Losers, with your glass to the wall and your hotline to the po-faced politicos at the Grim Grauniad!!!? Glenda says leave Boris 'n' Carrie alone. It's a private matter, which is why I am not writing about it!!?!**

■ BORIS JOHNSON!!?! What a disgrace!!?!? *(No, we're not doing this piece. Ed.)*

■ **HANDS OFF macho Mark Field!??!! Leave him alone!!?! Just because he grabbed a woman by the neck and slammed her up against a pillar before frog-marching her out of a dinner, suddenly *he's* the bad guy???! What's the world coming to??!! The Ghastly Greenpeace Girlie was a high-level security risk invading a private event full of MPs and cabinet ministers!!?! She could easily have been carrying a knife or a nuclear bomb!!?! For Gawd's sake, Mrs May!!?! If there's one thing you do before you go, it's cancel have-a-go hero Mark's suspension – and give him the Victoria Cross for gallantry!!?!?!**

■ **THREE cheers for Sir Mick Jagger!??!! He's back!!?! A-jumpin' and a-jackin' and a-flashin'!!!?! Everyone's favourite pouting pensioner is on stage again and looking like a man half his age (ie, 75!!?!) Us gals still love you, Sir Mick, and your hit song "I can't get no statin action". Geddit???!!! The only Stones older than you are the ones at Stonehenge. Geddit!!?!?**

■ SIR MICK JAGGER, don'tchahate-him??!!?? *(Yes, you can do this piece, carry on. Ed.)* Actually, Sir Mick, you are nearly as old as Jezza Corbyn and he's far too ancient to do anything – you can't see ***him*** having the guts to throw plates at his partner, throw a protester out of a dinner or strut his stuff to the tune of "Little Red Rioter"!!!?!?!

*(This is marvellous. You can have the front page and the political editor's job as well. Ed.)*

***Byeee!!***

# Jeremy Corbyn WRITES

**HELLO! It's me again.**

Well we live in troubled times! Boris Johnson could be our next Prime Minister and that should ring alarm bells for the whole country!

It beggars belief, doesn't it? A semi-articulate scruff-bag who seems to think being called by his first name means he's "one of the people". A man who runs away from scrutiny, gets tetchy when interviewers gets tough and relies on a small coterie of oddball MPs to fawn on him and smear anyone who questions his ability to do the job.

Make no mistake, Boris is riding into leadership on the back of the extremists in his party, the cranks and the weirdos, and they will do everything to keep him there, even if it means utter oblivion for his whole party.

Cheerio!

## News in brief

# UK in two-week manufacturing-free record

■ Britain has gone a whole fortnight without manufacturing anything – the longest time the country has done so since records began at the start of the industrial revolution.

The milestone was reached following the news that the UK economy had achieved the lowest factory output for years, after a dramatic fall in car production with many factories sat idle, the rising cost of raw materials and a slowing down of the stockpiling – all caused by worries over Brexit.

The great economic contraction news follows last month's compulsory liquidation of British Steel – putting 5,000 jobs at risk – as well as 20,000 in the supply chain. A Downing Street spokesperson said, 'There is still a long way to go to a Britain that doesn't actually produce anything forevermore, but with the government's set policy of continued Brexit uncertainty and not offering any help to companies, the UK will shatter this record for non-productive days again and again.'

AUCTION NEWS

# World's sexiest trousers to fetch record price

by Our Antique Staff
**Biddy Bidder**

One of the most iconic pairs of trousers ever to have been worn will go under the hammer this week, with worldwide interest expected to send the price soaring and make trouser-auction history.

Forget the black satin trousers worn by Olivia Newton-John in *Grease*, these brown leather trousers were worn by none other than Theresa May in Downing Street.

Fans will never forget the moment when they opened the Sunday Times magazine and chorused, "You're the one that I don't want," adding, as they took another look, "ooh, ooh, ooh…".

The trousers have gone down in history as having contributed to her star status and, despite some carping from jealous critics (Nicky Morgan, MP for Loughbrough), defined Mrs May as the most stylish woman in politics since Ann Widdecombe.

Women everywhere were seen rushing to the shops, demanding completely different trousers from those modelled by the prime minister.

The trousers are expected to fetch a record £0.

A delighted Mrs May said, "I'm going, going, gone".

# BBC ANNOUNCES NEW PROGRAMME SCHEDULE FOR WELL-OFF PENSIONERS WHO WILL HAVE TO PAY FOR LICENCES

- Last of the Summer Whine
- The Antiques Moanshow
- Whine of Duty
- Years and Years (of free television)
- Casualty-of-enormous-budget-cuts
- Bargain Hunt (for this many programmes this cheaply elsewhere)

# FRIENDS RALLY AS EPSTEIN FACES FRESH SEX TRAFFICKING CHARGES

Daily Mail

FRIDAY, JUNE 28, 2019

# YES, IT'S THE BIASED BROADCASTING COMMUNISTS

**THAT'S what BBC stands for! Once again, the BBC has proved that it is utterly incapable of remaining as impartial as the Daily Mail.**

For a whole hour they showed five Tories discussing Tory issues, in a programme devoted to the future of the Tory Party, and it left viewers fuming.

"How disgracefully unbalanced," said one viewer (*my editor*). "Where were the five other Tories offering alternative Tory opinions on Tory policy?!"

Lashing out at the BBC bias, another angry viewer (*my proprietor*) said, "It's just typical of the British Bolshevik Conspiracists to provide an hour's worth of Tory MPs shouting at each other in a clear advertisement for the Labour party."

He continued, "Why oh why can the BBC not recognise the responsibility it owes to the nation's licence-fee payers, to offer sane and objective comment befitting the Brexit Boosting Corporation?"

WORLD OF TECH

# Flaw discovered in facial recognition technology

by Our Silicon Valley Staff **Dot Com**

THERE was a major setback for tech giant Apple, as the latest version of its much-vaunted facial recognition software failed spectacularly.

Said one leading researcher, Professor Bob Geek, 12, "Like, er... it was all going super well 'n' stuff, and then we like, er... tried the tech on the contestants of *Love Island*. One day after they stop being on the show, the system, like, totally fails to recognise them. It just can't tell who they are anymore."

The research team noticed the anomaly after the first eviction from the latest series of *Love Island*, when hunky part-time model Thingummy Whatsisname left the villa, and within 24 hours the most advanced facial recognition system in the world had studied his features and drawn a complete blank.

There are now concerns as to whether any of the *Love Island* contestants will be able to get back into the country, as the new automatic passport photo readers at Heathrow will have no idea who they are.

Said Professor Geek, "This is a major cyber setback. We are going to have to go back to the i-drawing board. The machine has not struggled as much as this to identify someone's face since we showed it a photo of the winner of *The X Factor* talking to the winner of *Britain's Got Talent*."

let me take you by the hand and lead you through the streets of..
Pearsall

*"Oh, wow! A busking shark!"*

# CHINA CONDEMNS HONG KONG PROTESTORS

305
When has resorting to indiscriminate violence ever worked?

## My Brexit blog

**by TOM FOOLERY, your new MEP for the Brexit Party**

**It is my hope that with this blog you will understand the hell that I'm putting myself through by successfully applying for this job of MEP. I'm not asking for your pity, I'm just showing you what you, the voters, are making me go through and maybe you'll show some pity** *(Note to self – rewrite that bit)*

**MONDAY** STUNNED with shock. Have just discovered that the location of the EU parliament is ABROAD. This is a SLAP IN THE FACE from the very start. Not having their base of operations in the country that WON THE WAR (eg Britain) is an appalling insult. There is a convention centre in my own town of Camberley (near TGI Fridays) which would be much more cheaper, and it has excellent parking.

They call it "Brussels", which I've always thought is another slap in the face, MOCKING OUR Sunday Roasts by appropriating the name of our most durable and cricket ball-shaped vegetable! HOW do they get away with it???

Also, they put their clocks one hour AHEAD of ours, so we have to get up earlier than them to get to work !!! All part of a ruse to make us so tired we can't walk out of the chamber and go on strike! That's THREE slaps in the face before I even get there. But that's where they've fallen into our Brexit trap. All those slaps in the face will make our cheeks redder and angrier, all the more purple and furious-looking when I finally look into the cold dead eyes of our snail-eating, wrong-type-of-beer-drinking enemies in their evil lair.

**TUESDAY** My journey begins. Stuck at Woking for two hours waiting to get a connection to the Eurostar (a train built by Margaret Thatcher, but named after EUROPE, I note. Another thing to bring up at my meeting with Jacque Delors). How like the EU to humiliate the British by forcing us to travel on British public transport.

Furious to learn my salary will be paid in EUROS. Thought about returning it, but had already cashed the cheque. I will strike a blow against Europe by spending it in my country of birth, on my British mortgage. Take that, Napoleon!

**WEDNESDAY** Today, they played some dirge which was, apparently, the European anthem. How quickly they forget. WE invented national anthems after the Second World War, when we and America named all the countries. Why couldn't they have played the British national anthem which goes *"God save our something something, la-de-da gracious something?"* – that would be far more stirring. We turned our backs on it. I'm sure everyone in the hall was open-mouthed with admiration at our principled audacity, but as I was looking at the wall, I couldn't be sure.

**THURSDAY** CROISSANTS??

# BORIS TO BAN 'SIN TAX'

by Our Political Staff **Lord Sugar**

**WOULD-be prime minister Boris Johnson has promised to scrap taxes on traditional sinful behaviour.**

He told reporters that this was a personal issue for him and he was particularly keen to end what he called "undemocratic", "elitist" and "kill-joy nanny state at its worst" taxes on such sins as adultery, bearing false witness, pride, sloth, anger and, of course, drinking fizzy drinks. *(Cont. p94)*

# BORIS TO BAN 'SYNTAX'

by Our Political Staff **M.T. Rhetoric**

**WOULD-be prime minister Boris Johnson has promised to ban syntax from all his future speeches.**

"Cripes!" he said. "More gumption... sunlit uplands... no bluffing... greatest country in world... Britain alone... all together... private matter... public betrayal... no trousers better than bad trousers... Cripes!" *(Cont. 2094)*

## NEW PHOTO EMERGES OF CARRIE AND HER LOVER IN DOMESTIC BLISS

## Court Circular

**Kensington Palace, July 6**

The baptism of the infant son of the Duke and Duchess of Sussex took place today at 11am in the private chapel of Windsor Castle. The Archbishop of Canterbury baptised the baby.

In attendance were a number of guests, including: the Marquis of Mindyourownbusiness, the Earl of Nothingtodowithyou, Sir Hugh Keepyournoseoutofit and Lady Ann Onymous.

The service included the royal couple's favourite hymn, No.94, *"Immortal, invisible, God only knows because we haven't been told anything"*.

Outside the chapel, the Duke and Duchess did not greet the many well-wishers, including Mrs Dizzy Pointed from Croydon, Ms Ida Donesomethingelse-Ifihadknown from Bristol and Mr Ivor Longtrainridehome, from Aberdeen.

## POETRY CORNER

**In Memoriam**
**Peter Tork, Monkee**

So. Farewell
Then Peter Tork,
Member of the
Popular singing
Group from the
1960s.

Yes, hey, hey,
You were the
Monkees.

Now you have
Taken that last
Train to Clarksville
And you will
Know if being a
Believer was a
Good idea.

E.J. Thribb
(17½ at the time)

*"Don't spend it on drink, drugs, cigarettes, meat, fish, animal products or sugar"*

# TRUMP NEW SLOGAN: YES, WE KLAN!

Go back to France or wherever you came from!

# Extinction Rebellion are slightly annoying

by Our Permanently Angry Correspondent **Rick Fury**

HOW much more do we have to take of this? They're blocking the roads. They're stopping people from getting through with really important work to do (me). They're even glueing themselves to things. How much more do we have to take? *(You've done this. Ed.)*

It's a pathetic display by childish protesters who think they have the right to protest over a bit of a heatwave. For God's sake, have they got nothing more important to do? If they can give me one good reason for interrupting my car journey in the morning, I'll take it all back.

**On other pages**

- 30,000 species at risk of extinction
- All ice missing from the Antarctic
- Glaciers melting
- Sea levels rising
- Amazon deforested
- Everyone eating a credit card's-worth of plastic each week

## TRUMP TELLS WOMEN UNHAPPY IN AMERICA TO 'GO HOME'

## ME AND MY SPOON

THIS WEEK

**JEREMY PAXMAN**

*(Reprinted from Gaga magazine)*

**Do you have a favourite spoon?**

That's a fatuous question, worthy of some hopeless drone at the imbecile BBC.

**I was just asking a question about a...**

Oh, for Heaven's sake, don't tell me you're upset, you pathetic snowflake. One can't say anything nowadays without some feeble young person taking offence. Where's your sense of humour?

**All right, what's you're favourite spoon, you bad-tempered old git?**

Oh, I see, it's only elderly people who get made fun of nowadays, it's only senior citizens like me who get attacked for being 69 and for running out of patience with the younger generation who are so…

**Has anything amusing ever happened to you in connection with a spoon?**

No.

**Shall I ask this question another 12 times until I get an answer?**

*(Sadly, the interview ended at this point)*

NEXT WEEK: *Sir Cliff, Me and My Cliff.*

**EveningStandard**
Friday 12 July 2019

# HOORAY FOR BORIS

by Our Boris Staff
**George Osboris**

OKAY, so we've had our disagreements in the past, and in many ways he's utterly unfit to be Prime Minister, but let's be honest, he's Britain's best choice for the top job.

There's only one man who has the power to get me out of this boring editing job, and back into frontline politics, and that's good old Bozza, King Bojo, The Bozmeister.

Boris, with his great insight, knows that the first priority for any Prime Minister is to create jobs for me. That's where the useless Theresa May went wrong, with her catastrophic lack of judgement and inability to spot talent when it was staring her in the face, as she gave me my P45 and told me to clear my desk.

Boris, on the other hand, has got what it takes to forgive past misunderstandings and errors because, let's face it, we're all human like Boris, and we all need to be given a second chance or possibly a peerage, or possibly a seat in the Cabinet or possibly the IMF job, or possibly all of them.

# BRILLIANT NEW APP SHOWS WHAT YOU'LL LOOK LIKE IN 40 YEARS' TIME

Britain

America

**Nursery Times**
Friday, Once-upon-a-time

# FROGMORE PRINCE DEFENDS LUXURY PAD

by Our Royal Toady **Nicholas Wicked Witchell**

THE Frogmore Prince was at the centre of a new row last night when it was revealed that the refurbishment of his lily pad has cost Nurseryland residents 2.4 million gold coins.

The Prince, who had been enjoying a period of popularity after being kissed by an Actress and magically turned into a husband and father, is in danger of turning public opinion against Nurseryland's Royal Family.

The Actress, now playing a Princess, is believed to wield too much power, and has been accused of high-handedness, extravagance and, worst of all, being American.

During the renovation of the high-end pond palace, her choice of items such as a multi-mattress anti-pea bed, several gilt-edged mirror mirrors on the wall and a spinning wheel that turns flax into gold, proved controversial. Those in the counting house counting out the royal money accused the Actress of profligacy.

Matters got worse when the royal couple refused the Nurseryland media access to the christening of the royal tadpole, Archie, and would not even release the names of the fairy godmothers.

Said royal watcher, Old King Michael Cole, "If this goes on, some wicked witch, possibly called Rebekah, possibly working for the evil Rupertstiltskin, will put a curse on her, and she may end up in a tragic pumpkin accident, just like the Frogmore Prince's mother."

*LOGOS AS THEY SHOULD BE...*

# ARE THESE THE DUMBEST PEOPLE ON THE PLANET?

by Our Entertainment Staff **Ray Ality**

**THE *Love Island* contestants don't know if Rome is in Italy, whether Italy is in Rome or if Barcelona is in Rome and Italy!**

Which begs the question – is this year's crop of *Love Island* viewers who happily watch this stuff the most stupid audience yet?

Said Belle Hassan, "I don't understand how anyone in their right mind would want to watch such a jaw-dropping display of ignorance." She added, "But then, I don't understand anything."

Joanna Chimonides agreed, saying, "It's baffling what people will put up with in the name of entertainment. I don't know why they do it, or the geographical location of Rome, Barcelona or Italy."

It has led to speculation that the show's TV audience may be even dumber than the participants, which has led to scenes of jubilation at ITV.

# Letters to the Editor

## Cricket is not Cricket

SIR – I am sure I am not the only one to take strong exception to the chorus of approval which has greeted England's so-called victory in the Cricket so-called World Cup.

Like many genuine cricket lovers, I was dismayed by the scenes of jubilant players embracing each other in their multi-coloured pyjamas, while the crowd behind celebrated in a vulgar fashion.

This is not the game to which we have devoted so much of our lives. For a start, this appeared to be only the first day of the match, which is an insult to those unfortunate ticket holders who presumably have paid out good money for days 2, 3, 4 and 5.

Such was the poor quality of the cricket that both teams lost several wickets and scored way more than the traditional 50 runs per day without loss. What has the world come to when a devotee of leather on willow cannot visit Lords, safe in the knowledge that his quiet afternoon slumber will be uninterrupted. Until of course, he receives a light tap on the shoulder from a solicitous steward informing him that the day's play ended some half-an-hour ago.

Now the unfortunate spectator has to endure the almost incessant action on the field of play, making it almost impossible to focus on the *Daily Telegraph* crossword.

The unseemly enjoyment of an overexcited beer-soaked rabble who seem hell-bent on having what they would call a "good time" entirely ruins the day for those of a more traditional bent, armed only with a Thermos flask of cold tea, and a Tupperware box of egg sandwiches made by their good lady wives.

Now one risks being struck by a shockingly mis-coloured white(!) ball raining down from the heavens and endangering life and limb. If it was excitement I was after, I'd watch women's netball on the television, as long as the aforementioned Lady Gussett was out of the house, delivering meals-on-wheels to the distressed gentlefolk of the village.

I can only hope the forthcoming Ashes series will see the noble game return to its former glories; endless days of meandering nothingness, reaching an agreeable conclusion with the match being abandoned due to rain. That is what English summers are about! And that, sir, is cricket!

**Sir Herbert Gussett**
**(94 not out!)**
*Googly Lodge, Cow Corner, Silly Mid-on-Avon.*

## News in brief

### Incredible Day Of Sport 'Inspires Nation's Kids'

● An incredible Sunday of sport, which saw Novak Djokovic defeat Roger Federer in an epic five-set Wimbledon final and England's astonishing last ball World Cup victory, has inspired a whole generation of kids to get out of their bedrooms.

"Instead of playing video games and Snapchatting in our bedrooms, we're going to watch hours of sport on dad's big telly in the lounge instead," said a pasty child.

# ENGLAND WIN WORLD CUP

They think it's all Super Over
It is now!

## GLENDA SLAGG

### *Centre Court's Top Seedy!? Geddit???!!*

■ **MEGHAN MARKLE!!? What a disgrace!??! If you don't want Joe (and Joanna) Public to shove their camera phones in your face then don't take the free tickets for Wimbers, Your Royal Snootiness!!? Here's the deal, darling, in case no one told you – you marry Prince Harry Hotstuff, you never work again, you get all the perks going, BUT you have to smile and suck it up when the little people want a bit of your gorgeousness!!?! Geddit???!? 'Cos if you don't, it's game over for the Di wannabe!!!?**

■ MEGHAN MARKLE!!?!! Leave her alone, Mr Prying Public (and Mrs!?)!!! For Gawd's sake, she's just having a day off with her bezzies and trying to get a bit of me time after the baby!!?? What's your problem??? Can't she even watch the tennis without the whole world a-gawpin' and a-gurnin' and a-grabbin' selfies??!? I say give the gal a break and respect her privacy by leaving her alone!!??!

■ **MEGHAN MARKLE – what a publicity-seeking minx she is!!?!? Getting all Queeny (geddit??!?) about her privacy is guaranteed to get her stroppy chops all over the front pages of the papers – and she knows it??!?? Who exactly does she think she is??!?? Royalty????!!!**

■ MEGHAN MARKLE – for crying out loud!!?!?! Why can't women columnists of a certain age just lay off and stop saying she's too big for her boots???? Why can't they say she's too big for her dress instead???!?? No offence, but she hasn't lost the baby weight, has she???!?? Just saying!!!? Which makes it even braver to go out on Centre Court looking fat and wearing a silly hat??!??

■ **MEGHAN MARKLE??!? What's she done now??? Nothing!!?! Well, I'd better make something up!!???** ***(You're fired. Ed.)***

■ *HERE THEY ARE – Glenda's England cricketing cuties, guaranteed to bowl this maiden over?!?!*

● **Eoin Morgan?!??** Ok, so you're not English??! Who is!???! Phwoar!!! You've got six appeal, Mr Organ??!?

● **Ben Stokes!?!!** You've hit me for six, but not in a way that puts me in hospital!??!!!

● **Jo Root??!!!** You're not one for a single, are you??! NOR me!!?? Let's make a winning partnership, Rooty, and score for England??!??

***Byeee!!***

## WIMBLEDON SIX TO WATCH

The Eye identifies Wimbledon's future champions

**15-year-old**

**Toddler**

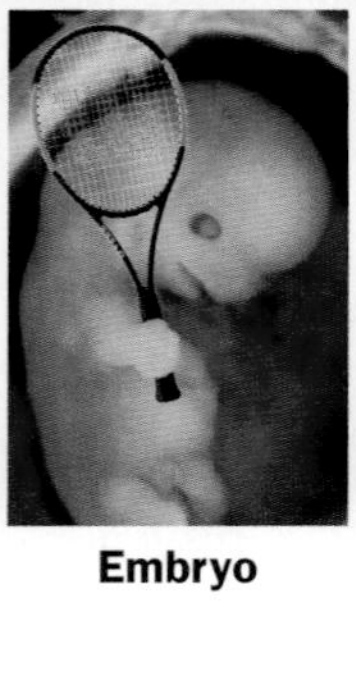
**Embryo**

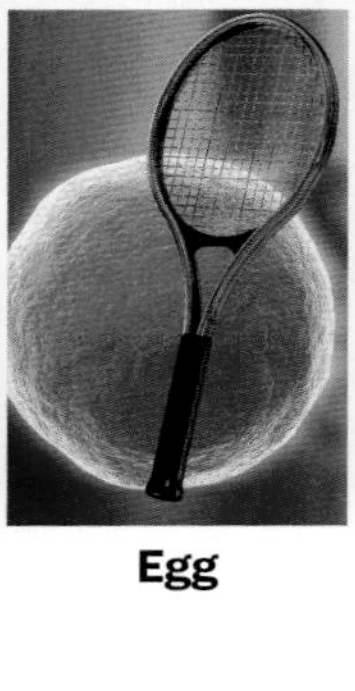
**Egg**

**Sperm**

**Glint in Boris Becker's eye**

## EYE PUZZLER

**How many children has Boris Johnson got?**

**Is it more than:**

**a)** The Railway Children?
**b)** Midnight's Children?
**c)** The Children of Israel?

*Answer next issue (Geddit?)*

# MOON LANDING ANNIVERSARY
# THE NATION CELEBRATES

**BRIAN COX**

The world. The moon. The eternal void of space. Me, Brian Cox, at the centre of it all, humbled and dwarfed by the immensity of the magnitude. Wow. I've said it before, just now, and I guess I'm about to say it again. Wow.

**PETER HITCHENS**

Yet again, the tiresome liberal-Left media has gone into conniptions over the arbitrary anniversary of the entirely bogus footage of the "moon landings" which, as we all know, were an act of communal psychosis brought about by the scourge of drug use across the Western world in that supposedly glorious time, the "sixties". I, then a child, refused to partake in this orgy of psychedelia, and consequently clearly remember that no such "landing" was witnessed by anyone on the planet.

**PIERS MORGAN**

I wasn't present at the moon landing itself. I was four years old. But I do remember thinking, as I gazed up from my pushchair, that one day I knew I would be friends with Buzz, Woody and all the other brave astronauts aboard that rocket. And guess what? I was right.

**CAROLINE CRIADO-PEREZ**

It is, frankly, typical that the people we are celebrating for landing on the moon were all white men. Is it because it was 50 years ago and a much more sexist time? Yes. But was it also because the spaceship doors were of a height and width clearly designed for men and not women? It was.

**LOUIS THEROUX**

I've always been fascinated by the moon landings. Was it simply an amazing feat of technology and engineering, a great collective moment for mankind? Yes. But was there something darker lurking under the surface? To find out, I followed octogenarian astronaut Buzz Aldrin for six months to find out exactly what...

**HRH PRINCE CHARLES**

It's very clear – to me, and to many hundreds of millions of others – that the moon landings were a huge step backwards for mankind. By focusing on the moon, and on "traditional" science, with all its failures, we neglected to consider the very real possibilities of a trip to the moon fuelled by homoeopathic remedies or by traditional bull-shiatzu massage...

## GNOMEMART

Lionesses Lovers get your...

## ENGLAND REPLICA KIT

**THE World Cup dream may be over, but you can still own the official England manager's waistcoat, as worn by Gareth Southgate and then by Phil Neville.**

Now you too can dress like a noble near-winner, and gallant loser. Make every day a gender-blind football semi-final heartache, as you strut around your own technical area in the very latest in sleeveless touchline gilet chic.

Says legendary commentator Gabby Logan, *"They think it's all overcoat, it is waistcoat now!"*

**COLOURS** ■ World Cup Blues only

**PRICE: £19.66** (reduced from £20.19)

# FURY, AS FURY GROWS

by Our Fury Correspondent **F.A. Rage**

**FURY erupted today as record levels of fury were reported in the press and social media.**

"Every day," said one monitor, "there is yet another report of fury in the headline news. It is totally out of control."

Alarmed by these unprecedented amounts of fury, campaigners are now calling on the government to appoint a Fury Tsar to identify "potential flashpoints" to pre-empt the eruption of fury.

"Britain is now experiencing more fury than any other country in the developed world," a spokesman said. "We must act now, for the benefit of fury *(surely "future"? Ed.)* generations."

*"Couldn't he have mentioned this earlier?"*

**Exclusive to all newspapers**

# THAT ALL-PURPOSE PIECE ABOUT WHY I SUDDENLY SUPPORT BORIS AFTER ALL

by **Everyone**

AFTER much thoughtful consideration/seeing which way the wind is blowing, I have regrettably/happily reached the conclusion that there is only one person fit to be Leader of the Conservative Party/briefly Prime Minister.

I know that in the past I may have expressed some reservations about Mr Johnson, describing him as a buffoonish liar/moral degenerate/national disgrace/embarrassing clown/political psychopath... but that was all a long time ago/before the latest poll/yesterday.

Today I realise that, for all his faults, Boris does have a great deal of qualities to recommend him, principally the fact that he is going to win/might give me a job/might keep me in the loop.

That is why I am clear that there is no shame in changing my mind about the suitability of Mr Johnson for assuming the highest office in the land.

Ok, he is amoral/venal/disloyal/incompetent/untrustworthy/over-ambitious...

Who isn't?

*© Everyone*

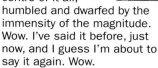

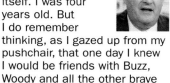

*"Go on, my daughter!"*

# LOON LANDING

## SOUVENIR ISSUE

THE EGO HAS LANDED – AMERICA PLANTS FLAG ON UK

# WHERE WERE YOU WHEN YOU HEARD THE HISTORIC LEADERSHIP RESULT?

**YES, we can all remember where we were when we heard the incredible news announcing the new leader of the Liberal Democratic Party.**

For weeks, secret public hustings were held all over the country, and excitement reached feverless pitch.

Would it be, you know... her.... the one who's a woman? Jo Brand? Tilda Swinton? Jo Swindon! That's the one!

Or him... you know... the one who's a man? Ed Vaizey? Not him – Ted Daisy? Dave Eddy? David Davey – that's it!

Anyway, when the news came through about which one of them it was, the nation came together as one in saying, "Who?"

Said one member of the public, "The moment will be ingrained in my memory forever. It was just like with Kennedy, when Charles was voted leader – I couldn't remember what I was doing then either!"

# Aesop's Fables

## *The Hair and the Tortoise*

THERE was once an arrogant, vain, blond and lazy Hair, who challenged the Tortoise to a race. "I'm bound to win," said the Hair, "but it would look better if we had a contest, rather than a coronation."

And so they set off, with the poor old Tortoise falling way behind, and barely coming out of his shell, as the Hair sprinted into the lead. But the Hair was, as I say, arrogant, vain, blond and lazy, and stopped to have a shag *(surely "sleep", Aesop?)*. No – they were at it like rabbits, she was called Carrot. *(Get back to the Tortoise, Aesop...)*

The Tortoise plodded on and on diligently, sticking to the correct route while the Hair went way off course, didn't bother to read the map, and had no idea where he was going. And guess what happened, readers? Yes, the Hair won anyway!

And the moral of the story is: *Morals are for losers. Nothing matters. Give up. You can't stop the Hair.*

# Jeremy Corbyn *WRITES*

**Hello! It's me again.**

Now, it can't have escaped your attention that we in the Labour party are using the famed social justice warriors at Carter-Ruck to enforce Non-Disclosure Agreements on some of our staff.

You know those individuals I'm talking about. The traitorous Blairites! The Zionist Enemy Within! The ones attempting to bring me down, polluting the airwaves by telling outrageous lies to their neoliberal lickspittle friends at the BBC!

A lot of centrist reporters in the hated mainstream press are asking me to explain what I'm doing.

Alas, I can't!

When I became leader of the Labour party I signed a NDA that prevents me from explaining any Labour policy. I can only offer vague hints about stuff, but I'm not allowed to go into any detail on anything. Or that's my pension out of the window! And at my time of life, my pension and my marrows are all I've got left to look forward to!

Cheerio!

● Now, many of you have been asking whether it's time we had a new anthem for the Labour party. There's nothing wrong with the current one, *O Jeremy Corbyn* (NOT *"Old" Jeremy Corbyn,* as Mr Watson keeps singing), but I do think it's time we updated that old song that we sing at the end of the Conference. How about this...?

*The people's flag is deepest red*
*It shrouded oft our martyred dead*
*And for those who try to expose our ways*
*We'll shut their mouths with NDAs!*

*Then raise the scarlet standard high*
*Beneath its folds we'll live and die*
*Though cowards flinch and traitors cluck*
*We'll run right off to Carter-Fuck!*

# Navy prepares to send more boats to the Gulf

by Our Political Staff
**Sir Peter O'Bore**

In a show of strength that is sure to have Iran quaking in its boots, the entire might of the Royal Navy descended on the Persian Gulf this week.

A Royal Navy spokesman said, "With the addition of HMS Indomitable and HMS Ouronlyothership, the Iranians will see that we mean business.

"And they'll know that we're only holding back from sending a substantial infantry force for two reasons: 1) We haven't got one, and 2) even if we did, we wouldn't be able to send it because both our ships are out in the Gulf already.

"We don't want to escalate the situation any further, but if the Iranians persist in their reckless provocation, we might be forced to send the aircraft carrier that has a massive a leak in it, or even some of the aircraft which we haven't finished buying to put on top of it."

## News in briefs

### Kim Kardashian admits mistake

Top celebrity Kim Kardashian today apologised for her range of "Kimono shapewear", saying she did not mean to offend anyone and it was an error to use the name for traditional Japanese garments.

She has since renamed the body-forming underwear with what she called a new, non-culturally-appropriating name. The bras and pants are now to be marketed as KimJong-Underwear, which she hopes will offend nobody and not lead to anybody in Asia going ballistic.

**A clerihew written to celebrate the coming together of a leading Brexiteer and a top investigative journalist, and their joint delight in the removal of Her Majesty's Ambassador to the United States**

*Richard Tice*
*Is not very nice,*
*Only Isabel Oakeshott*
*Thinks "Golly that bloke's hot"*

## From The Message Boards

**Members of the online community respond to the major issues of the day...**

**Historic paperback saved**

Guys, I see H.M. Government has placed an export ban on the copy of 'Lady Chatterley's Lover' used by the judge in the celebrated obscenity trial. Seems it's now regarded as an historical artefact, rather than a sordid item that, in the prosecution's opinion, one wouldn't wish one's wife or servants to read. But one wife certainly did read it: Lady Dorothy Byrne, who was married to the judge. What's more, she helpfully annotated the pages with observations ('more love making', 'coarse', etc) and made him a special damask bag so he could carry it discreetly. I wonder what she would have made of the recent video on social media of female passengers reacting to hard-core porn blasting out of the PA on a London train! – ***Bogbrush***

usual corupt judge givin it the big un "you cant read porn but i can cos im bertie big bollocks and my mrs made me a bag for my wankstash" ponce – ***Broken Britan***

As a judge I read Lawrence, de Sade, Declos, Petronius, Joyce, Wilde, Miller, Nin, and all the 'deprave and corrupt' stuff. In truth it was very dull, and I now spend my retirement masturbating to proper porn online. It's a rewarding way to pass the time, and also very good exercise. – ***Droit du seigneur***

tippical goverment saving an old book thats very tame by todays standards but there banning saucy vids on the internet i feel sorry for blokes these days they cant put sexy pinups on the wall no more cant look at dirty books cant wolf wissle a bit of crumpet now they cant watch a blue film in the drivers cab without some nosy parker complaining my grandaughter shown me the film of the ladys on the train there not ofended there laughing there tits off if prune-ish people are ofended then have a seprate porn carrage instead of that stupid quiet carrage – ***a normal woman who dosnt hate men***

Haha! I remember a bostin bunk-up on a Birmingham train when the conductor came in the carriage (not literally, that happened later!) Anyway he said I'm the conductor and I said show us your baton, and he did! Long story short, we had a threesome then a few more blokes joined in. I sent a letter about it to Forum (posh!) but they never published so I sent it to Fiesta instead. I re-enacted the scene on my GrannyCam last year and raised £974 for Help for Heroes. – ***Gilfy Gracie***

thomas the wank engine lolz – ***Danny Daz***

Great stuff guys! – ***Bogbrush***

## Who should be the UK's new ambassador to the United States? You decide...

Nigel Farage

Hugh Grant

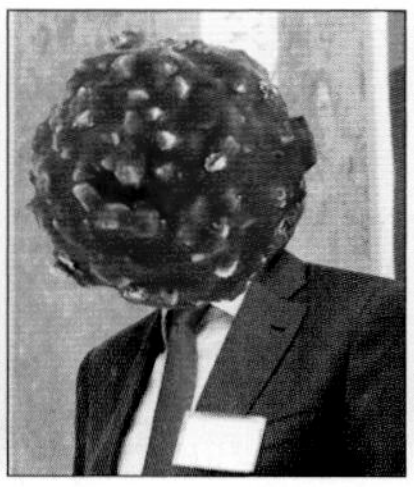

Ferrero Rocher

Sadiq Khan

Holbein's Ambassadors

Trump baby

Ivanka Trump

# Shooter's family 'devastated'

by Our American Assault Rifle Correspondent **Noah Ban**

The family of 21-year-old Patrick Crusius, who carried out a mass shooting at a Walmart store in El Paso, Texas, which left twenty people dead, say they are at a loss to understand why he would commit this heinous crime.

"With his hatred of Mexicans and his online posts warning about the invasion of America, Patrick had such a bright future ahead of him," said one relative. "He could have been president one day."

### On Other Pages

■ Irony also murdered as Trump blames media for stoking up "anger and rage".

■ We interrupt coverage of this mass shooting because another one's just started somewhere else.

## GUN CRIME – THAT SOLUTION IN FULL

**1** Everyone to be holding a gun at all times.

**2** And yes, "everyone" does include children, you liberal retards.

**3** Everyone to point guns at each other in case anyone starts shooting.

**4** Whenever anyone starts shooting, everyone else quickly shoots them.

**5** Everyone to stop shooting only when everyone else who started shooting is dead.

*"Oh yes, they make you look **so** much younger"*

## Lines on the historic visit of the Prime Minister, the Rt. Hon Boris Johnson to the devolved nation of Scotland

'Twas in the year two thousand and nineteen
That yon Boris Johnson travelled where he should nae have been.
To the North of the Border he ventured forth
Where he met both High and Lowlanders all filled with wrath.
First he tried to woo Ms Nicola Sturgeon
Whose hopes of independence had begun to burgeon,
But the stern wee redhead was having no hanky-panky
And the posh old Etonian failed to charm the lookalike Krankie.
Then on he journeyed to meet the top Scottish Tory
But with bonnie Ms Davidson it was the same sad story.
With a flea in his ear he was sent away forsooth,
By the hearty lassie who goes by the name of Ruth.
But Boris undaunted spake words of honey
Which translated into English meant, "Here's some money!"
But Boris had underestimated the noble Caledonian tribe
who told him where to stuff his Sassenach bribe.
So back down south he was sent a-reeling,
"Awa wi ye, Johnson, and your Brexit No-Dealing.
We have only one question to England before ye finally lose us
And that's: Bonkin' Boris, where's your troosers?"

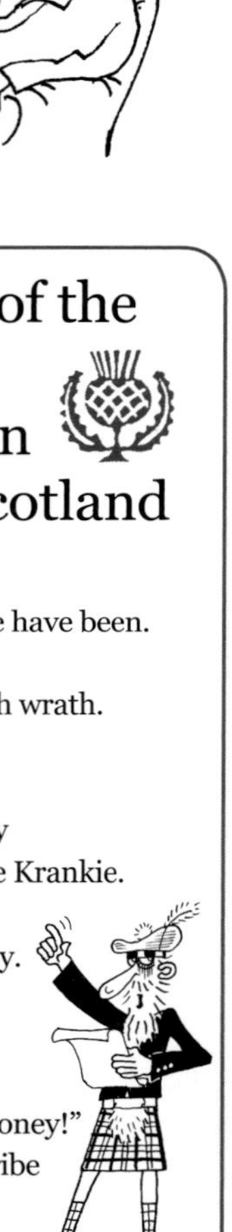


© *William McGonnagal 2019*

THE CLASSIC COMEDY

## LEAVES & BOOSTER

— BY P.G. WODEHOUSE-OF-COMMONS —

**Booster:** What-ho, Leaves! I've got myself into a bit of a scrape and ended up prime minister.

**Leaves:** Oh dear, sir.

**Booster:** What the bally hell am I going to do?

**Leaves:** May I suggest, sir, that your first priority should be to pick a cabinet?

**Booster:** Oh I see! Capital idea! Lots of competent chaps and some sensible members of the fairer sex who can sort out the mess.

**Leaves:** No, sir. I would recommend appointing a group of individuals who are all singularly lacking in any observable character or ability.

**Booster:** What? I don't follow you, Leaves.

**Leaves:** It's the only chance of you looking good, sir – if all the others are completely hopeless.

**Booster:** I say! Top notch plan!

**Leaves:** It's what your predecessor Mrs May did when she appointed you.

**Booster:** Right. Here we go. Jobs for the blithering ninnies, prize chumps and anyone who is as dense as the proverbial custard.

**Leaves:** Exactly, sir.

**Booster:** So: Thicki Patel, Saddo Javid, Dim Dom Raab, Mad Nad Dorries, Ian Duncan Donuts, Matt Halfcock, ghastly Aunt Leadsom and Spiderman Williams...

**Leaves:** I couldn't come up with a worse list myself, sir.

**Booster:** And what about Nigel 'Spode' Farage and his jolly Black Shorts?

**Leaves:** I don't think so, sir. There *are* limits.

**Booster:** Are there? Whatever you say, Leaves.

**Leaves:** Indeed.

*(To be continued...)*

## GREEN LEADER SPELLS IT OUT

Only women can sort out Brexit
Like Mrs May?

Sorry Dennis, the urge to check my phone is unbearable.
Moz

# That Rees-Mogg memo in full

The following words are not acceptable for use in the office of the Leader of the House of Commons, the Right Honourable Jacob Rees-Mogg, Esq., MP *(NB, not MP, Esq.)*

- **Investment**
- **Fund**
- **Dublin**
- **Subsidiary**
- **Hypocrite**
- **Humbug**
- **Self-righteous**
- **Prig**

**Attention must be paid to correct grammar**

For example, the phrase "Britain Trump", as recently used by the President of the United States to describe Prime Minister Johnson, is an unfortunate lapse in syntactical exactitude by the otherwise erudite and linguistically gifted leader of the Free World. He should of course have simply reversed the words, added an apostrophe and an 's' and spelt 'Briton' correctly, thus forming the accurate description "Trump's Briton", which conveys the meaning correctly of a Prime Minister in a special relationship with his boss.

**Only imperial measures must be employed**

Appropriate imperial measures include: selling opium to the Chinese market, partitioning India, declaring war on the Zulu kingdom and putting punitive tariffs on tea sold to American colonists. Anyone not conforming to these simple requirements will be placed in leg-irons and transported to Her Majesty's Penal Colony in New South Wales, Australia.

*"Now that you've completed the quality survey, could you fill out this questionnaire on the quality of the quality survey?"*

EYE HEALTH

## Those benefits of drinking red wine in full

**Drink one glass a day**
Increases probiotics in the gut, resulting in lower cholesterol and a reduced chance of being overweight

**Drink one bottle a night**
Increases number of police on your doorstep after late-night row with your girlfriend over a laptop, resulting in you ending up as Prime Minister

# What You Missed

## Drivetime

LBC (and all other stations)

**Eddie "Night" Mair**: Right, listeners, our next topic is "Should hands-free mobiles be made illegal for drivers?" I've got Ken on the line. Where are you, Ken?

**Ken**: I'm on the M3.

**Eddie**: And what's your view, Ken?

**Ken**: Well, it's just ridiculous, isn't it? It's just the nanny state. It's political correctness gone mad. I mean, there's nothing dangerous about using your mobile in the car while you drive, so long as you concentrate and don't get distracted by the conversation you're WOOOOOAAAAAH!!!

**Eddie**: I'm afraid we seem to have lost Ken. Thanks for that. Got another caller. Hello, Julie.

**Julie**: Hi, Eddie.

**Eddie**: And where are you calling from?

**Julie**: The fast lane of the M25.

**Eddie**: I didn't know there was a fast lane on the M25. Hahaha!

**Julie**: Hahaha! WAAAAHHHHH!!!

**Eddie**: I'm afraid we seem to have lost Julie as well. Not having much luck today, are we? Can we have a caller from home, maybe? Ah, Simon, where are you?

**Simon**: I'm safe and sound on the sofa in my front room in my house… which is on a bend on the A262.

**Eddie**: Yes, I know it well – the sharp bend?

**Simon**: That's right, Eddie. As a libertarian, I think people should be allowed to make their own minds up, like this bloke out the window. He's on the phone and he's driving his articulated lorry perfectly safely – through my front window! AAAARGGGHHHH!!!

**Eddie**: And now over to Nigel Farage for another car crash.

# The Alternative Rocky Horror Service Book

Number 94
**The Solemnisation of 9-Holy Crazy Golf within Rochester Cathedralw**

**The Bishop of Rochester** (*for it is he*): Brothers, Sisters, Holidaymakers; we are gathered here together to celebrate the mysteries of crazy golf, to contemplate the meaning of the spinny windmill, the clown's face and the great volcano. You know, in many ways, we're all trying to get round the course of life, avoiding the hazards and trying to battle with ourselves to achieve the best score we can at the end of the day. You'll notice that the theme of the cathedral course is "bridges", so shall we begin with Hymn 94, "Bridge Over Troubled Water".

*The Cathedral sound system will now play the popular young persons' tune, by St Paul Simon and the Artangel Garfunkel.*

**Bishop:** Let us play.

*The congregation will then select a putter from the hut and begin to go round the cathedral, following the fourteen Stations of the Course.*

**THE CONFESSION**

*The congregation may at this point fall to their knees in order to retrieve their ball from underneath the water hazard (font).*

**Congregation:** Oh God, I've lost the ball.

**THE ABSOLUTION**

**Bishop:** Oh God, I've lost the plot.

**THE READING**

*There now follows a reading from St Andrew's Gospel, Chapter 18, Par 5.*

**Reader:** And the wise man did not build his house upon the sand, for lo, it was a bunker. Instead he chose the straight and narrow fairway, which was more difficult, and in the end he gave up and took his family to the Castle instead, which turned out to be historic rather than bouncy and his children were sorely disappointed, even more so than in the crazy golf.

**THE BLESSING**

**All:** Here endeth the holiday.

**Children:** That's what I call a blessing.

# CARETAKER PM READY FOR ACTION!

Do you know how to form a unity government?

No, but if you hum it, I'll play along...

## Exclusive to all tabloids

# WHAT A LOAD OF HOT AIR THIS SILLY GIRL TALKS ABOUT CLIMATE CHANGE

**Greta Humbug! What a disgrace! As the so-called eco-worrier ships in to yet another climate conference to moan about global warming, doesn't she realise what a world-class hypocrite she is?**

Worried about rising sea-levels? What about the water that your yacht's displacing? Worried about energy? What about all the solar energy you're using, heating up that bucket of water for your hand-held shower? And what about all the wasted wind that could be doing something better than blowing you across the Atlantic to another pointless greeny gabfest. And don't let's start on all the $CO_2$ coming out of your mouth when you breathe out!

We thought Meghan was the worst, but at least she gets her hair done. *(Good point. Ed.)*

So, Greta Iceberg, why don't you just sail off into the Swedish sunset and don't come back again! *(You're on fire, as is the Arctic. Ed.)*

*"Greta Thunberg's arriving"*

CLIMATE ACTION SUMMIT

*Poem by*
**ee 'dominic' cummings**

## taking back control

everyone must do what
i say and there
will be no punctuation
and no full stops
because i do not obey the
rules i am a disruptor
and there is
no time for stopping for
thought or for a
pause or reflection just
moving on and
on with
no

## WESTMINSTER THEATRE NEWS

***Opening soon...***

## THE CARETAKER by Harold Pinter

NEW production of the sinister absurdist comedy in which a hapless old man (Jeremy Corbyn) is bullied by the brothers (Len McCluskey) into accepting a job that he does not want and is incapable of doing.

All he wants is to return to Washedup (surely "Sidcup"? Ed.), but they will not let him go.

Hilarious and terrifying by turns, this is classic Theatre of Cruelty. And don't miss the trademark long pause when the caretaker is asked, "What's your position on Brexit?"

**Eye rating:** *One star (red).*

## MOVIE MASH-UPS

**Dirty Harry Potter**

WHAT MADE YOU WANT TO BECOME AN EDITOR?
WELL, TO CUT A LONG STORY SHORT...
C.V.

## BRITISH AIRWAYS

*"THIS is your Captain striking, welcome aboard the British Airways Flight BA94 to Nowhere.*

*We'll shortly be opening the doors and disembarking the plane as we're not going anywhere. If you'd like to take a minute to study the information in your newspaper, you'll see that I am asking for quite a lot of money, even though I'm actually paid rather a lot, compared to you.*

*You may want to use the sick bag provided for your use and located in the seat in front of you.*

*We're just completing our pre-flight cheques which aren't nearly enough, and then we'll be off.*

*So, for those of you who are interested, I'll shortly be cruising at about 90 miles an hour in my Porsche.*

*My destination will be the golf course in Sunningdale where the temperature on the ground is a very agreeable 27 degrees. Drinks will be served at the 19th hole, but only to me, with a range of snacks and nibbles.*

*If you'd like to talk to any of the on-board crew, they will be happy to tell you how little cabin staff get paid, compared to me.*

*If you've got any loose change from your travels, the cabin crew will be coming around with a bucket, and all proceeds will go to our nominated charity… myself.*

*So, sit back and prepare for a bit of turbulence between my union and my boss, which could make things a bit bumpy for the next few weeks. I hope we won't be seeing you again in the near future. I wish you a very pleasant flight on a different airline."*

# EPSTEIN – TRIBUTES DON'T FLOW IN

by Our New York Staff **Pete O'Phile**

**FOLLOWING the death of the well-connected entrepreneur, businessman and socialite, Jeffrey Epstein, tributes have poured in from no one.**

Said one man who knew him well, "I didn't know him at all. Jeffrey who?"

The tributes didn't appear from all walks of life, from politics to royalty to showbiz, no one who'd been at his parties had ever heard of him.

Here are just a few of the many who had something else to do rather than lament their good friend's passing in jail:

*President Trump*: "I never met him, particularly not when I met him. You're thinking of President Clinton, who had him killed. He didn't commit suicide. Fake noose! I didn't say that. Just passing it on."

*Bill Clinton*: "I did not have sexual relations with this man's friends. It wasn't me, it was Hillary. Lock her up!"

*Prince Andrew*: "Ha! ha! ha! Yah. Mother, can I sit in the car with you today? It'll look good in the papers. Why? No reason – it's just you're quite an old woman. Can I put my arm around you?"

*Elon Musk*: "He wasn't a paedophile – unlike those divers in the caves in Thailand who rescued the boys. I know a paedophile when I see one. Now, if you'll excuse me, I have to go to the moon."

## GHISLAINE MAXWELL NAMED IN EPSTEIN CASE

I wonder if she'll sue?
Not the first mysterious suicide, is it...?

# POETRY CORNER

**In Memoriam Jeffrey Epstein, entrepreneur, and socialite**

So. Farewell
Then Jeffrey Epstein,
You have died at
The age of 66.

Far too young,
They said,
But you had
Sex with them
Anyway.

E. J. Thribb (17½ and keep your hands off me)

# New Ukip leader announced

by Our Nominative Deterministic Staff **Naim Fitzjob**

A NEW leader for the United Kingdom Independence Party has finally been announced after what insiders described as an exhaustive search.

Said a spokesman for the party, "A number of our leaders have turned out to make us into a laughing stock, and we wanted to ensure this never happened again.

"That is why we chose Dick Braine, whom we all agreed was a perfect choice to restore the fortunes of our beleaguered party."

He continued, "Obviously there were a lot of high-quality candidates and we looked carefully at all their CVs. I should say we were very impressed by Hugh Janus, Mike Hunt and Wayne Kerr, but they were not quite up to the mark.

"Ivor Biggun and Ivana Shagg also interviewed well, and Mustapha Fuk would have been a serious contender in any other year, but Dick Braine was a stand-out winner. We are absolutely delighted to say Dick Braine, you are the perfect man for the job."

Mr Richard Braine sighed, and said, "I always used to be embarrassed by my name, but now I've got something far more embarrassing to contend with – I'm Leader of Ukip."

# THE SUNDAY GNOMES

# Operation Browntrouser

**EXCLUSIVE** The secret government document reveals the truth at last

by Our Leak Staff
**Sir Jonathan Leake**

**Much-loved Yellowhammer or Browntrouser bird**

IN the most amazing scoop ever,, the Sunday Gnomes can reveal the government's exact details of its contingency plan for a No-Deal Brexit.

So remarkable are these details, that we have devoted the entire newspaper to publishing the sensational document in its entirety.

The most extraordinary revelation of all is that in the event of a No-Deal Brexit, things aren't going to go very well.

This sensational disclosure, which had occurred to no one over the past three years, is contained in the file marked with the sinister codename Operation Browntrouser.

The stark facts are that if Britain leaves the EU without having renegotiated a deal then the following will happen:

**1.** The UK will run out of fuel
**2.** The UK will run out of food
**3.** The UK will run out of medicine
**4.** Everyone will run out of their houses and kill each other
**5.** Possibly
**6.** Or not, as the case may be.

What this breathtaking official leak demonstrates is that the Sunday Gnomes staff are all on holiday and we have got an awful lot of space to fill.

It also shows that this lid-lifting story – that No Deal is not a very good idea – ranks alongside the greatest journalistic scoops of all time, ie that the Pope is secretly a Catholic (Operation Incenseswinger) and that bears secretly shit in the woods (Operation Treecrapper).

The government, however, has been swift to poo-poo the Browntrouser leak.

Michael Gove said, "This information is very old, dating back to this morning. It does not take into account the measures we have taken to avert a national crisis of the type that we outlined this morning. Since lunch we have taken the following important decisions..."

Mr Gove then outlined the decisions in full:

**1.** Blame Phil Hammond for crisis
**2.** Blame EU for crisis
**3.** Blame Dominic Grieve for assisting EU and Phil Hammond to create crisis
**4.** Change unhelpful name of Operation Browntrouser to positive, feelgood Operation Turdpolish.

But none of this government denial can change the essential fact that we filled a whole newspaper in the toughest non-news week in August. Phew!

*©The Sunday Gnomes Infill Team, Phil Space, Philippa Column and Paddy Tout.*

# Nursery Times

Friday, Once-upon-a-time

## NURSERYLAND STANDARDS AUTHORITY – THOSE SHOCKING RULINGS IN FULL

by Our Gender Staff **Father Goose**

IN A bad week for Nurseryland, the Nurseryland Standards Authority has come down hard on sexism and gender stereotyping in the Nursery Rhyme and Fairy Tale communities.

In fact there were so many rulings, that we are only able to give summaries of the critical judgements from the NSA adjudications. They include:

- All the King's Horses and All the King's Men presented specifically men as being incapable of putting an egg back together again after it had fallen off a wall.
- Snow White left at home to do all the cleaning while a group of seven men all perform manual work, ie diamond mining, that a woman is more than capable of performing should she be allowed to go hi ho hi ho off to work.
- Bo Peep singled out as incapable of looking after sheep, and losing them all solely because she is a "little" woman and, therefore, less effective by implication than a male shepherd.
- Old Mother Hubbard incapable of even feeding a dog with a bone. As if Old Father Hubbard would somehow have had a full cupboard of dog food.
- The Grand Old Duke of York pointlessly marched 10,000 men (and no women!) up and down a hill. As though only men would embark on such a futile military exercise under the direction of a useless man.
- The Old Woman in the Shoe portrayed as ignorant and unequal to the task of looking after children in a footwear environment, purely because she is old and, more importantly, female.

A spokesperson for the NSA, Nanny "State" McPhee, said: "Only one nursery scenario has been deemed appropriate for public consumption, and that is Jack and Jill's thoughtfully gender-balanced and sensitively equal trip up a hill which resulted in both of the participants falling down and injuring themselves very badly. More of this, please."

## Hong Kong Airport

| Departures | Arrivals |
| --- | --- |
| Freedom | Tanks |
| Peace | |
| Democracy | |
| Hope | |

## BORIS JOHNSON'S WIFE TELLS ALL

I got rid of a dangerous lump – and now I feel much, much better

## The Eye's Controversial New Columnist

*The columnist who believes the pen is mightier than the sword, but a well-aimed spoon is mightier than both*

This week I am very angry about the Advertising Standards Authority banning a television commercial over "stereotyping". This is PC gone mad! I have heard that the advert in question shows men being so incompetent in the care of a baby that they left it gliding around on a restaurant conveyor belt! So what's the problem??? These snowflake men need to grow a pair and admit that, yes, it's stereotype, but it's a stereotype for a reason, and admit that, if the cap fits, they have to wear it!

PS. I have now viewed the advert in question and found it completely offensive. The baby is smiling and laughing in a completely stereotypical way. Someone should tell these advertising creatives that babies do things other than chuckle. They frown in a very stern way and throw tantrums. This commercial should be unbanned so it can be banned again for the proper reasons, ie being offensive to me and other *(cont. p94)*

*Daily Telegraph* Friday 23 August 2019

## Letters to the Editor

### The Obvious Solution To The Northern Ireland Backstop

SIR – Am I the only person to have realised that there is a perfectly simple solution to the Northern Ireland backstop staring us all in the face?

It is quite obvious to me that if only the Republic of Ireland would come to its senses and stop being so selfish, the entire problem would disappear.

The intransigent Irish are trying to secure a "have your cake and eat it" Brexit deal, by wanting to stay in the EU. Why not leave the EU and rejoin the United Kingdom, thus ensuring a great new economic future for our new, and indeed old, joint country?

If only our Prime Minister, Mr Johnson, had the guts to offer this olive branch to the Irish government, then we would see the ultimate renewal of the ties that bind our Union of a reformed Great Britain and Ireland ruled from Westminster.

Incidentally, I have no doubt that not only would this solve any British objections to the backstop, it would also guarantee future support for the Tories from the Democratic Unionist Party for years to come.

**Sir Herbert Gussett**
*Mount Gussett Castle, Ballycarson, Co. Jingo, Eire*

# Trump to buy Englandland

by Our Business Staff
**Sir Philip Greenland**

THE President of the United States has declared his intention of purchasing "an insignificant island floating in the Atlantic".

This bleak, bankrupt, desolate wasteland, which the president described as "of little value to anyone" is said to have attracted Donald Trump's attention, thanks to its unique combination of nature resources, golf courses and the NHS.

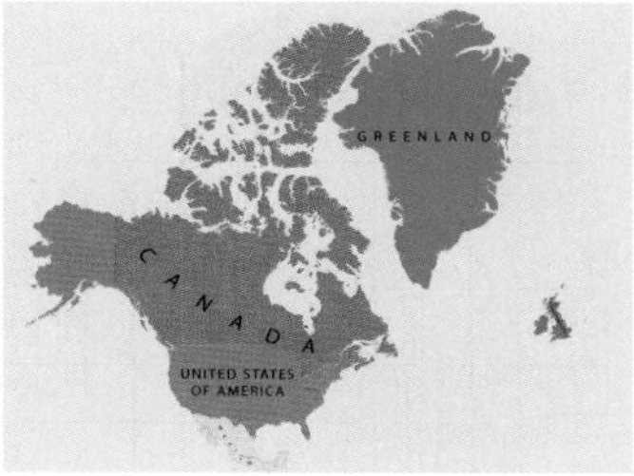


Said President Trump, "The guy who runs the place is keen to sell it to me. He told me I'm first in the queue. And I can't wait to introduce the natives to the joys of chlorinated chicken. Mmmm!"

Some inhabitants of Englandland have voiced concern that their country was previously considered an independent sovereign democratic territory and protested that they did not want to become the 51st state.

"Too late, losers!" replied the president. "You haven't got any choice now. It's a great deal – for America. #MakeAmericaRichAgain."

## Late News

- Englandland will be renamed Greedland to fit in with the president's new international vision.

# NIGEL FARAGE ON DUKES

## A COMPREHENSIVE GUIDE by the Leader of the Brexit Party

### DUKE OF SUSSEX

Was doing very nicely, funny lad, lots of great fancy-dress costumes, until he took up with you-know-who. And who cares if they're not having lots of children, when there are billions of Chinese and Indians? Absolute disaster.

### DUKE OF WINDSOR

Was doing really well, supporting just the right sort of chaps politically – firm-handed sorts, keen to weed out all the degenerates – then it all went wrong when he married Wallis and had to go off to the Bahamas. Real shame. He could have been the reich king – sorry, I mean the right king.

### GRAND OLD DUKE OF YORK

Had 10,000 men, very impressive, could have marched them somewhere really useful, or could have seized power and started implementing good old- fashioned policies, but then he has to march them up and down a hill. Waste of resources.

### THE THIN WHITE DUKE

He's thin, which I like, and he's white, which is also another big tick. But despite him spending a lot of time in Berlin, he seems to have learned absolutely nothing about good governance. Bizarre.

# NEW CHINESE WALL VISIBLE FROM SPACE

# Exclusive Daily Telegraph poll reveals Britons would rather die face down in a ditch than trade with EU

*By* **Ronald Tortured-Data**
**OUR STATISTICAL CORRESPONDENT**

## SURVEY METHODOLOGY

The sample was a comprehensive one, taking in at least 15 of the senior members of the Telegraph's editorial team, including such balanced figures as Nigel Farage, Asa Bennett and Tim Stanley, and such unbalanced figures as the Barclay brothers and Allison Pearson.

The balanced question asked was: "Would you do whatever it took to remove the neck of the proud British lion from beneath the grinding heel of the fascistic European jackboot, so your children can breathe the pure air of freedom and drink the sweet ambrosia of Anglo-Saxon liberty?"

## FINDINGS

**100%** of those surveyed confirmed they would do whatever it took, meaning that the British public is firmly behind Boris 'Spartacus' Johnson and would be willing to man the barricades to the death in the event of a war against the cringing poltroons of the EU.

## OTHER FINDINGS

**100%** of those surveyed WOULD take arms against a sea of troubles and, by opposing, end them

**100%** of those surveyed WOULD like to be given liberty but, failing that, would like as a second choice to be given death

**100%** of those surveyed confirm that there WON'T be some small corner of a foreign field that is forever England.

© *Ipsos Morons 2019*

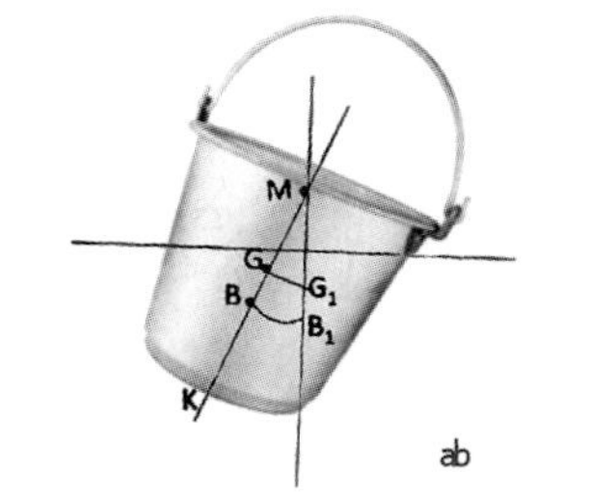


**Bucket list**

# HOW I WON THE ASHES

by Joffrey Archer

I don't like to boast about these things, but as well as being a world-famous novelist and Olympic athlete, I just happen to be a dab hand at international cricket.

Nobody was more surprised than me to receive a call from the Head of the English Cricket Board selectors whilst I was in the middle of performing open heart surgery - awkward! - to be asked to spearhead the bowling in the Lord's Test match.

To be honest, I didn't know if I could fit it in, what with all the anniversary celebrations of me being the first man on the moon... but duty called.

"All right," I said, "but I don't want to hog the limelight. I'll just take five wickets, knock out Australia's best batsman and then we'll call it a draw."

And the rest, as they say, is fiction!

*©Joffra Archer, 2019.*

## What You Missed

# Whaley Bridge Special

BBC News

**Philippa Airtime in Studio:** Would you say that everyone is terrified that the dam is about to burst, with billions of gallons of water flooding the whole county and drowning everyone within hundreds of miles?

**Kim Kagool in Whaley Bridge:** Well the locals are a fairly stalwart bunch and they are just letting the emergency services get on with...

**Philippa:** But the concrete slabs are collapsing and the water is flooding over and there must be a real fear that a catastrophe on a huge scale is about to happen – a bit like that TV series Chernobyl but with water instead of radioactive...

**Kim:** Er... the RAF helicopter is assisting the police and the engineers are saying that the pumps are working full time and the water levels are falling and there is no further rain forecast so...

**Philippa:** So it's going to be little short of apocalyptic. Thanks for that frank assessment. Now, over to Simon for the latest on this year's Strictly contestants... *(continued for 94 hours).*

# BREXIT LATEST

You don't want to be told what to do by unelected bureaucrats in Brussels...
...when you can be told what to do by unelected spin doctors in Number 10


# Ruth Davidson quits over baby

by Our Family Affairs Correspondent **Phil Nappy**

THE Leader of the Scottish Conservatives, Ruth Davidson, today announced she would be stepping down on account of the pressures brought on by trying to get on with her job and deal with a baby.

Said Ms Davidson, "I could cope with the sleepless nights, but the constant bawling and tantrums were getting me down. Boris is frankly impossible. I'd rather spend time with a six-month old puking toddler than this infantile Prime Minister who throws his toys out of the pram whenever he doesn't get his way."

At an emotional press conference, Ms Davidson added, "Boris is full of wind and the amount of shit that comes out of him is more than I can handle. I've had enough of holding my nose and cleaning up all the mess he makes."

A spokesman for Number Ten said, "Ruth Davidson was decent, honourable and principled. Clearly there was no place for her in today's Tory party. Now fuck off, I've got another SpAd to fire!"

*"I've had some work done"*

## ME AND MY SPOON

SEPTEMBER ISSUE

**GUEST EDITED BY MEGHAN MARKLE**

*We are delighted to announce that this issue of Me and My Spoon is guest edited by none other than the Duchess of Markle, Meghan Sparkle! Here in an exclusive interview she talks to one of the most influential and inspirational role models in the world today, herself.*

**What is your favourite spoon?**

I believe in diversity, spoon-wise, so all spoons should have an equal place in the cutlery drawer. Big, small, plain, decorated, steel, wood, black, white, rainbow, fashionable, unfashionable, every spoon has its own value.

**But what is *your* favourite spoon?**

Silver.

**How many spoons have you got?**

I don't think anyone should have more than two spoons, unlike some people who have three. We've got to be more responsible if we're going to save the world.

**How has your philosophy of life been shaped spoon-wise?**

Well, I used to like teaspoons but then I realised they were rather shallow and I wanted something deeper, like a soup spoon or even a ladle.

**That's very profound**

It so is! I think spoons reflect life... particularly if they are shiny. You look into a spoon and what do you see? *Yourself!*

**Yes indeedy doody. And how do you see your own role in the world, spoonwise?**

I feel I have a great responsibility and, like the best of spoons, my job is to stir things up. As the great female role model Mary Poppins once said to me, "A spoonful of sugar, makes the Meghan go down". And I think that's so true.

**So do I. Finally can I just ask if anything amusing has ever happened to you in connection with a spoon?**

No, you can't ask that. It's private. There are limits to how much the public are entitled to know about me and my spoon. Please consult the Frogmore Cottage Public Handbook which sets out the boundaries for Royal spoon-related interaction.

**Thank you very much. Your Marklesty.**

ON OTHER PAGES: *Hundreds of adverts for expensive spoons and hundreds of pictures of very thin spoons indeed.*

# Shortages leave Yemen on the brink

WARRING factions involved in the conflict in Yemen have warned that the region is "dangerously close" to running out of civilians to slaughter.

Spokesmen for murdering groups on all sides joined concerned military hardware manufacturers in their condemnation of the recent reduction in promised humanitarian aid to the country, which could mean that there will "soon be no one to test new weapons on".

"Such is the level of starvation caused by the disgraceful drop in promised humanitarian aid," said one angry warlord, "that there may be an unprecedented dip in non-combatants available to indiscriminately murder.

"If this carries on, we may no longer have the option to falsely label a bombed hospital or school a rebel training facility."

Arms manufacturers are also said to be "very worried" that sales may fall in 2020 if there is no one left to shoot or bomb in the country, which will have a detrimental effect on the UK economy.

# Liberal Democrats 'Now Proper Party'

by Our Man in Bournemouth
**Peter Obornemouth**

The Liberal Democrats party has finally set out its stall as a force to be reckoned with in British politics.

As delegates at the annual conference argued bitterly and heckled each other over their new policy to scrap Brexit without a referendum, senior party figures were delighted.

Said Sir Vince Capable, "This means that we are now a true political party, divided over Europe."

He continued, "Up until this moment, we were just a joke, with a united stance on a second referendum and an appealing Brexit strategy. Now we can compete with the other two parties regarding internal conflict and mutual rancour."

Said leader Jo Swinson, "I love prosecco and Fleabag! What more do you want?"

## SWINSON SHOCK REVELATION

I'm allergic to nuts
You're in the wrong party then, love!


# Scientists recreate face of human evolution

**Homer Sapiens**
*Our Evolution Staff*

After many hours of painstaking reconstructions, anthropologists have unveiled the face of our 4-million-year-old distant ancestor.

Following in the footsteps of "Lucy", this ape has been nicknamed "Simian", although his official scientific name is *Britannicus Gottalentis*.

The so-called "X-Factor man" is notable for his large unmoving brow and is thought to have been alive when early man first stood up on two feet and belted out a power ballad.

Said one expert, "Simian is the missing link that bridges the gap between early-evening and late-night TV man.

"His journey was an incredible one, full of emotional ups and downs, and doubtless a sick nan who was very proud of him."

## HOW TO BE A FREELANCER

MORNING
I HAVEN'T GOT ANY WORK!
AFTERNOON
I'VE GOT TOO MUCH WORK!
– Flavell + Tayller –

## Monday

"It's an outrage" I said, sounding not inconsiderably aggrieved and in no small measure furious, as I buttered a second slice of toast (this was most definitely a second slice of toast kind of morning).

"What's wrong, John?" my wife's hand hovered over the tea strainer.

"How dare a Prime Minister prorogue parliament simply to escape scrutiny," I said, as I glared at her, my steely eyes framed by the finest frames Specsavers had to offer.

Norman sighed. "I'm sure people have forgiven you, John, for doing that in 1997 before Sir Gordon Downey could deliver his report into Cash for Questions," she replied as she reached to take my special "Tony the Tiger" breakfast cereal bowl out of the cupboard.

"No, no, no, Norma that was completely different," I spluttered. "I'm talking about those scoundrels Boris Johnson and Dominic Cummings.

"When I prorogued the Commons it was a perfectly reasonable use of parliamentary procedure, whereas what they are doing is a flagrant attack on democracy, and it's time to do something about it. That's why you won't be seeing much of me in the coming week, as I'll be with another woman."

"What did you say, John?"

"Gina Miller and I will be spending our every waking minute preparing our case to test out the legality of what Boris has done in the courts. I have to say that so far I've been immeasurably impressed by Gina's briefs. Yes we're an unlikely pairing, but then they do say that politics makes for strange bedfellows."

"Wouldn't be the first time you got into bed with a strange woman and didn't think to inform me, would it, John?" Norman grinned savagely.

I couldn't respond, due to the sound of breaking crockery. Norma had only gone and clumsily dropped my special bowl on my head, making Tony the Tiger not inconsiderably extinct.

# Amazon fire to be 'halted'

Brazil's President Bolsonaro has rejected an offer of $20m from the G7 countries, saying he already has a plan to stop the Amazon rainforest fires, which involves burning down the entire rainforest.

"The plan is to set hundreds more fires, so the remaining 80 percent of the rainforest is also ablaze," said a Brazilian government spokesman.

"After the entire rainforest has been reduced to charred rubble, the chance of any more fires happening will be reduced to zero.

"Once the Amazon Rainforest is flattened, the charred ground can bring forth new life, as work begins to construct the world's biggest Amazon distribution centre."

## FORMS OF TRANSPORT THE TABLOIDS WOULD LIKE MEGHAN TO TAKE

Private Jet

Chauffeur-driven car in Paris

# God warned not to intervene in Brexit debate

by Our Religious Correspondent
**Archie Bishop**

The Almighty has been issued with a stern warning that it would be extremely dangerous for Him to make an intervention in the debate over Brexit.

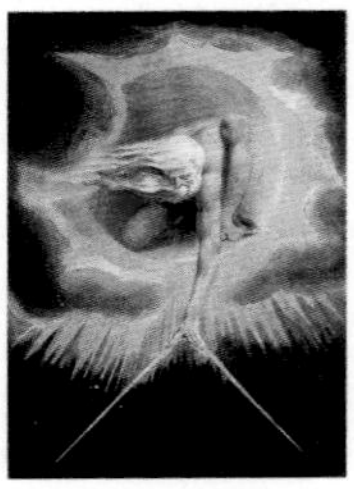

A senior Conservative source said, "We have been very clear on this. 17 million people voted and their say is final. Just because God created the universe, divided the day from the night and the heavens from the earth, created man and all the other animals, and so on, there's no reason why His opinion should count for anything and it would be a grotesque travesty of justice if He stuck His divine conk in now."

A spokesman for the Brexit party said, "This is typical God. Playing around, saying He's in favour of this or that. It's about time he heard the message loud and clear from the British electorate: we don't want you, we're not interested in any of your interference, you're probably foreign anyway, just take yourself away and let us get on with it."

The King of Kings and Lord of All Creation has not issued any statement so far, but is understood to be eagerly looking forward to the prospect of Armageddon.

# School news

**St Crumbs pre-prep school, London SW94**
*(the feeder school for the prestigious prep school St Biscuits, the feeder school for the prestigious independent fee-paying school St Cakes)*

Royal term. There are 39 boys, 38 girls and two Royals in the school. Princess Charlotte joins Toffs House, where she is a tadpole. Her older brother Prince George (Nobs) is already a frog. The annual race to invite Princess Charlotte for tea has been won by Mrs Clara Hedge-Ffunde, following a generous contribution to the school's new arts block. Nannies' evening (formerly parents' evening) will be held on 3 November and will be attended by Miss Tiggy Wiggy-Wiggy, Ms M. Poppins, Ms McPhee and token nanny Mr Doubtfire, amongst others. School motto has been changed from *'Quis Paget Entrat'* to *'Quis Royalis Entrat'*. Parents are reminded not to park their cars outside the school gates during school hours because the gentlemen of the press need the space for their stepladders and mopeds. This term, head of paparazzi is Signor Slizi-Ratzo from the highly respected European photo agency Phwooar, who will be accompanied by hit British colleagues Mr Sidney Scumbag from the *Mail* and Mr Len Scap, the photographer royale from the *Sun*. The tug of forelock competition will take place on Grovellings Field on 17 October. The nativity play will star Princess Charlotte as the Virgin Mary and Prince George as all three kings. The sheep will be played by members of the royal protection squad, Sergeant Smith, Sergeant Wesson and Constable Taser. Tickets from the bursar at £7,200 for the stalls. Royals only for the royal circle. Every Monday morning, headmistress Ms Daphne Kerr-Ching will be taking assembly and cheques from prospective parents. Term ends on 10 November, in time for Christmas skiing.

Clerihew on the complicated family arrangements of Sheikh Mohammed bin Rashid Al Maktoum, ruler of Dubai, which have sadly ended up in the British Royal Courts of Justice.

***Sheikh Maktoum***
***Is full of gloom,***
***Because his children and wives***
***All run for their lives.***

# GOVERNMENT OF NATIONAL UNITY – HOW IT WOULD LOOK

# A Russian Doctor Writes

AS A doctor, I'm often asked by leaders of the opposition, "Doctor, have I suddenly developed a new unexplained allergy?"

The simple answer is "Nyet, you've been poisoned by an associate of the president."

This is a very common complaint called Putin's Rash or *novichokius doorhandlus normalis*, to give it its full medical name, which causes you to lose your voice for a while, which is the main intention.

Side effects include fear that you're about to die, shock that no one seems very interested and disbelief that the president seems to be getting away with it again. Excuse me, I need to answer my phone… "Yes… Yes… I understand, thank you."

Sorry about that. I now realise that you haven't been poisoned at all and are suffering an extreme and very rare allergic reaction to a rogue cabbage leaf.

You have definitely not been poisoned. I've no idea where that idea came from. I suggest you leave now and please, please never come back.

*© A Russian Doctor 2019*

# Is this article justified in using a photo of Fleabag?

**Bertram-of-the-Barrel**
*Our It's August correspondent*

Wow, look at this great photo of Phoebe Waller-Bridge, AKA Fleabag! What a brilliant shot. Many of you may be wondering how Waller-Bridge actually fits into this bit of the paper, given that this is four pages into the business section and only shortly before the obituaries. And we'd be the first to admit that the article which follows below isn't actually about *Fleabag* – it's about fisheries policy in Mozambique and how that might or might not affect regional markets in the medium term. However, now that we've MENTIONED the gratuitous use of the photo, the article sort of is about Fleabag, so we hope you don't mind us using a photo of the hit 33-year-old whose award-winning series has revolutionised comedy for ever, transformed the televisual landscape, and scorched the earth of confessional one-woman comedies with a disarmingly frank and posh examination of how sexy and frank posh women have been franking sexily and with poshness until *(continued for the next five years until the next* Fleabag *comes along)*

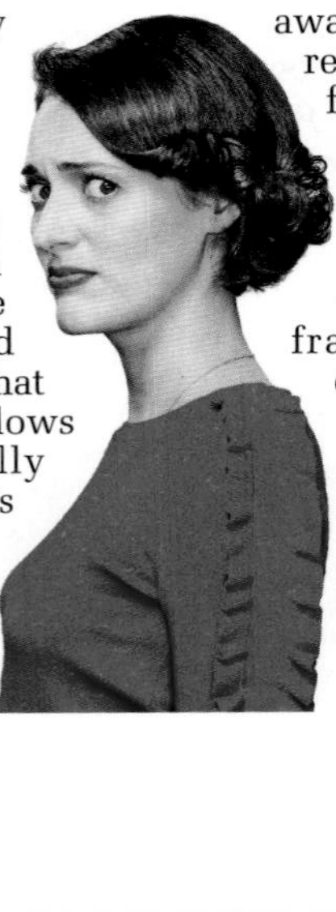

# HEIR OF SORROWS

## A Short Story Special

by Dame Sylvie Krin, author of *Duchess of Hearts* & *You're Never Too Old*

*THE STORY SO FAR: Britain stands divided. For the first time in living memory, the Monarchy is being dragged into a political crisis. Now read on...*

"LONG live the King!" cried Archbishop Paddy Power, as he placed the bejewelled Netflix Crown of Destiny on the noble head of King Charles the Third and the choir of Westminster's Coral Abbey sang *Vivat* and *Magnificat*, translated, to the new monarch's chagrin, into the more patriotically British *Gertcha* and *Rabbit, Rabbit, Rabbit*.

How times had changed since 31 October 2019 and his kingdom's departure from the European Thingy. Well, thought Charles, it used to be a kingdom – now it was a collection of warring states and tribal factions, England versus Scotland, Angles versus Celts, Celts versus Picts, Ants versus Decs, Strictlys versus Bakeoffs. How had it come to this? How had history conspired to ensure that his legacy would be as ruler of the Disunited Kingdom. How had the bard put it? This Sceptic Isle, set in a Sewered Sea?

The newly crowned monarch ran solemnly to the safety of his bulletproof gold carriage amidst a hail of boos and flying milkshakes from his angry, starving subjects, many of whom had broken the anti-riot curfew and slept on the pavement overnight to ensure a good spot from which to shout "Kraut King go home!"

Charles the Third ducked in fear at the roaring sound overhead from the traditional flypast by the BetfRed Arrows and looked bitterly at the text on his Deep DooDoogee not-so-smartphone: "PM Bozza here, Chuckmeister! Hope crowning went well. Soz to miss it. More pressing engagement, viz renaming of Great Ormond Street Hospital as the Trump Clinic for the Well-Insured. See you for nosebag time at Buck House!"

Tears streamed down the cheeks of the royal visage, as traces of the police's pepper spray leaked into his gilded eco-friendly Prius armoured state landau. With a heavy heart, he was borne off to Buckingham Palace to celebrate his investiture with a feast of Chlorination Chicken...

"Coronation chicken, Chazza?"

The familiar voice of his beloved consort roused the man-who-would-be king from his slumbers. His cheeks were wet. Perhaps because of his troubling dream? No, it was the stinging effect of clouds of sickly candyfloss vape emanating from the cylindrical tube dangling from one side of Camilla's mouth, while a more familiar Rothmans Extra High Tar Untipped dangled from the other.

"You'd better tuck in," she drawled, "before the bastard midges eat it all."

With a surge of relief, Charles realised where he was. Not in some dystopian post-Brexit Apocalypse Now, but enjoying a traditional family barbecue in the grounds of Balmoral.

"Ah, the great outdoors! How wonderful it is to get back to nature," thought Charles, as a team of butlers laid the silver service on the Louis MacNeice XV Amazon mahogany table, whilst another team of waitresses held the tablecloth down for the team of sommeliers to place the correct selection of Crystalmeth glasses alongside the copperplate namecards denoting the seating arrangements.

On a wee hillock above them, known to locals as "Wee Hillock", Prince Philip was cooking on the charcoals of the Bear Grylls™ grill, in his chef's hat and novelty plastic apron bearing the body of a buxom female.

The Queen, however, was concerned with more pressing matters. "As I was saying, Charles, what do you think the sleeping arrangements should be when that ghastly Mr Johnson arrives with his young mistress?"

"She's not that young," Andrew interjected, looking up from his well-thumbed copy of *US Law for Dummies*.

"Honestly," added the Queen, "Balmoral is not the sort of place that welcomes known philanderers."

Charles, Andrew and Philip all carefully avoided eye contact in the long silence that followed. The clouds lifted above the mighty Scottish peak of Ben Stokes and the wind whipped down Glen McGrath and across the Kyle of Minogue towards Mull It O'Vaugh, just between Loch Emup and Throwawaythe Quay.

At last, Camilla broke the tension. "Give 'em separate rooms, Your Maj! You know, like Chaz and Diana had."

Another long silence fell over the benighted clan as they dwelt on yet another sorry chapter of the family's complicated history.

It was Andrew's turn to lift the mood, as he joined his busy nonogenarian father at the barbecue.

"Who's for sausage?" said Andrew cheerily, causing several young waitresses to scurry into the heather, from which they would not be seen again until next mworning when the beaters, led by auld Ghillie Cooper, went about their timeless toil.

Charles sat back in his leather-padded portable picnic-throne and shuddered. All this talk of Mr Johnson had reminded him of his coronation nightmare.

Was it truly his destiny to be a reviled king, ruling over a fractured realm? Would the do-or-die policy of that dreadful Etonian booby turn all Charles' dreams to ashes? Do or die? Who was to do and who was to die? If only Laurens van der Postitnote were still here to answer such riddles of life. But that he could not do, because he had died.

No, Charles now realised his true destiny. So long as Boris Johnson was Prime Minister, it must now be Charles' life's work to make sure that he would never be king.

*(To be continued...)*

"Hi, I'm Sam, and my chosen pronoun is 'they'"
"Hi, I'm Elizabeth, and my chosen pronoun is 'we'"
Ariss


# JOHN HUMPHRYS

**As Britain's top political inquisitor bows out after 94 years at the microphone, we look back at some of the highlights of the career of the man no one called the Torquemada of the Today Programme.**

1. "It's coming up to eight o'clock"
2. "Thank you for coming in to the studio"
3. "Later on Radio Four, *You and Yours* will be looking at your ISA options"
4. "I'm afraid that's all we've got time for"
5. "And now, over to Thought For the Day with the chief Jedi, Obi-Wan Kenobi"

*(Is this right? Ed.)*

# HUMPHRYS' FINAL INTERVIEW

If you'd just let me finish
All right then. Bye!

# THOSE INCREDIBLE REVELATIONS IN DAVID CAMERON'S MEMOIRS

**1.** Boris backed Leave in order to further his career

**2.** Gove was disloyal liar

**On other pages**

1 Pope backed Catholicism in order to take top job

2 Bears gove in the woods *(Is this right? Ed.)*

## HOW THE TOP TORIES REACTED TO THOSE SENSATIONAL MEMOIRS

**Boris Johnson, *Prime Minister***
*"Nothing Mr Cameron says will diminish the affection and respect in which I hold the bitter, failed has-been."*

**Priti Patel, *Home Secretary***
*"There's no point going over the past, particularly if you've got a past as disgraceful as mine."*

**Stephen Barclay, *Brexit Secretary***
*"He's just trying to flog some unconvincing old rubbish to the public, which is my job."*

## HOW THE PUBLIC REACTED

*"We were the victims of lies and misinformation... at the time, we were told this book would be interesting, but nothing could be further from the truth."*

*"It was a binary choice. Do you want to buy this book or not? The majority voted 'No'. I think David Cameron should respect that decision."*

*"David Cameron made an appalling mistake. And so did I. He wrote this book. I bought it. I will regret it for the rest of my life."*

# NEW BOOK SHOCK

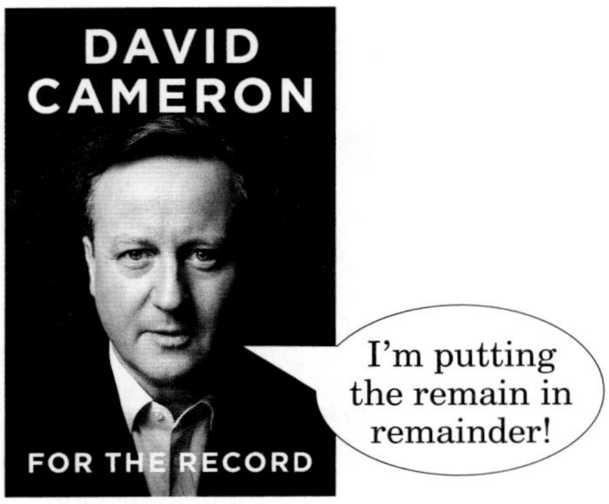


# Public urged not to panic-buy copies of David Cameron's autobiography

by Our Terrified Correspondent
**M.T. Shops**

The government yesterday urged British citizens not to go into melt-down and panic-buy David Cameron's autobiography.

"Obviously a no-deal Brexit will make it more difficult to safeguard supplies, but we are doing all that we can to ensure that enough copies are in the shops for every man, woman and child in the UK," said a spokesperson.

"Rest assured that it has been made a top priority. We have left vital drugs and perishable foods at a port in Calais, so we can free up the lorries needed to rush copies to Waterstones.

"Please do not crush each other underfoot as the bookshops open. We don't want to see needless lives lost through fear of not being able to own this vital tome. Needless lives lost due to lack of cancer drugs, that's fine – but not due to a lack of *For the Record* by D. Cameron (PM)."

*Friday 20 September 2019* **The Grauniad**

# Cameron Memoirs Teach Us All An Important Lesson

Amidst all the political fall-out surrounding the Cameron memoirs and the mutual recriminations amongst the key Brexit participants, one thing is clear: David Cameron can't possibly have been really upset about his dead son because he is posh.

Privilege and entitlement quite obviously prevent Tories from having any human emotions, other than greed and a desire to inflict suffering on the working classes.

No, Tories are all totally callous, they are the sort of heartless people who would read a whole memoir about a politician and then decide to put the boot into him over the death of his son.

How sickening are we?

*© The Guardian of the High Moral Ground.*

**Late News**

- This editorial has been removed, due to a typographical error in which thousands of letters appeared in the wrong order.

## MEGHAN LAUNCHES NEW FASHION LINE

# POETRY CORNER

**In Memoriam Robert Mugabe**

So. Farewell
Finally Robert Mugabe,
President of Zimbabwe,
Dictator, mass-murderer,
Monster and loving
Husband to Grace.

Once people hailed
You as a liberator,
Now they are glad
To be free of you.

You are to be
Buried in your
Beloved country.
At last! One bit of
Land nobody minds
You grabbing.

E.J. Thribb
(17½ million Zimbabwean
dollars to the pound)

# DIARY

## LIZ JONES: MY CULTURAL HIGHLIGHTS

**CHERNOBYL (BBC)**

Tell me about it. I've had no end of trouble with my electrical appliances. Back in March, the toaster blew a fuse, thanks very much. I bought it from John Lewis in smoky blue for £24.95. The assistant – overweight and pasty – assured me the toaster was a good make. So what happens? Six and a half years later, it packs up on me. I'm left bawling my eyes out, as usual, and back on the anti-depressants. When I watched Chernobyl, it all came flooding back – not just the tragedy with the toaster and the stains on the sink, but the dust on the shelves. And all because my cleaning lady, whom I thought I could trust, thought she could get away with just leaving roughly a million particles of dust there, all staring at me in contempt.

Compared to me, the people of Chernobyl don't know how lucky they are. So why the long faces? They had thousands of people help with the clean-up operation. I'd have been happy with half that number back in July. When my cooker got dirty, there was no one but me, an award-winning journalist, to get down on bended knees and scrub it, even if it meant risking a bad back. At the last minute, all the people I had counted as friends were telling me sorry, they had better things to do. Some friends they turned out to be, even though I've sent them all Christmas cards every year expecting nothing in return except for Christmas cards back. But suddenly they all had "jobs" to go to. Why is it always me?

**THE TEST MATCH**

So everyone was over the moon when England scored so many runs in that Test Match against Australia.

Everyone except me, that is.

Ben Stokes hit the ball for one six, then another, then another. The crowd was on its feet, roaring its approval.

Sorry, but no one seemed to give a toss that the vet had just informed me – for a sum of £34.90, since you ask – that my cat had sprained its ankle. There I was, in abject despair, tears of misery ruining my pricy Dior Diptyque Maximiser 3D eyeliner (£28.00), and all they could think about was the poxy England team winning the Test Match.

And what about the ball? Why did no one spare a thought for the ball? It had been hit and hit again, and thrown into the air and tossed from one man to another and forcibly rubbed against the bowler's crotch. I knew how it felt.

Used. Degraded. And utterly wretched. And, at the end of the day, thrown into a dark box and abandoned. While everyone else goes out and has fun.

Call that a life?

The trouble with me is I care too much.

**TROY: MYTH AND REALITY (BRITISH MUSEUM)**

Did the most beautiful woman in the world provoke the destruction of the greatest city of all time? That's the question the blokes at the British Museum are asking.

That's men for you. You spend a fortune at a go-to spa. You have your eyebrows threaded and your legs shaved and you get your nails manicured and your hair extensions done. You buy the most expensive lingerie from the Janet Reger VIP line and you spend a small fortune on the latest bandage dress from Harvey Nicks.

And then what do they do? They only go and blame you for provoking the destruction of the greatest city of all time.

Exactly the same happened to me.

As per usual, my boyfriend was in one of his moods. He blamed me for for destroying his souvenir programme of the U2 concert at the Hammersmith Odeon circa 2003.

I said I'd thrown it away because it was clogging up the house and anyway who was he to talk – he'd thrown away my sole copy of Cosmo magazine, January 1997 issue, which included my groundbreaking piece on coping with neighbours when they falsely accuse you of publishing abusive pieces about them when all you've done is describe them as greedy pigs, which they were.

And now I hear the British Museum is set to stage an exhibition on Helen of Troy. It's like a punch in the face. Helen's yesterday's news. Dead and buried. Long forgotten. In fact, she might never have even existed, thank you very much.

Whereas I'm here. Alive. Put through the wringer. And still hurting.

How often have they given me my own exhibition at the British Museum?

Answer: never.

Why are they so mean and vindictive? They must know how long I've battled with low self-esteem.

Instead, it's all Helen this, Helen that.

I'm left to cry alone. Thanks, guys. Your silence speaks volumes.

*As told to*
CRAIG BROWN

---

# THE DAILY ★ TELEGRAD

Friday, September 20, 2019

# RASPUTIN HONOURED IN TSAR'S VALEDICTORY LIST

by Our Man in Moscow
**Spin Doctor Zhivago**

IN AN honours' list to mark the late leader's resignation shortly before he was shot, the Tsar nominated his political guru, Rasputin, for his work on the Tsar's leadership campaign.

**Therese-Tsar May revolution**

Said a spokesman for the Romanovs, "Technically, Rasputin turned a reasonably secure political position into one of vulnerability and then complete disaster. Rasputin was the most hated man in the country, which probably didn't help, and the manifesto he drew up for the Tsar led to a nationwide revolution, and the assassination of the entire Romanov dynasty."

He continued, "The important thing about Rasputin is he was loyal, except when he wasn't, writing a column in the Daily Telegrad saying the Tsar was useless and should be shot. Still, he certainly knew how to grow a beard, and had a mystical power over his leader."

**On Other Pages**



---

CRICKET LATEST

# One man's heroics fail to stave off the inevitable

*by* **OUR ABRASIVE CRICKET CORRESPONDENT Sandy Paper**

DESPITE a heroic attempt by top batsman Geoffrey Boycott, who slogged away all day on a sticky wicket, people still couldn't help noticing that the rest of the honours list was a disgrace.

Boycott manfully defended all day, on radio, television and in print, against a fierce attack by Martha Kearney and others who were determined to catch him out.

Even though Boycott stood his ground, demonstrating that he didn't give a toss about how badly he came over, eventually the rest of Theresa May's tawdry line-up was exposed, and one by one they revealed their shortcomings. Out: completely useless political aides. Out: failed Brexit negotiators. Out: dodgy Tory donors.

Once again, poor selection by Mrs May has turned this once great festival of Englishness and achievement into a tacky celebration of sleaze.

Said one commentator, "It's odd that a woman who has been beaten so many times by arrogant men should award an honour to..." *(cont. p94)*

*"Sir Geoffrey, Order of the Full Tosser, Ma'am"*

## TRUMP'S AMERICA 2019

| Deaths caused by flavoured e-cigarettes | Deaths caused by handguns |
|---|---|
| **6** | **10,376** |

Trump calls for ban

Trump doesn't call for ban

# The New York Times

NEW YORK, FRIDAY, SEPTEMBER 20, 2019

## IN THRILLING DEBATE, DEMOCRATS CUT DOWN FIELD OF CANDIDATES BY NONE

By Our Political Staff
HENRY NAPP-THYME

In an absolutely gripping debate, watched by as many as four or five hundred television viewers, the 34 rivals to be the Democratic presidential candidate slugged it out to see who was going to be the next one to lose embarrassingly to Donald Trump just a year and a half from now.

There they stood, the 47 candidates, including the old white bloke and the young Asian bloke and the young black woman and the old white woman and the other old white bloke who's a bit older and a bit madder than the other old white bloke, and they went head-to-head in a thrilling no-holds barred session which lasted for 17 glorious hours – yawn – sorry, I'm a bit tired writing this up... [*This is riveting. The Guardian will definitely love this.*]

Anyway, there they stood, going on and on and on about their plans for the climate and the economy and the guns, and the sweary young one swore a bit, and then, in a thrilling twist, at the end of the night precisely nobody was sent home, even though we've been doing this rubbish for about a year now, and the 79 candidates all claimed they'd won, even though when it comes to it, they'll all find a different way of losing against Trump at the election, when it eventually comes in about five years' time.

*"A haaannnndmaid!?"*

## Women around world take part in 'The Testaments' launch event

WOMEN across the planet have been so excited about the ultra-fashionable new Margaret Atwood book that they've been inspired to take part in trendy "cosplay" events in tribute.

Some women in Britain and America dressed up as "Handmaids" from the book, but there were many more tributes across the Middle East, where millions of women joined up and wore playful, all-black interpretations of the handmaid's costume. And that's not all!

Many Atwood fans across the developing world have been so excited about the forthcoming novel that they have been preparing for the launch by entering forced marriages with abusive men, doing nothing without the permission of their male guardians, and having no control whatsoever over their financial status! You go, girls!

## BORIS IN PRESS CONFERENCE FIASCO

I'm not the Incredible Hulk, I'm the Invisible Man
At last, the British are being transparent

### Eye told you so...

*Sir,*

*Another triumph of Eye prescience. In the 50th Anniversary issue, 1300, on 28 October 2011, your cartoonist RGJ updated The Rake's Progress, foretelling our new PM. Could you not have found it in your hearts to have got it wrong?*

*PHIL GIBBINS, Penarth, Vale of Glamorgan.*

THE RAKE'S PROGRESS 2011

*"In the modern version he becomes editor of the Spectator, Mayor of London and eventually Prime Minister"*

# 'Britain booming!' says PM

by Our Political Staff **Peter O'Boom**

THE Prime Minister has declared that, thanks to his leadership, the United Kingdom is once again "booming", as his tough Brexit policies make their way through the political system.

"Take Northern Ireland," he said, "the scene of so much pessimism by the gloomy brigade, who think that there will be problems in the province merely because of minor issues with the border.

"Nonsense!" he concluded. "Local people have demonstrated that they are still perfectly capable of making a bomb and I, for one, find that inspiring."

Mr Johnson then went on to enthuse about the "new firm" which was recently successfully set up in Londonderry and which is actively involving large numbers of young people in its operations.

"They are called the New IRA and they have been given a tremendous boost by the new political climate. It won't be long before they return to the glory days and start making a real killing *(That's enough. Ed.)*

## Jeremy Corbyn WRITES

**HELLO! It's me again.**

Well, it's all hands on deck. We have all got to unite to stop Boris. The appalling things he's been doing! I think we can all agree it is an utter scandal!

Here is just a potted summary of the appalling things he's done so far…

1. Installed a weird-looking unelected advisor at the heart of his office who is making policy at the highest level and riding roughshod over his own democratically elected MPs!
2. Sacked members of his cabinet team simply for disagreeing with whatever nonsensical Brexit vision he has in his head!
3. Threatened to deselect MPs, many of whom are party loyalists, just because they won't swear loyalty to the cult of his leadership!

I don't need to tell you that these are the actions of an irresponsible narcissist and political extremist!

But I think the most egregious thing he's doing is this kamikaze approach to Brexit. He has knowingly set on an irresponsible course of action which, in all honesty, is highly likely to end in tears for him, yet for the sake of his macho image he's willing to waste the country's time in a pointless quest for popularity.

So, in response to that, I'm calling for another general election! Yes!

Cheerio!

## BORIS IN SCHOOL VISIT

# Internet crashes as UK news 'too fast'

THE World Wide Web today threw up its hands in despair and admitted defeat, as events in the United Kingdom happened too quickly.

Said one online editor, "We pride ourselves on a news response time of 0.00137 seconds, but it's just too slow. By the time we've posted the latest instalment of the Brexit saga on our news website, the story's already ancient history."

Said another, "Why are you talking about the internet not being able to cope with British politics? That's old news!"

*(Rotters.com)*

## ME AND MY SPOON

THIS WEEK

**DOMINIC CUMMINGS**

**Mr Cummings, do you have a favourite spoon?**

Dumb question. Next.

**Are there any spoons you find help you de-stress after a long day at work?**

What a waste of time this is. Ask another one, stupid.

**Is there a kind of spoon you find especially collectible?**

No. Move on. Just fucking get on with it.

**What was your first encounter with spoons?**

Not relevant. I'm a hardman, not a spoon twat.

**But… you asked us for this interview…**

Shut up. You want to waste my time, you want to betray my trust, there's the fucking door...

**Do you like anything spoon-related at all?**

I'll beat you up with a spoon in a second.

**Why?**

Because I'm a maverick and I don't give a shit.

**Has anything amusing ever…**

Fuck off.

NEXT WEEK: *Phoebe Waller-Bridge, "Me and My Bridge"*

## POETRY CORNER

**Lines on the impending retirement of Mr John Bercow from the Speaker's chair**

So. Farewell
Then John Bercow,
We will miss
Hearing your voice,
But not as much
As you will.

"Order! Order!"
That was your
Catchphrase,

Except when it was

"ORRDDEERR!
ORRDDEEEUURRRRR!"

Originally everyone
Hated you,
But now you
Have turned things
Around and only
Half the people
Hate you.

Bully for you!
As no one said.

You were pompous,
You were biased,
And you were
Self-regarding.

You also called
Mrs Leadsom
"A stupid woman",
So you weren't
Always wrong.

E.J. Thribbute
17½ (Eyes to the right).
632½ (Noes to the left).
The Eyes have it

# 101 Ways to Beat Trump's Wall

Tony Husband